THE CHRISTIAN SACRIFICE

Christus quotidie immolatur in Sacramento

St. Augustine

Quoted by St. Thomas (III^a p., q. 83, a.1)

EUGENE MASURE

Director of the *Grand Séminaire*, Lille

THE

CHRISTIAN

SACRIFICE

Translated with a Preface by Dom Illtyd
Trethowan, Monk of Downside Abbey

LONDON

BURNS OATES & WASHBOURNE LTD.

Publishers to the Holy See

PERMISSU SUPERIORUM O.S.B.

Nihil obstat   Georgius Can.Smith, S.T.D., Ph.D.
                                   Censor deputatus.

Imprimatur   †Edwardus Myers.
                                   Vic. Cap.

Westmonasterii, die 29a Septembris, 1943.

From the French of
LE SACRIFICE DU CHEF

THIS BOOK, FIRST PUBLISHED 1944 AND REPRINTED
1947, IS PRODUCED IN COMPLETE CONFORMITY WITH
THE AUTHORIZED ECONOMY STANDARDS

CONTENTS

		PAGE
PREFACE		7
INTRODUCTION		12

CHAP.   BOOK ONE : Sacrifice in General

i. Sacrifice in History	17
ii. A False Trail and an Unfortunate Definition . .	27
iii. The True Idea of Sacrifice: a Transfer of Property .	33
iv. The True Idea (continued): The Return to God . .	41
v. The True Idea (continued): The Return in Two Stages	48
vi. The Greatest Sacrifice (the result of sin) . . .	54
vii. The Place of Immolation in Sacrifice	60
viii. The True Idea (concluded): The Sign . . .	60
Conclusion	78
Note on the history and use of the word "Sacrament"	79

BOOK TWO : The Sacrifice of the Son of God

Part One : The Mystery of the Incarnation

Introduction	84
i. The Human Nature of the Divine Person . . .	94
ii. The Divine Person in the Human Nature . . .	107
iii. The Eternal Person	128
iv. The Glory of the Son	130
Conclusion	142

Part Two : The Mystery of the Redemption or
the Sacrifice of the Cross

i. The Only Son's Return	147
ii. The Son's Return and its Two Stages . . .	154
iii. The Perfect Sacrifice	163
iv. The Sacrifice of Christ Our Head	170
v. The Sign of the One Sacrifice	176
Conclusion	185

6   CONTENTS

                                                          PAGE
          BOOK THREE : The Sacrifice of the Mass

   i. Christ's Institution of the Sacraments   .   .   .   188
  ii. Christ's Institution of the Eucharist   191
 iii. The Eucharistic Tradition up to the 16th century   .   204
  iv. The Break with Tradition   221
   v. The Return to Tradition   226
  vi. Synthesis   235
 vii. The Sacrifice of the Church in the Mass   .   .   .   243
viii. Christ's Immolation in the Mass   259
  ix. The Sign   269

      Conclusion—Christ Our Head   280

PREFACE

A TRANSLATION of a book written a dozen years ago by a Frenchman practically unknown in England will cause some surprise. The explanation must be given in the first person. Two or three years ago I took *Le Sacrifice du Chef* from a library shelf in a moment of idle curiosity. I had seen the title in a general list but had met no other reference to it—nor have I discovered any since apart from favourable reviews of it in two French periodicals. A sentence caught my eye and I read on. In the next months I read it twice, becoming more and more impressed by it and more and more puzzled by its apparent failure to win recognition. I started to collect opinions and found that theologians, better qualified to judge, were enthusiastic. Scarcely anyone had read it previously. The one available copy became the object of a competition; there was no means of getting others. An English publisher could hardly be expected to pirate an edition in the French; translation therefore was the only remedy.

The book's importance, as it seems to me, lies partly in the reconciliation of de la Taille's *Mysterium Fidei* with what may be loosely called "official Thomism" on this supremely vital subject. I don't mean by speaking of reconciliation that there are no differences, but that in the wider canvas which Masure has used the differences prove to be rather aspects of a single mystery which comprehends them. Others must justify or reject that rather sweeping statement; this is not the place for detailed argument. The book has other claims in any case. No one, I think, can question that it is also a sort of general introduction to Christianity of quite unusual value. The author brings to his task a very full equipment. Much in the earlier chapters would win respectful interest in intelligent circles even of the most sceptical kind; some of the later ones might be conferences for contemplatives. But only at two points will a lack of technical theology on the reader's part be any serious hindrance, and the following brief survey of the ground will indicate them in their proper places.

A glance at the Contents will show a full-dress scheme, organized with an artist's love of symmetry. The first impression given is of a close-packed book; actually it is diffuse, sometimes (a philosopher might feel) *ad nauseam*. But the less philosophically-minded will be grateful for it. Masure works on the whole on the broadest lines (though with admirable and fascinating excursions into scholarship) and constant repetition of his general principles drives them deep into the reader's mind. This is indeed, I think, one of the book's great virtues. The chief mysteries of the Faith are expounded here with a freshness and consistency which make them a living organism; the bare bones of theology (as they so easily seem to us) take on flesh and blood. The author's Introduction obligingly provides a sort of *précis* of the entire book—which is one reason for saying little or nothing about his conclusions in the Preface. This Introduction, to the less discerning reader, may seem a trifle bare and disappointing. It is obviously the merest sketch and the filling out of it in which the book consists provides the real excitement. It will be found at least a most convenient guide and is worth rereading when the book is finished.

The first of the three books into which the work is divided (on Sacrifice in general) gives us the general context of the whole; nothing need be said about it here. But for the second book a note is necessary. The discovery that nearly a quarter of the work concerns the mystery of the Incarnation may be at first a little startling. The explanation is two-fold. First is the author's most legitimate desire to show us the Mass as the very centre of Christianity, the focal point of our entire religion. The Incarnation leads up to it, explains it and is itself further explained by it. We cannot understand the Mass without a knowledge of Christology (and therefore without Trinitarian theology); nor can we understand theology at all in any real sense without the Mass. But it remains the fact that the first part of this second book goes into details which are not strictly necessary; of this there seems to be a further explanation—*Le Sacrifice du Chef* contains materials which had already seen the light as

articles, and at this point the unity of the·design, elsewhere
so perfect, is a trifle weakened; we see the paste and scissors.
These pages (I gather from a French review) were written
originally for the *Revue pratique d'Apologétique* under the
title of *Aux origines du Chrétienté*, a title which more than
justifies the hopes it raises. To have abridged them would
have been a thousand pities; nevertheless it is in this section
that the reader unfamiliar with the ground may first feel the
strain, and if he is compelled to skip he may do so without
real danger to the argument. Masure makes skilful use of
this material later on, but on the whole only for purposes of
illustration.

The section following on the Redemption must certainly
be read entire. Not only is it part and parcel of the whole, but
it contains one of the finest theological syntheses in a book
peculiarily rich in them. Masure is a metaphysician, to my
mind, of no small merit. His language is either quite un-
technical or, when technical terms are unavoidable, technical
only after suitable preliminaries and with the necessary
subsequent expansions. In this section speculative theology,
that Cinderella of the sacred sciences, comes into something
like her own. Implications indeed remain to be drawn out, as
also later in the theology of the Mass, but that general dis-
satisfaction which we so often feel with the methods of
theological enquiry is absent. No one knows better than
Masure the limits of pure reason in theology; but when
there is something which we *ought* to understand, some
seeming arbitrariness, anomaly, or mere obscurity per-
petuated unintelligently by the text-book writers, a relentless logical analysis is brought to bear on it in a way which
can be followed and appreciated by the non-specialist.

The second point where comfort may be offered the faint-
hearted is towards the middle of the third and final book on
the Mass itself. The reader who feels stuck may move on
from the sticking-place to the sixth chapter where he will
find what matters most. Later he may be stuck again but only
for a line or two; the splendid commentary on the Common
of our Roman Mass and on the Missal prayers will amply

compensate his perseverance. The penultimate chapter on Christ's immolation in the Mass, though most straight-forward, is also perhaps the most controversial. I should be tempted to say that even if S. Thomas did not mean exactly this he should have done so, and in particular that Masure's view effectively rules out any supposed *special* act of Christ's in the Mass-Sacrifice. That (as Dr. Moran showed us recently*) is a quite modern theory. At Mass we have the whole Christ, and so His Sacrifice. But that is breaking ground forsworn.

P. Héris O.P., in a review† otherwise almost wholly laudatory, complained of Masure's language. It is, he says, untheological. It is true that there are a few loose phrases. But P. Héris was not at home, perhaps, with a writer who quotes Baudelaire as readily as Bossuet and who has an eye on his agnostic friends as well as on the seminarist. And it is significant that Masure in his own most respectful reference to the work of P. Héris in this field hints delicately that it will not be to everybody's taste. Masure's style, it can (I think) hardly be contested, has nearly always some distinction and rises sometimes to the heights of eloquence. We hear that deep note which seems to make us touch the very soul of the true France, the strong and tender theological piety to which we owe so much: we think of great Dominicans and Jesuits such as Gardeil and Clérissac, Rousselot and de la Taille himself.

This will have largely evaporated no doubt in the transla-tion. Masure is at times quite extraordinarily untranslatable. Faced with the recurrent dilemma of losing the flavour of the original almost altogether or writing rather awkward English, I have chosen normally the latter horn. I can only hope that it will not be too uncomfortable for the reader. To keep the English in some kind of flow I have allowed myself small omissions or additions which make no difference to sense or emphasis. Masure breaks out sometimes into "affections." These are impressive in the French; in transla-

---

* *Irish Ecclesiastical Record*, Nov., 1942.

† *Revue des Sciences Philosophiques et Théologiques*, 1932.

tion they are inevitably less convincing. The writing is often in what might be described as "conference" style; sentences need stressing heavily in certain places. This applies also to the English. I can only ask that the defects of the translation should not be fathered on the original, and I can claim only to have conveyed the author's thought and to have respected, so far as in me lies, his own expression of it.

May I conclude by going back to where I started? Isn't it true that we in England are more than ever interested in the Mass, but still hesitant (many of us) about its meaning? People are so often fascinated by popular accounts of de la Taille, but frightened by the disagreement with him which they know exists, and which they very properly respect. Yet the "official" views are hard to grasp. A sort of cloud hangs over the proceedings. How often, for example, do we hear sermons on the Mass which really tell us *why* we offer sacrifice and what, precisely, it is all about? The hope behind this production (Masure has all the answers, I believe) is that it may help to remedy this state of things. Nothing matters more.

INTRODUCTION

THE Mass is a true sacrifice. The Council of Trent has defined this essential dogma, in conformity with all previous tradition, and all Catholics agree in proclaiming a doctrine which lies at the heart of their liturgical worship. But how is the Mass a true sacrifice? For in spite of the commentary provided by the Council, modern theologians and devotional books which follow them often yield to the temptation of discussing the explanation: Vasquez, Bellarmin, Lessius, de Lugo, to name only the most famous, appear to-day in the manuals, accurately or inaccurately, as leaders of so many little schools, leading by narrow paths to dead ends or dangerous short cuts or mere goat-tracks in the wilderness. How shall we regain the highway, the road of tradition? Perhaps it would be enough to consult the Fathers and the Doctors, S. Augustine and S. Thomas, interpreting Scripture and the liturgy in the light of origins, clarified further by the oldest longings of the human race. If we return to these principles, we shall have the joy of meeting on our way to the altar all the great Christian dogmas, the Incarnation and the Redemption, the Divinity of Jesus Christ, and the mystery of the world's salvation by the Saviour's Cross. Thus the Eucharist sums up all our faith, even as it has within it all our wealth. The theme round which our enquiry will turn is the idea of sacrifice. We shall study in turn Sacrifice in general, the Sacrifice of the Cross and the Sacrifice of the Eucharist.

In speaking of Sacrifice in general we must look not only to the tradition of the Church but to that of the whole human race. For Sacrifice is as universal as religion itself; it lies at its centre, is the very kernel of it. It is an institution which demands our fullest understanding.

When a man first sets himself to this problem he is at first crushed by the weight of the evidence, or repelled by the apparent oddness of sacrificial rites and ceremonies. But he realizes on reflection that the main stream of these strange liturgies is almost always the same; we present it as the work of de la Taille has restored it to us in accordance with S. Augustine and S. Thomas.

When he offers sacrifice man has his purpose to *make sacred* (*sacrum facere*) that is to make a profane object divine, so as to unite himself with the Divinity itself by subsequent communion with the victim. This broad religious undertaking implies a whole series of significant actions, showing varieties of arrangements in the rituals, but with the following operations, more or less underlined, appearing throughout their course. Man must first make renunciation of some personal possession, profane or imperfect like himself, and that is immolation. Then he must offer this object to the Divinity, and that is oblation; and then he must make the oblation acceptable, otherwise the victim would not be really sacred. Finally he must reclaim his offering and make it somehow return to him, charged with the divine acceptance, in order that the victim may be a sign for him of his heavenly alliance. That is communion.

The word *sign* must be heavily underlined. For the object offered and immolated is in all this business a true symbol, or, as S. Augustine said, a visible sign, in which a whole series of spiritual realities is bodied forth: first the religion of men, who into that victim set apart from among their possessions have poured as it were all the strain and substance of their adoration, their repentance and their petitions. In their victim men immolate themselves, offer themselves to heaven, strive to reach God, and, in every sense of the word, to touch Him. Then, in return, all divine blessings and favours are contained in this victim, so that to communicate with this object (originally the proof of our own religious attitude) is to guarantee the heavenly alliance of which it has become the pledge.

This analysis has already shown us why the decisive events which occurred between the evening of Maundy Thursday and Easter Sunday (and indeed Ascension Day) form the perfect Sacrifice in the eyes of Christians. That sacrifice, it is true, is written not in the figures of ritual but in the pages of history. But this realism makes it the more precious. Christ, our divine Founder, was then truly the victim of the Sacrifice of the religion instituted by Him, the religion which is also ours.

He makes the renunciation of His life and He offers Himself to His Father; thus He immolates Himself. Certainly He does not put Himself to death, but He accepts the only way which would lead us to God after sin had come into the world, the road of suffering and death. The death which He offered is an immolation. God the Father receives this Sacrifice, and He grants to the body and soul of Christ at the Resurrection and Ascension that glory to which the Sacred Humanity of the Son was entitled from the first, but did not yet enjoy. Thus He shows and proves how acceptable to Him is His Son, how splendid the welcome He prepares for Him. Immolated by reason of our sin, this Son is now glorified by reason of His merits: in virtue of this double title, He appears to us as the victim in which perfect religion finds its supreme expression and its most assured reality.

But how is Christ to become *our* Victim? How are we to unite ourselves with Him, to find in Him the effective sign of our heavenly alliance? Perhaps a mere moral and spiritual communion of men with their Saviour might have sufficed. But Christ willed something more—a sacramental union. That was the Eucharist.

*　　　*　　　*

What then is the Eucharist? In the Sacrifice of the Mass the Church takes bread and wine and first seems to use them as the sign or symbol of her adoration. But she can never make them acceptable as such: however pure and beautiful these oblations may be they have no power to please God.

But when God changes them into the Body and Blood of the sole Victim acceptable to Him, then, by an inconceivably triumphant transformation, our Sacrifice receives the perfect proof of the divine appeasement. For the Church, by means of this transubstantiation, is put in possession of the one efficacious victim, as the victim of *her* Sacrifice, and with this of all the religious achievement which she sought:

the Church shares in an upward movement that perfect adoration of which the Sacred Humanity of Christ is the temple; downwards she sees coming to her through the accepted Victim all divine favours, all the Father's good pleasure.

The spring of all this great action is the Transubstantiation which brings with it the Real Presence of the Body and the Blood and which forms in truth the most glorious of Sacrifices. Sacrifice consists in changing the profane into the sacred, in making our religion incarnate on the one side, in gaining communion with the Divinity on the other. Here the consecrated victim exists already. But it must turn our impotent offerings into its own self so that our poor religion may share in the richness of its own. All is then accomplished.

* * *

The work which we here present to the public has as its purpose to develop, to explain and to prove the insufficient summary which we have just set out, giving way to the dangerous ambition of outlining a book in a single page. If we wished to sum up this page too in a single phrase we might perhaps venture with all necessary reservations to write the following:

The signs instituted by Christ contain and make real what they represent. The Eucharist was instituted by Christ as the Sign of the Sacrifice of the Cross. Thus the Eucharist contains and makes real the Sacrifice of the Cross.

And finally could we gratify our impatience to the furthest limit by trying to reduce even that syllogism in its turn to a single definitive expression? Perhaps, provided that the reader will give the word *sign*, one of the richest in the theological and sacramental vocabulary, its full, absolute sense, that of the Council of Trent: *sub SIGNIS visibilibus Christus immolandus*. We should then say, using the pregnant language of scholasticism: *the Mass is the SIGN of the Cross*.

BOOK ONE: SACRIFICE IN GENERAL

CHAPTER ONE: SACRIFICE IN HISTORY

THERE are great occasions in the history of families, of peoples and of Churches when men and the Divinity greet one another at the climax of a system of rites, often magnificent, sometimes distasteful. Priests and levites in our history, sorcerers, magicians or witch-doctors elsewhere, preside over those rites and perform them, bound to the service of holy things, consecrated by the biblical anointing or the wild chant of some savage initiation. The liturgy begins with traditions of previous generations weighing on the will of living men, enshrined in grim or weird prescriptions. It is as if the dead were speaking, issuing their orders. These traditional gestures and inherited formulas enable man to reach God, almost to touch Him. Then the incense crackles and smokes; libations are poured; the victims are brought forth.

"*Grand Dieu! voici ton heure: on t'amène ta proie.*" For it is the divine moment of sacrifice.

At the risk of contamination among these dark pools where our feet slip in the blood of goats and heifers, we must spend some time in this religious shambles if we are to understand it. However gloomy and sanguinary the spectacle may be, rational animals have spent too long here for us to refuse to breath an atmosphere so charged with the psychology of mankind, though so strangely mingled. If I do not approve of all that my distant ancestors have done—Jews, Greeks and barbarians—at least I must realize their inmost longings.

After these scenes of slaughter and butchery the ceremony is completed by a real or symbolic communion, by a sacred meal, in which the offered and immolated victim, suddenly inverting its meaning and value, seems to return over the course which it had run when charged with the adoration, the repentance and the prayers of men. Now it comes down from heaven to earth as the pledge of divine blessings and eternal favours.

What does all this mean? To understand it better I pick up

B

at random and reread certain descriptions evoking those strange rites, horrible or gracious, splendid or repulsive.

The Bible gives me the patriarchial account of venerable sacrifice in the distant past:

> Abel was a shepherd of sheep, and Cain was a labourer. At the end of a certain time Cain offered the fruits of the earth as an oblation to Jahve: Abel in his turn offered the first-fruits of his flock and their fatness. Jahve regarded Abel and his offering but did not regard Cain and his gifts (Gen. iv, 2–5).

> Noe built an altar to Jahve and having taken of all clean animals and of all clean birds he offered holocausts upon the altar. Jahve smelt a sweet savour and He said in His heart: I shall no more curse the earth (Gen. viii, 20–21).

> As Abram returned victorious over Chodorlahomor and the Kings that were with him, the King of Sodom came to meet him in the valley of Save, that is the valley of the King. Melchisedech, King of Salem, brought bread and wine; he was a priest of the Most High God. He blessed Abram and Abram gave him the tithe of all (Gen. xiv, 17–20).

> Abraham took the wood of the burnt-offering and laid it upon Isaac his son; and he took in his hand the fire and the knife; and they went both of them together. Isaac said to Abraham his father, "My father!" He replied, "Here am I, my son." And Isaac said, "Here is the fire and the wood; but where is the lamb for a burnt-offering?" Abraham replied, "God will provide a lamb for the burnt-offering, my son." And they went both of them together. When they came to the place which God had appointed to him, Abraham built the altar and laid the wood; then he bound Isaac, his son, and laid him on the altar. And Abraham stretched out his hand, and took the knife to slay his son. Then the angel of Jahve cried to him from heaven: "Abraham! Abraham!" He replied, "Here am I." And the angel said to him: "Lay not your hand on the child and do nothing to him; for I know now that you fear God and that you have not refused your son, your only one." Abraham, lifting his eyes, saw behind him a ram caught in a thicket by its horns; he went and took the ram and offered it as a burnt-offering in the place of his son (Gen. xxii, 6–13).

> Moses rising early in the morning built an altar at the foot of the mountain, and set up twelve stones for the twelve tribes of Israel. He sent young men, children of Israel, and they offered burnt offerings to Jahve and sacrificed oxen for thank-offering. Moses took half of the blood, and put it in basins, and he sprinkled the other half on the altar. Then, taking the book of the Covenant he read it in the presence of the people, who replied, "All that Jahve has spoken we will do and we will be obedient." Then he took the blood and sprinkled the people with it saying: "This is the blood of the Covenant which Jahve has made with you on all these conditions" (Exod. xxiv, 4–8).

We shall ask the witness of classical antiquity from Virgil's religious soul. Æneas is to descend to the lower world, but first he must placate the gods:

> Four sable bullocks, in the yoke untaught,
> For sacrifice the pious hero brought.
> The priestess pours the wine betwixt their horns ;
> Then cuts the curling hair; that first oblation burns,

Invoking Hecat hither to repair—
A pow'rful name in hell and upper air.
The sacred priests, with ready knives, bereave
The beasts of life, and in full bowls receive
The streaming blood: a lamb to Hell and night
(The sable wool without a streak of white)
Æneas offers; and, by Fate's decree,
A barren heifer, Proserpine, to thee.
With holocausts he Pluto's altar fills:
Seven brawny bulls with his own hand he kills:
Then, on the broiling entrails, oil he pours;
Which, ointed thus, the raging flame devours.
Late the nocturnal sacrifice begun,
Nor ended, till the next returning sun.
Then earth began to bellow, trees to dance,
And howling dogs in glimm'ring light advance,
Ere Hecat came.—"Far hence be souls profane!"
The Sibyl cry'd—"and from the grove abstain!"*

Let us now move to the opposite side of the world and of history, to the Temple of Heaven at Pekin. There is nothing in the centre of the monument but the Emperor's throne; There is no idol, no statue, no inscription. Vast chafing-dishes are smoking, ready to consume the bodies of animals offered to heaven as holocausts.

In this magnificent temple the Chinese Emperors of the two last dynasties presented themselves three times a year, from 1420 onwards, to adore Heaven, to implore its favours and to give account of their stewardship. The first ceremony took place at the the beginning of winter; the second was to ask heaven for the power of government throughout the year; the third, which took place at the end of spring, begged for a bountiful rainfall and a rich harvest.

The monarch, assisted by the princes and great mandarins, made three genuflections and nine adorations on the terrace. Under the Ming dynasty, while the Emperor offered the traditional lapis-lazuli, the choir chanted:

May this offering climb into space, and be known on high! May it obtain for us what we desire! I am come to this Mount, with my officers, to ask the August Heaven to grant earth the ripening of crops, a fruitful harvest.

Then the Emperor made nine more prostrations and the choir continued:

* Æn., VI, 243–259. [Since a literal translation is not required, the chance to use Dryden was irresistible.—Tr.]

By my offerings, I make my reverence known on high. May their smoke, following the path of the thunderbolt and of the nine dragons, rise aloft, and may blessings descend upon the people. That is what I, a little child (the Emperor), ask by these offerings.

When the offerings were consumed by the fire, the choir went on

The tripods and the censers smoke, the pieces of flesh and silk are blazing, their smoke rises, higher than the clouds, to show the pains of the people. May our music and our chants make known the devotion of our hearts.*

The races which we call savage offer us detailed examples of these ancient practices of mankind. P. Schebesta gives the following account of sacrifice among the primitives of Malaya :

The following is a brief description of the first sacrifice which I attended. It was a dark night: I was sleeping in my cabin, in the middle of an encampment which contained about ten shelters. I woke towards midnight with the threat of storm. All was quiet.

Suddenly there was a terrible crash, a thunderclap so close that everyone was roused. Great fires were lit. I saw women running from one shelter to another. At first I did not realize what was happening. Then I remembered the great sacrifice of blood, of which I had learnt previously from books about the Semangs. At once I rose. I drew near in the torrential rain to see the preparations for the sacrifice more closely. What was my surprise at the sight which met my eyes!

With their bamboo knives in their hands they were cutting their flesh. The blood flowed. It was collected in a bamboo cane where it was mixed with a little water. The liquid was then thrown into the air, while words which I did not [that night] understand were uttered.

The author later put the words together, and they amounted to this :

I pay my debt. Behold my sin! My debt has lessened. Cease then. Behold my blood! I pay my debt. My debt is no more.†

Let us now watch a horrifying but very instructive scene, which takes place among the aboriginals of ancient Mexico before the Spanish conquest.

On the eve of the sacrifice the captives and their masters spent the night in a temple. Towards midnight, when sleep was forbidden, the master cut off before the fire long strands of the captives' hair, the sign of his warlike profession and military honour. They were kept as relics, that is as a

* Excerpted (freely) from the *Revue Illustrée de l'Exposition Missionaire Vaticane*, published officially August 15, 1924. Bibliography : Mgr. Favier, *Pekin*, and the works of P. Wieger, S.J.

† *Semain Internationale d'Ethnologie Religieuse*. 4th session, *Milan*, 1925. Proceedings published in Paris by Geuthner, 1926, p. 188.

protective talisman, by those about to perform human sacrifice. In the morning the victims, covered with red and blue paper, the emblems and colours of the god, were led into the great sanctuary of Mexico. The masters too had their arms and legs festooned with white down and their heads with feathers, as though they also had been prepared for sacrifice. They handed over their captives to the priests who made them climb the steps of the pyramid which served as temple. The victim was laid upon the stone of immolation; one man held his head, two his legs and two more his arms. The priest, seizing his knife, opened the breast, tore out the heart, raised it in the air to offer it to the Sun, and then cast it into a cup. The body of the victim was thrown down the steps of the pyramid and rolled to the terrace at the foot. There the bodies were collected and skinned. The victim was hacked to pieces and the remains carried to the house of his master, except for a joint which was reserved in honour of the King. The flesh was cooked with maize, and each received in his dish a portion of the meat and the savoury. It is said expressly in the case of some of these victims, who were immolated with special solemnity after a ritual combat, that the master alone of his family did not share the meal. The reason was that the victim, who had been fed for some time at the master's house, was his own flesh, and he did not wish to eat himself; but he ate without qualms the flesh of a victim offered by another when presented to him.*

And finally this is how S. Nilus the Sinaite in the fifth century (or the writer who bears his name) saw the sacrifices of the wild and piratical nomad tribes who occupied the seed-ground of Islam from Arabia to Egypt.

They offer their prayers and adorations to the morning-star. To this they immolate their richest booty, when their brigandage has brought them prey which can be slaughtered. For this they seek out especially young people in the flower and beauty of their age, and sacrifice them at dawn upon an altar. If they have none of these they place on its knees a white camel without blemish, and all walk round it together three times. One of them leads the procession and the chant in honour of the star, a chief or a priest of venerable age. After the third circle has been made, with the last words of the chant still upon the lips of the people, the priest draws his sword, strikes a hard blow and hastens to be the first to taste the blood. The others rush up in the same way and cut with their swords a small piece of skin and hair, or take what flesh they can bear away. Others take even the entrails and the intestines, so that nothing remains to be seen intact at sunrise.†

What, again, is the meaning of these gestures? Why is this victim, separated from the rest of the booty or the herd, both blessed and cursed, execrated and consecrated? Why is it put to death? Why, after being slain, is it offered to the

* From Bernardino de Sahugun, *Histoire Générale des choses de la Nouvelle-Espagne*, trad. Gourdanes and Siméon, Paris, 1880. Cf. Pinard de la Boullaye, S.J., *L'Etude comparée des Religions*, Beauchesne, 1925, vol. III, pp. 57–58n.

† P. G. de Migne, vol. LXXIX, col. 612–613. Cf. Lagrange, O.P., *Les Religions Sémitiques*, Paris, 1905, p. 257.

divinity? Once offered it returns in joyful communion as a ratified pledge, ratifying itself the blessings of the barbarous or Olympian God. What justifies this great change? What explains this reversal of the roles?

The inhabited earth and the history of the world have been filled with such spectacles. To escape them we should need to be no longer men. Mortals born of woman and sons of our far-off fathers, we carry with us an inevitable heritage which controls and lies in wait for us. I shall never be wholly my own self, if I cannot understand the weight of the past which is always mastering my present life. I try to pass back in imagination across the centuries to find the meaning of these strange harmonies imposed on me in the furthest depths of my personality.

So then as a soldier of Vercingetorix waiting upon the incantations of the Druids before the gathering of the sacred mistletoe—as a son of Greece, a victor of Marathon or an athlete—as a soldier of Rome, faithful to the eagles, to the people and the Senate, I join in the sacrifices in the forest, on the Acropolis or on the Capitol. And during the sacred ceremony I dream of impossible unknown lands, unconquered by the imperial legions, distant islands placed by the poets beyond the columns of Hercules. Here other men, if they are worthy of that name, grouped round their monstrous fetishes, pile up scalps in fearful pyramids, or climb to high places to shake them with their shameless, self-tormenting dances. But everywhere, in woods and deserts alike, by mysterious lakes and in Egyptian palaces, I hear the double rhythm: grief rises to heaven in plaintive appeal and the shedding of blood, and reaches its consummation in an apotheosis of communion and of joy. This is sacrifice with its two aspects, one provisional, of suffering, the other the conquest of joy, final and definitive.

The name Christian which I bear does not forbid me to gaze into these sacred depths; quite the contrary. As a disciple of Christ, I have the right and the duty to try to understand these ancient human things. In history as in apologetics there are two shoals to shun: bringing Christianity too near other religions at the risk of denying its transcendence and exclusiveness; and sundering it too far from them on the pretext of exalting it, emptying it therefore of its humanism. On the one hand it becomes a human invention like its predecessors and ceases to be divine; on the other it does not meet our real needs, or rather its privilege comes to seem a monstrous thing, since it abandons millions of reasonable creatures to the abyss of total error. As a solution Christianity alone is true, all other religions false: *omnes dii gentium dæmonia*. But on the road of truth which leads to God the smallest progress must be respected; and even if it is mingled with strange and dreadful horrors, its value is not negligible. In the clumsiest gesture of prayer there is a movement to the one true God; and Christianity takes over and purifies this movement. In that sense this religion, although of divine origin, is also human. It corresponds to our needs, it supplies what is lacking. Other religions then, which also represent our needs even in perverted forms, will have points of contact with Christianity.

It would be too much to say, wrote M. Grimal, that all immolations and communions, except those of the Tabernacle and of the Temple of Israel, were nothing but orgies of sacrilege and superstition. Even in the Greek cults with their fundamental idolatry and sensuality we seem to see at times the shadow and more than the shadow of true religion. In the two great tragedians, Æschylus and Sophocles, whose dramas come so close to worship, do we not see beneath the invocatory formulas the attitude and accent of the adoring soul? And why should the religious sentiment have been less alive than other noble instincts which survived in the heart of darkness and corruption? God, who tries the reins and the heart to discover the least tarnish upon virtue and also the smallest germ of good intention, half-buried beneath error and incomprehension, must have disentangled sometimes from these perverse purifications and communions something like a desire and stirring after homage, expiation and true sanctity, an appeal for a perfect victim, a witness of the *anima naturaliter Christiana*.*

In words of even higher inspiration P. Laberthonnière expressed similar ideas.

We still give absolute approval to Bossuet's idea, in the *Discours sur l'Histoire universelle* of making Christ the centre and truth of history, and of using history to shed light upon the truth of Christ. Only instead of taking as the subject of history external events, the rise and fall of Empires, the exploits of great commanders . . . we now take the very life of humanity

* I. Grimal, *Le sacerdoce et le sacrifice de Notre Seigneur Jésus Christ*, Paris, Beauchesne, 1911, pp. 77–78.

seen from within in its aspirations, its beliefs and hopes, its denials and
distresses, its strivings and its failings . . . in the tremendous discontent
which is always renewed and always the same, giving it no rest. It will be
possible to show that Christ is present in all this diversity, unknown,
known or misconstrued, desired, accepted or rejected, but always the
spring and centre of the movement.*

But to realize the coincidence between false religions and the
truth, we must always go behind their poor appearances to
find their innermost desires; or rather beneath the rubbish
heap of myths, rites, systems, weird confusions and hideous
practices, we must find the hidden line of Godward movement. Many historical manuals of religious history give too
much the impression of a more or less well-informed ency-
clopedia, while the reader is looking for analyses of living
souls and human consciences. Yet Christianity, in proportion as we live it, disposes us to grasp the value of these
tentative approaches, or rather it gives them by reason of its
own achievement an intense interest which is the fruit of its
own richness. It enables us to understand these gloomy
religions better than they understood themselves. Thus we
can try to guess how our heavenly Father looks upon this
vast religious epoch from Adam's sin to the conversion of the
barbarians, though so motley and sometimes so horrifying.
If we consider its doctrine, it is an immense accumulation of
errors, and the truth is indeed in Christ alone. But if we take
it as an expression of minds and wills in search of their end,
it becomes the huge conflagration of a burning bush covering
all the globe, with every tongue of fire a witness of adoration.

That holocaust may have been some times only a disgust-
ing bonfire; but in the leaping of its flames it already sings
God's glory. *Domini est terra, et plenitudo eius.*

True, we are putting deep truths into the brains of human
beings darkened by sin, separated from their divine origins,
parted too by millenaries of barbarism from the Redeemer
and His Revelation. But do not refuse these rational animals
a remnant or an earnest of moral worth and intellectual
dignity. Admit for example a primitive revelation which has
never been completely obliterated: that is the traditionalist

* R. P. Laberthonnière, *Pages choisies*, Friedel, Paris, Vrin, 1931, p. 181, n. 1.

hypothesis on which the Roman Church has never wholly smiled, but which is convenient as well as edifying. It has charmed Christian philosophy in France for so long; it has prepared us to meet the shock of prehistoric anthropology. . . . Or at least admit a continuity of natural truths even in the heart of the grossest errors in virtue of that essence of rational animality which exists in all men and drives us in the end, if we follow the rational instinct of our nature, to largely identical solutions. Think too and above all of those eternal designs of universal redemption which have shed abroad the rays of a providential preparation in the distant centuries of man's youth. And through these various explanations, which one day perhaps must be gathered together in a modern *Discours sur l'Histoire universelle*, you will discover a religious idea embodied in the ritual of sacrifice, in which death and life, grief and triumph, trial and victory, succeed one another like winter and spring, weeping and laughter.

Simplify these institutions more and more bringing them on to broader and broader lines; and you will be less astonished at the obstinacy of mankind in seeking contact with God by the blood of victims and final resurrection and true salvation by a previous death.*

Go further again and sift the matter to its foundation. When you give substance to this magnificent metaphysic by appealing to human psychology you will see guilty men substituting the most monstrous anthropomorphism for the great divine laws of creation and, on the pretext of adoring God, destroying His creatures, torturing them, shedding their blood on loathsome smoking altars where the acrid smell of burning flesh affronts the glory of the author of life and youth and beauty.

But you can also cast over these horrors the transparent veils of the myths and the intoxicating clouds of symbolism.

---

* ". . . . Behind all rites of initiation there are always two complementary ideas, those of death and resurrection . . . among certain Australian tribes the neophyte is considered dead . . . After the initiation he returns to the world of the living. . . ." R. Allier, *La Psychologie de la Conversion chez les non civilisés*, Payot, 1925, vol. I, p. 310.

We are now in Greece, in the freshest and most luminous of countries, and in the East, in lands of ease and grace. Then all this great system fades into incense-smoke, an outline of unsubstantial beauty. Sacrifice becomes a theme—its two aspects are called mysteries, mysteries of winter and spring, of death and life, of Adonis who dies and rises again to the sound of tambourines and castanets waved by Bacchantes drunk with wine and love.

Interpretation, in a sense, does not matter, since at bottom it is always eternal man, a great child telling himself his own history and his inward drama; whether he be mystic or temple-servant, fetish-worshipper or hierophant, he takes up his double journey once again, this movement on two planes, where the mysterious being that he is faces the two sides of its divided nature. Renunciation is translated psychologically by grief, privation and mortification; the other side, the clinging to existence, by joy, triumph and mystical intoxication. If sacrifice is summoned to make these two successive states a living reality for us, to show more clearly the two facets of our journey, we realize that it is costly only for our profit, grievous only to bring blessing— let us reach the heart of it, death-dealing only to be life-giving. Such was the vision of the distant past which Pierre Termier saw.

> I believe that there have always been worshippers, suppliants and lovers. . . . That has been enough for God. As the earth turns around the sun times without number, many crimes are committed on its surface, many bestial cries, shouts of grief and despair, even blasphemies, rise from this strangely fated planet to the horror-stricken skies; but the holy murmur from retreats where simple good men are praying easily drown the shouting and the blasphemy; and the smoke of sacrifice, a thin blue column rising into the calm air of dawn or dusk, bears a perfume so keen that it destroys the stench of crimes.*

But we must go beyond these descriptions to understand them fully; we must seek a definition of Sacrifice, metaphysical as well as psychological, from the philosophers and the theologians.

---

* Pierre Termier, *La joie de connaître*, Paris, Nouvelle Librairie Nationale, 1926, p. 305. (Conference, at Louvain, on the antiquity of man.)

CHAPTER TWO: A FALSE TRAIL AND
AN UNFORTUNATE DEFINITION

IT is unfortunate that the formulas in manuals, in the attempt to clarify the essential notions of a science for beginners, often reduce the richest realities to a dry and empty scheme. A scholastic commentator seizes upon this dead formula and proposes to explain it; to explain it, he pulls it to pieces according to certain conventional methods; and (crowning misfortune) stereotyped examples selected for purposes of elementary instruction ossify the subject still further. As a result some great reality is unrecognizably mutilated by too much cutting and drying. The pupil learns the definitions for examinations, gains his honours by an exercise of memory and understands almost nothing of the subject.

We must gain an intelligent grasp of our tradition from the real Masters; but in part it is the common heritage of mankind. For thousands of years men have offered sacrifice; what do they think to accomplish in thus obeying their ancestral rites and rational instincts? Do they themselves really know? Yes, if we do not hold them up, as they are all tempted to hold themselves up, at the mere formalities of ritual which lie upon the surface, if we grant them their deepseated motives, if we distinguish, in virtue of this hidden understanding, between what is essential and what is accidental; and if in virtue of Christianity, recognized at least as the summit of man's religious experience, we understand better than primitive peoples themselves what they believed themselves to be achieving even if they attained no formulation of it.

For three centuries the necessity of defending religion and our lamentable quarrels with the Protestants dragged almost all authors in the wake of a definition proposed by de Lugo, clear and exact but foreclosing a really metaphysical or even psychological enquiry into sacrifice by the implications of its logical structure.

Yet this is the definition which still remains with unimportant variations in almost all the manuals; *Sacrifice*, it runs, *is the oblation of a sensible object, and its immolation by destruction or otherwise, these performed by a legitimate priest, to the honour of God, to recognize the sovereign power of the Creator and to obtain from Him pardon for our sins, this immolation being normally followed by communion;* Or: *Sacrifice is the immolation of a victim offered to God by a legitimate priest,* etc. . . . In any case, in all these formulas and the explanations given of them, the accent is on the word *immolation.* God, they say, is the sovereign master of heaven and earth, of life and death. How can we express our recognition of his prerogative except by putting to death a living being? Or, less crudely, how can we offer to the invisible God something which belongs to us without destroying it to show that we renounce our right to use it? etc. . . . In short, the *genus proximum* of the definition thus formed and explained is immolation and even destruction.* Now, for our Western minds, the *genus proximum* is all important; it controls the whole philosophy of the subject. Here, then, is sacrifice conceived from the start and essentially as a putting to death, its existence and with it that of religion depending upon the previous existence of sin, as if religion were not in history, and above all in metaphysics, anterior to sin. The deadlock to which such a definition must lead is easily foreshadowed. Yet there is not a word in the *Summa Theologica,* nor therefore in the Council of Trent, to recommend such a method. It is a description rather than an analysis; it is an extrinsic definition. We do not lack descriptions of sacrifice. The History of Religions, we have seen, has put hundreds of examples at our disposal. It is the understanding of this human and divine mystery that we want. We need to grasp it, and, by seeing into it more deeply, to grasp ourselves, engaged in it as we are by our most inevitable legacies from the past, the most disturbed and disturbing movements of our secret selves. This great rite of sacrifice dominates our civilization to such an extent, the tang of human nature is so

---

* Cf. de Lugo, Disput. XIX *de Eucharistia ut est sacrificium,* sect. i *de sacrificio in communi,* Edit. Vivès, Paris, 1868, vol. iv, pp. 181, sq.

sharp around these far-flung altars, that we must try to find out the significance of ancient practices and gestures on pain of renouncing our own nature and its deepest and most insistent instincts. Our morals are declining; we shall soon have to admit that we are but a topmost branch on the great tree of mankind, since the finest European races, the French above all, are on the eve of dying, like the Redskins, the Bushmen and the Pigmies. Isn't it because in our superficial civilizations the altars are destroyed, the sacred fire of the ancient city put out, the sacrifices of the New Law deserted? No incense rises to the sky, no victim reconciles us with our End, and the spirit of sacrifice has disappeared. Then death comes down on us.

It is high time to think and understand; otherwise we perish.

Now we possess in our traditional theology a definition of Sacrifice more ancient than de Lugo's and built on different lines. It had been sketched by S. Augustine and is taken over by S. Thomas. In the *Summa* it is expressed in a formula so complete that, as often happens with the great Doctor, its riches are not realized. The careless reader overlooks this perfectly balanced masterpiece and prefers to it the poor imitations of the manuals, as unperceptive buyers in the *rue Bonaparte* prefer colourful plaster statues to the pure and simple lines of less superficial subjects in more genuine materials.

The theology of de Lugo puts the immolation of the victim in the forefront as the *genus proximum*. And for an immediate justification of so daring a step without involving too much spiritual and religious reflection, it hastily constructs a doctrine, fine enough in principle, of God as sovereign Lord of life and death: to recognize the absolute sway of God over all creatures, His power of creating and annihilating, His rights over life and death, we destroy victims and oblations to His glory, since we cannot make material transfer of the object which we offer.

There are large elements of truth in this summary account, but the perspective is narrow and lacks depth. This rapid indirect method of approaching a formidable problem rules out from the start any wider metaphysic of the subject. It is a way of getting there, but a close and stifling one. At a pinch pious submissive souls might be constrained to it. But one seems unlikely to succeed in making the broad stream of modern ideas pass by such a path or the sufferings of proud and grieving souls. Ancient and primitive sacrifices may seem to have been explained; but sacrifice becomes almost impossible of acceptance for the modern mind. If we are content with an insufficient philosophy we may perhaps explain what savages and Israelites thought they were doing, but we do not explain what at bottom they were trying to achieve. We do not understand them better than they understood themselves; and straightway we really fail to understand them—we do not relate their hidden desires to the Christian sacrifice; and this in its turn, forced into the mould of this narrow metaphysic, this hasty psychology, loses something of its transcendent richness. Reduced to being only one sacrifice among so many, following upon so many, it ceases to replace and surpass them, to accept them and bring them to completion.

From all these points of view the definition is a failure. Who will give us back the ancient institutions of mankind still with their vague penumbra of mystery, and the Sacrifice of Christ with its infinitely spreading glories? Who will give us a formula powerful enough to embrace these desires of offering and bestowal which rise from East to West, from North to South, on the vast altar where mankind has revealed its most inevitable movements of soul, its most insistent heart-burnings and its eternal destinies?

Well, we shall see that the formula is in S. Thomas, who himself is continuing S. Augustine.

Meantime, de la Taille, in his great work on the Holy Eucharist,* seems to have destroyed the conception of Cardinal de Lugo once and for all; after reading the relentless words of the learned professor of the Roman College,

---

* Mauritius de la Taille, S.J. *Mysterium Fidei de Augustissimo Corporis et Sanguinis Christi Sacrificio atque Sacramento*, Paris, Beauchesne, 1921, cap. 1. Cf. M. de la Taille, S.J., *Esquisse du Mystère de la Foi suivie de quelques eclaircissements*, Paris, Beauchesne, 1924.

another Cardinal, Mgr. Charost, Archbishop of Rennes, accepted his conclusions enthusiastically and wrote in a pastoral letter to his diocesans:

> Let us try . . . to gain a true idea of sacrifice. Many books dear to your piety, which deserve your regard because they enhance your generosity to God, have nevertheless drawn a notion of sacrifice from a theology of relatively recent date (its author is Cardinal de Lugo) which seems to us unsatisfactory. It corresponds neither with the inmost tendencies of human beings nor with the glory of the living God. For that is not found, as so often with human glory, in carnage, but in the good wherewith the Creator would saturate His creatures. Yet they tell us in these modern books that the destruction of human life is itself a means of glorifying the Lord! It would even appear the absolute homage due to His supreme majesty and the most striking expression of His sovereign sway over life and death. But, they add, since man is not allowed to destroy himself, he offers to God instead of his own life some creature which nourishes it and can be considered as a part of it.
>
> Does then the highest religious act, so far from raising man to his highest perfection by bringing him as near as possible to God, reduce him to nothingness? God is "He who is" . . . He has placed in all His creatures a continuous movement towards Himself, to display, as St. Paul says (Rom. ii, 4), "the riches of his goodness". He has ordained all things that man might anchor his restless, wavering being to the changelessness and the infinite and blessed peace of His divine Being. Would He set His glory in the sight of man's withdrawal in a sort of savage self-annihilation from this centre of vigorous and radiant life? Would He take pleasure in the extinction of the living spark, the projection of His unfathomable goodness. . . ?
>
> The doctrine of St. Thomas Aquinas is far truer and far humaner than this.[*]

Perhaps the spirituality of the Gallican Church for the last two or three centuries has yielded too easily here to a destructive pessimism under the real or merely verbal influence of Jansenism. M. Lepin, studying the doctrines of the French Oratory under the old order, has been constantly forced to rectify and to contest the theory of annihilation-sacrifice.[†] An insufficient metaphysic of sacrifice in the obscurity of Latin manuals or the purely academical splendour of pompous exordia and flamboyant perorations can do no great harm. But when it is taken over into a system of the moral and spiritual life, it can speedily set the poison at work throughout a great Church and separate it from the deep-seated rational desires of mankind. In his all too famous

---

[*] Mgr. l'Archevêque de Rennes, *Lettre pastorale* (10) 1922, Rennes, Vatar, 1922, p. 9.

[†] Lepin, *L'Idée du Sacrifice de la Messe d'après les théologiens depuis l'origine jusqu'à nos jours*, Paris, Beauchesne, 1926, e.g. pp. 471, sq

Eclaircissements sur les Sacrifices, published as an appendix
to *Soirées de Saint Pétersbourg*, Joseph de Maistre propagated
these deadly exaggerations of Gallican pessimism. He must
be corrected by his friend, the Vicomte de Bonald, in his
Théorie du pouvoir politique et religieux or, better still, by the
restorer of the Oratory in the 19th century, P. Gratry, who
in the fourth book of his *Connaissance de l'âme*, sketches
in a highly romantic setting a conception of sacrifice both
thoroughly sound and thoroughly Thomistic.

Joseph de Maistre is responsible along with many others
for the forbidding and truculent attitude which the finest
elements of the French clergy felt it necessary to take up in
face of the admittedly ill-regulated humanism of the 19th
century. The Vicomte de Bonald would have been perhaps
a better guide.

Faguet, who was not a theologian but was well-informed
and clear-minded, wrote as follows:

> Christianity, for de Maistre, confirms and completes that pessimistic
> system of philosophy of his which we have just described, in that it is
> itself *that very system*. . . . This then is his complete philosophy: a pessim-
> ism which finds its term, its resting place and its satisfaction in Christi-
> anity; a belief in evil which finds its confirmation, its explanation and its
> consolation in the Christian Faith. . . . His opponent, de Bonald, is an
> optimist; he sees order and good immanent in the world, sometimes a little
> spoilt, but never intermitted. . . . Christianity is creation. Perhaps there
> have never been two minds which reached the same conclusions along
> such opposite lines. Their intelligences are diametrically opposed. . . .
> "*My thoughts have never been at variance with your writings; my writings
> have never been at variance with your thoughts*," wrote J. de Maistre to the
> Vicomte de Bonald, and the latter added in the margin: "*The claim, so
> flattering to myself, yet admits here and there of some exceptions.*" "It admits
> of so many that it leaves nothing," said Faguet.*

Is it rash to think that these two masters of 19th century
French Traditionalism embodied in their differing theories
of Sacrifice the two tendencies which this great Catholic
century was to see opposing one another in the bosom of our
Church in the form of two competing schools joined in a
lamentable rivalry? The exigencies of a necessary redemption hide from the eyes of one side the original creation,
which was good: they eye nature and what they call "liberty"

* Emile Faguet, *Politiques et Moralistes du XIX siècle*, 1st series, Société
Française d'Imprimerie et de Librairie (1890).

askance in the name of a severe and suspicious religious pessimism. In the eyes of the others Christianity is first and foremost the exploitation of a good creation, and they tend to forget that need of a redemptive activity which applies to present fact. It is permissible to think that a firm Thomist theology would have reconciled these warring tendencies and brought these generous souls into unity, from Cardinal Pie to Mgr. Dupanloup, from Veuillot to Montalembert . . . to mention no more recent names.

CHAPTER THREE: THE TRUE IDEA OF SACRIFICE: A TRANSFER OF PROPERTY

THE Ancients were lucky. Closer to Christian origins, closer also to life itself, they communed with reality with an intellectual passion which we no longer have. Our modern manuals in the attempt to be clear and convenient drain the goodness out of the venerable formulas which rose to the lips of the old Masters packed with the reality of everyday life and glowing with the warmth of intimate experience. These old and ever-living thoughts lie to-day arranged in synoptic tables like dried flowers in museums. We must escape from these lifeless relics in their glass cases, forget these all too neatly written labels, throw away our catalogues, and make our way out of the galleries on to the mountains, to find these same flowers by the torrent-beds, with their sap and colour in them, breathing their scents, face to face with the sun which nurtures them.

S. Augustine belonged to the ancient world. He did not belong like ourselves to a laicized society. He knew what religion means and how rich are its mysteries for souls, whether weary or fervent. He is a man for whom God exists and the inner world of divine love, but also the outer world of living symbolic rites. He knew their meaning and the value of their ceremonies.

c

S. Thomas also belongs to the ancient world. Behind his scholastic Latin lies a passionate overflowing life, charged with the thought of eternity. When we think him distant and distracted he is really absorbed. He is a contemplative first and a scholastic afterwards. We, poor wretches, are always trying to make summaries of him. We should do better to try to hear what he is really saying.

A first glance at the institution of Sacrifice reveals or recalls to these holy Doctors that it is an action. As they put it, there is a *doing* or a *making* in Sacrifice.

> Sacrificia proprie dicuntur quando circa res Deo oblatas aliquid *fit*. . . . Et hoc ipsum nomen sonat: nam Sacrificium dicitur ex hoc quod homo *facit* aliquid sacrum.* . . . *There is a sacrifice properly so-called when something in the oblations (or, about the oblations) happens. . . . The name itself shows it. . . . Sacrifice means : making sacred.*

The last phrase is traditional, coming from S. Isidore of Seville.

If then we pursue to their source these obstinate desires of men in their splendid and costly ceremonies, we shall see clearly enough that sacrifice is a *religious transfer of property* for the greater profit of him who makes the renunciation of his goods. It may be some ordinary profane object taken from the wealth of a tribe or individual. It is to pass into the possession of God or the Gods so that it may become sacred and a means of communion or of obtaining heavenly favours. The meaning of the word has remained true to its etymology, a rare occurrence, throughout the centuries: a sacrifice is an object made sacred: *sacrum factum*. To sacrifice is to *obtain something divine*.

At what price, on what conditions, for what ends? First, at what price? By means of a renunciation by man of his property, a relinquishment carrying with it a privation, the passing of the object, always troublous for man, into God's hands. For living creatures this passage is normally death as the only possible route to God's ownership.

On what conditions? The divine acceptance of the object, for it cannot be forcibly imposed. It must therefore be implored. Here prayer and supplication have their place, and,

* IIa IIae, q. 85, a. 3, ad. 3.

since the result is nearly always invisible, confidence, if not faith, in the granting of the petition.

For what ends? That the object, partly at least restored to man, may be the pledge of heavenly blessings and may thus grant him entrance to communion with the Divinity.

We must be excused for using the simplest words of the human vocabulary just because we are at the very origins of our most ancient institutions, at the source of our most universal experiences. It is a question then of having something divine in order to put it to a use. To have it, if we have it not already, we must make it. To make it we must pay the price, give up a profane object and obtain from God its sanctification by His acceptance of it as His own. At this happy moment the cause is won. Such is the great religious movement, the cycle of decisive and significant actions in which sacrifice is found. *It is a liturgical offering in which we pay the necessary price, and which, once accepted by God, becomes a means of communion with Him.*

And when once this governing principle is established, we may safely shift the emphasis from side to side. If I am a sinner and wish to expiate my sins I shall underline especially my renunciation to the point of making it cruel and distressing. If I desire rather to proclaim God's greatness I shall shower offerings upon Him and shall humiliate myself in bringing them to Him with endless adoration. If I hesitate or feel shame or fear I shall turn all my energies, all my prayers, to obtaining the divine acceptance. If it is God's protection and confidence in this that I chiefly need I shall make careful preparation for my final communion, which will then become a banquet of alliance, a feast of friendship with my heavenly Protector.

In fine, this is the whole of religion, as another Augustinian definition is going to tell us—translated into a living symbol in which our gestures are pregnant with our feelings and in which the victim in its turn bodies forth all the movements of our souls.

But this analysis shows, too, that the contrasts underlined in our elementary manuals, between oblation and immolation, between bloody and unbloody sacrifice, have not the essential importance which we have come to assign to them, as though the true understanding of the mystery sprang merely from their interplay. That understanding smiles at our superficial categories and surpasses them by plunging deeper into mankind's experience.*

Immolation, for example, which we have come to conceive of as a distinct liturgical gesture, with the oblation or victim as its subject, does not take place originally at the point at which we put it nowadays for convenience of exposition. It lies in the man who performs the sacrifice far more than in the slaughtered animal. It is man who makes renunciation of his property and deprives himself of his wealth; the victim, living or otherwise, only changes its master, and it loses nothing by the change, since it passes to God's service. The prisoner of war who is butchered on the altar dies only for him to whom he belongs by right of conquest; he himself goes to the other world to serve a greater master. And when, later, domestic animals are substituted for the vanquished and for slaves, the original pattern is continued: to become the property of God is not a *diminutio capitis;* what is diminished is the flock of the patriarch and therefore the patriarch himself.

But the faithful servant of Jahve does not possess only rams and bulls. He also cultivates his fields and the vine. When he offers the fruit of his harvests in ritual burnings and sacred libations, he is still materially impoverishing himself, although in order to obtain for himself the favour of heaven in good exchange. It is the same movement; the same actions are performed. Blood does not flow, because there are now no arteries or veins to be cut. But the essential

* Have we not lost the precise meaning of the catechism expressions : bloody sacrifice, that of the cross ; unbloody sacrifice, that of the Mass—which we are tempted to make two kinds of sacrifice, the first including an immolation, the second a simple oblation ?—M. Lepin has given much importance to this distinction.

Although the Bible never uses the word *zebah* for unbloody sacrifice, Leviticus does not seem to make much distinction between sacrifices where blood flows and those where it does not. So the Old Testament is not a great authority in favour of the theory of simple oblation without immolation. The Council of Trent, session XXII, cap. i., does not consider bloody and unbloody sacrifice as two species of the same genus, but it opposes them *Sicut repræsentativum repræsentato*, as Billot well says (*De Sacramentis*, vol. 1, 1924 ed., p. 602).

end remains the same. It is no fresh institution obeying new laws or a different psychology. So we find in Leviticus (i–vii) following immediately upon one another without distinction and under the same rubrics the rites which we have separated too sharply in the interests of our superficial theology into the two categories of bloody and unbloody, and in which we find—unjustifiably—the respective types of immolation and oblation.

In the most ancient and elementary religions, therefore, what was really immolated was, in men's minds, not the victim but the offerer. He, recognizing his wrong-doing or his obligations to the Divinity, deprived himself of some of his personal wealth in favour of the latter; he relinquished his claim to a creature which he feared to retain as a superfluity, or he punished himself for having been too much attached to it and made a violent renunciation of it into the hands of the offended God. In that sense he immolated himself. The victim entered through death into the possession of the Divinity, and thus was neither destroyed nor annihilated. Far from having its being diminished, was it not rather magnified and exalted in these men's vague belief? Joseph de Maistre (*Eclaircissements sur les Sacrifices*, chap. II), in order to lessen the horror of human sacrifices, thought that originally the victims were criminals publicly condemned. That is a confusion. It would be too great an honour to the criminals to choose them as victims, and an injury to the Gods. Prisoners of war, by all means !—they are prizes, and will therefore be shared with the protecting deities, who will receive the firstfruits of the prey now that they have shown themselves the warrior's helpers.

Undoubtedly immolation and oblation, considered in the man who performs them in sacrifice, are only a single religious movement, the same essential undertaking. For to give my property I must renounce it. It is the obverse and reverse of a single action. In depriving myself I immolate and to some extent immolate myself. In giving to God I offer and indeed offer myself, since these riches which I have relinquished were the extension of my personality, of my

enjoyment of ownership. Let us say simply that these riches
are immolated in so far as they leave me, and offered in so
far as they reach God.

Later a more searching religious analysis will show in the
light of Biblical and Christian Revelation that there is between these two aspects of a single sacrificial act, the negative
and the positive, all the distance which separates the state
of sin from the state of innocence. In God's original design,
as also in the fulfilment of our destiny, immolation, conceived of as the return of creation to God, is reabsorbed,
absorbs itself, in the offering, which at present it must be
content to prepare for (in making it possible) or to follow up
(in making it effective). In our present psychology, as in
our financial accounts, it is opposed to oblation, because
to-day it is a means for which we have to pay a heavy price,
whereas the divine acceptance is the end in view, a source of
profit. But in good metaphysics, as also in the Gospel
promises, *to abandon ourselves to God is to find our true selves,
and to lose ourselves in Him, to save ourselves*. It is because of
sin that death now precedes and conditions life, and that
without shedding of blood there is no remission. But, *in the
beginning it was not so*.

In view of these final coincidences, we must not give too
high an importance in our descriptions of sacrificial ceremonies to the difference between rites of oblation and rites
of immolation. Custom may invert these symbols and sometimes identify them in a simple gesture. The history of
liturgies is in fact full of such things. One rite can absorb
another without thereby destroying it. There are many
sacrifices, among which the holocaust is the most famous, in
which the final communion, the return (that is) of the now
consecrated victim to its original owner, seems entirely suppressed, because it takes place in the invisibility of faith: it
is, if you will, purely spiritual, or rather considered as enclosed within the sensible rites which come before it. Conversely, there are sacrifices which give the impression of
being reduced to a sacred meal, to the final communion
which this time has drawn to itself and swallowed up all the

previous rites. The camel eaten by the Bedouins of the desert of whom S. Nilus speaks would be an example. Yet these are all true sacrifices in which the caprice of custom has brought in variations which will not fit the bed of Procrustes provided for them by the Manuals.

After these instructive digressions we must turn back to the essential idea of this analysis. To make a sacrifice is to make an object sacred, to renounce some part of our property for this purpose, to offer it to God and to ask Him, in taking it for Himself, to divinize it; by means of this object, the value, meaning and (above all) ownership of which are henceforth new, we shall communicate with the Divinity. Sacrifice is thus *something to be done*, *a making sacred*. It is an object as much as a gesture, for it is *material upon which liturgical gestures are directed so as to change the nature of it*. Let us note this formula carefully; with certain additions it would already cover the Catholic definition of the Eucharist and the Mass.*

Modern languages then have made too great a distinction between sacrifice and victim. The sacrifice is nothing without the victim, or rather the two are blended. In any case in New Testament Greek the word which we have translated sometimes by *hostia* (Luke ii, 24), sometimes by *sacrificium*,

---

* There is no doubt that for S. Augustine sacrifice is a thing rather than an action or more precisely a thing to which an action is being or has been directed. See in the *Civ. Dei* (X. 6) the commentary on the famous definition which we shall be discussing: *Omne opus quod agitur*, etc. . .

"Although sacrifice is done or offered by man, it is nevertheless a divine thing (*res*): the old Romans called it so. Thus a man consecrated to God and vowed to his service is a sacrifice in so far as he dies to the world in order to live to God. And this applies also to the pity a man has on himself. That is why it is written: *have pity on your soul so as to please God*. Our body itself, when we mortify it by temperance, if we do it (as we ought) for God, so as not to deliver our members to sin as instruments of iniquity but to God as instruments of justice—our body is a sacrifice. If then our body, which the soul uses as a servant or an instrument is a sacrifice, when it is turned to God by a proper and legitimate employment, how much more is the soul when it is turned to God so that, inflamed by His love, it may be stripped of the concupiscence of this world, reform itself upon its incomparable model and please Him by the beauty which He has given it? . . ."

Cf. also S. Augustine, *Sermo de Sacramentis in die Paschæ* (*Sermo III ad infantes*, Migne, XLVI, 827–8; or Ed. Dom Morin, Rome, Typog. Vatic. 1930, pp. 18–20): non nunc ovis aut hircus divinis altaribus admovetur, sed sacrificium jam nostri temporis corpus et sanguis est ipsius sacerdotis: *Our sacrifice to-day is the body and blood of our Priest Himself*. So too the Fourth Council of the Laternan (1215): in qua (Ecclesia) idem ipse sacerdos est *sacrificium Jesus-Christus*, cujus corpus et sanguis in sacramento, etc. . . . (Denz.-B., 430).

refers rather to a thing, an object offered, than to the gesture of offering or immolation. When we speak of making a sacrifice we mean making an object sacred and not only performing a religious gesture or merely executing a ceremony.

How can we fail to notice that in the Epistles of S. Paul and S. John the words ἱλασμός (I John, ii, 2; iv, 10), ἱλαστήριον (Rom., iii, 25), προσφορά and even θυσία (Eph., v, 2), are applied not to the death of Jesus nor to His oblation nor to His immolation but to Jesus Himself ? Thus to renew the sacrifice of Christ is less to immolate Christ again than to employ the sacramental means to possess the immolated Christ as the object of our sacrifice.* But we must find the metaphysics hidden behind this psychology of sacrifice. We must also follow in more detail the secret links which bind these successive movements together, and discover beneath the welter of the numberless liturgies in the history of religions the course of the great highway which Christianity will follow to its final goal.

* I owe the following note to the kindness and competence of M. Lepin: "There is no doubt that the word which we translate 'sacrifice' means in Hebrew as in Greek 'the thing sacrificed' as much as the ' sacrificial action'.

The text which you quote, Ephes., v, 2, refers to Exod., xxxix, 18, only for the subsidiary ideas in the final words in odorem suavitatis ; these ideas occur in the same way in many other passages.

The chief part of the text προσφορὰν καὶ θυσίαν refers to Ps. xxxix (Hebr. xl), 7 : Θυσίαν καὶ προσφορὰν οὐκ ἠθέλησας quoted in Heb., x, 5.

The Hebrew terms corresponding to θυσία and προσφορά are respectively zebah, generally translated 'sacrifice', and minehah, regularly translated 'oblation', the first designating bloody sacrifice, the second unbloody.

Zebah (θυσία, sacrificium) comes from the root zabah, 'to immolate'. It means 'immolation', or 'sacrifice', or 'immolated flesh' or 'victim of sacrifice'. Eg. Ezech., xxxix, 17 : Concurrite ad victimam meam (Gk. ἐπὶ τὴν θυσίαν μόυ; Hebr.: 'al Zibehi i.e. zabah. Cf. 1 Cor., x, 18).

Minehah (προσφορά, Oblatio) comes from the root manah, 'to give as a present', and means 'present', 'gift', not precisely 'the action of giving' but 'the thing offered as a present' (L'Idée du Sacrifice, pp. 676–677).

This being understood, it must be noticed that in Hebrew as in Greek and Latin the act of offering sacrifice is expressed by a general term hiqrib, which exactly corresponds to προσφέρω and offero.

If then it is true that in the New Testament as in the Old προσφορά and θυσία are used to refer to the victim, it is no less true that there is always an active verb to express precisely the offering of this victim. It is not the victim but the offering of the victim which makes the act of sacrifice strictly so called. In the N.T. we find προσφέρειν (Act., vii, 42 ; Heb., v, 1 ; viii, 3 ; x, 12), or ἀναφέρειν (Heb., vii, 27) or again ἀνάγειν (Act., vii, 41). The last two verbs have the idea of ascending movement, of elevation."

CHAPTER FOUR: THE TRUE IDEA
(continued): THE RETURN TO GOD

THIS profound reality, the substance of sacrifice, seen in its eternal bearings, in the conditions true for every state, that of nature and that of supernature, that of sin and that of innocence, is the final meeting of the creature with the Creator, the return of the creature to Him who has made it for Himself so that it may find its end and therefore its happiness in Him and for His glory:

> Verum sacrificium est omne opus quod agitur, ut sancta societate inhæreamus Deo, relatum scilicet ad illum finem boni, quo veraciter beati esse possumus.*

Sacrifice is the movement or action by which we try to bring ourselves to God, our end, to find our true beatitude in our union with Him. *To sacrifice a thing is to lead it to its end.*

Creation is a vast divine undertaking unfolded in time. Time itself is only one of the many aspects of our contingent state. The fact that we do not hold all our being at once and cannot realize ourselves in an instant, the necessity upon us to wait for what is to come, to win our way to ourselves by conquering ourselves, the obligation to be in movement to our final cause and to possess ourselves only in hope in our life on earth, all this is a poem, a tragedy, a journey, and, since we are speaking of the life of religion, better still a pilgrimage.

Sacrifice is essentially the decisive effort and imploring prayer which is imposed on us if we would reach our end; it is the attitude of adhesion to God by which we deliberately ratify our destiny; above all it is the attainment of the goal, when the creature makes the final act of casting itself into the Creator's arms, losing itself there in a complete abandonment.

Do you remember those wooden hoops which we used to throw ahead as children in the Luxembourg or in our own

---

* S. Augustine, *De Civ. Dei*, bk. X, cap. 6. S. Thomas takes over the definition IIIª p., q. 48, a. 3; and in IIIª p., q. 22, a. 2, with the precious variant: *Omne illud quod Deo exhibetur; ad hoc quod spiritus hominis feratur in Deum.* The same doctrine is found in the *Summa Contra Gentiles*, bk. III, cap. 120 (med.).

gardens with a twist of the hand which brought them obediently back to our feet after a few yards' run? It seems that
the whole Creation, cast by the Lord with a great sweep into
space, as the Bible describes it, as Michael Angelo painted
it, is controlled by an inner law to flow back towards its
Creator, and the world of bodies, spirits and souls is a vast
cycle of coming and going, in which God has His glory, and
creatures their happiness in Him, the happiness of returning
to His embrace: "The whole constitution of human life, its
supreme law and universal end, is that we who have come
from God should one day return to him."*

The casual reader who takes de la Taille to mean that
sacrifice consists in an offering, understanding the word in
the narrowest sense, at once removes all the strength and
stability from this splendid metaphysic of reunion with the
final end. Certainly offering something to God is directing
it to its final end, but assurance is needed that God accepts
and receives it, for otherwise it will be an empty gesture:
telum imbelle sine ictu. And then we must avoid at all costs
thinking about children offering flowers to their mothers on
feast-days, for such actions, however charming, are feeble
compared with the vision of the creature as it gains its goal.
We must think rather of the impact of an arrow shot from a
mighty bow at the moment when it quivers in the mark.
Sacrifice is an offering, yes, but only in its preparation and
its drive towards the goal. Its drive is not its end. It goes to
it, leads to it. "Omne sacrificium est oblatio, sed non convertitur," says S. Thomas, IIa, IIae, q. 85, a. 2.

The confusion between offering and union with God is the
more disastrous in that the Jewish and Christian liturgies
accept the word offertory in the sense of a preliminary action,
previous to the actual immolation and designed to pave the
way for it. This initial presenting must not be confused with
the final encounter, the supreme *tête-a-tête* with God, the

---

* Leo XIII, Encyclical *Tametsi Futura*, Nov. 1, 1900, on Jesus Christ the
Redeemer. This form of expression and the doctrine which it enshrines are
classical in the tradition long before Scholasticism. They appear in the Greek
Fathers. Cf. G. Horn, Amour divin (Eros) dans saint Grégoire de Nysse, in
Revue d'Ascétique et de Mystique, Oct., 1925, p. 381.

direct confronting of the approved, accepted, sanctified victim, which follows the immolation and is consummated in communion, unforgettably described in the vision of the Epistle to the Hebrews of the "entering" of Christ: *introivit semel in sancta.*

In meeting its God, the creature countersigns and ratifies its own being and its own true worth. It declares itself as God had wished it and framed it to be. It finds at this supreme point all that God had placed in it from the beginning, neither more nor less; and in achieving its course and being reunited to its principle it exhausts all its internal powers, which pass completely into act. It adds nothing to its nature, but it realizes it to the full; the two extremes touch or rather interlock, both the great creative act which has given us existence and the noble sacrificial act of the creature which, recognizing itself, submits to God's will and finds its whole self in Him.

This achievement creates nothing which God has not first created. Man recovers nothing in the consummation of his sacrifice which God had not placed in him when He cast him forth into existence. But it is indeed enough that man (and through man all things in the world) should be able to ratify God's work, although nothing can be gained in the end save His will and their true natures.

Yet, thanks to sacrifice, man plays a part in the issue of his own destiny. He becomes God's collaborator in the work of his salvation. And, if he adds nothing to creation, he establishes it by a deliberate act in the order proper to it, an order achieved according to divine decree. That is why sacrifice is an action, accomplished through the creature's effort, making its own drive to its end under the almighty act of God.

Thus there is an essential dynamism in the movement shown in sacrifice. Man puts to it his inmost power and in it he carries himself onward. In the measure in which his free consent is necessary to the realization of God's designs upon the world, within the limits in which he can increase the glory of the one and only Master, he offers the concurrence of his will to the accomplishment of these high purposes. We need not pronounce upon the Thomist and Molinist conceptions of human action to say that sacrifice is this action in its full deployment; it mingles with God's work whatever man can so mingle, and it has power and value, the power of life and the value of existence; it represents, if you like, the accord of created wills with the sovereign will, and we are entitled to think that this adhesion has its worth in the eyes of Him who could dispense with our values and our collaboration, but who at this time lays claim to them from His free creatures.

But this effort of adoration does not succeed unless God accepts it; and in this sense it is God who brings to its conclusion the great movement roused in earth and heaven by sacrifice at the moment when it is received by Him. This religion of man, this love and this submission, do not obtain their end, do not find their realization unless the Lord ratifies them by His acceptance. The analysis of the idea of sacrifice ends then in the language of union and encounter, of a social compact, at the moment when God and man unite in the great embrace in which God's child falls into his Father's arms and finds there his true self: *ut sancta societate inhæreamus Deo*.

The liturgy in its external and symbolic side has as its essential plan the representation and, so far as human means allow, the realization of that encounter. The oblation, the victim or host, is the being chosen by us to make the course in our name, going before us to represent, herald and substitute for us. As such it reaches God and, once accepted, finds rest in Him.

Unfortunately men have had such insufficient and fragmentary ideas of God in the course of ages that this symbolic gesture of union has been too often performed in conditions which shock our Christian feelings and the religious refinement which we owe to the Gospel's purifying influence. God has been conceived as jealous, carnal and influenced by passions, but always men have thought it their duty to make offerings to Him, and to present wrapped in them the clan, the family and the entire tribe. According as peoples have seen in the Divinity a powerful ally for whom a part of the prey must be reserved, or a sort of super-adversary against whom precautions must be taken, or a sort of Absolute into which after the necessary purifying we must be absorbed, so sacrifice has adopted differing styles in extravagant and (it might seem) contradictory rituals. The day after victory the God of Hosts has been offered the tithe of the booty as if one could give His due to the Creator. Men have wished to appease His anger. They have thought to satisfy His jealousy by a lavish share of goods as if won by common effort. They have recompensed Him as a collaborator in partnership or business association. They have thought that after filling and satiating Him with spoils they could better enjoy the remainder of the plunder while He was engaged in glutting Himself with the first-fruits. . . .

But why need we be troubled with the horrible abuse of a thought which after all is legitimate? Thanks to Jesus of Nazareth the thought will end by mastering and illumining. Sacrifice will become more and more the symbol of complete surrender. This, too, humanity has glimpsed. An official ceremony ritually accomplished at set times by men forced to spend the rest of their lives upon their inevitable material needs is a declaration that they would indeed think always of their God; but, having neither the power nor the purity necessary for this, they would at least acquit themselves from time to time of their essential duty in a great and solemn act by means of a symbolic liturgy. Formalism seized straightway upon this rite, making it mechanical; men thought to satisfy God's exigencies at little cost by empty gestures. Again why need we be troubled?—since the deep-seated direction of this desire was originally right and, by and large, showed the true path, the road of Justice, the way to the End. This road is also that of adoration. On this essential point S. Thomas's analysis is decisive. In authentic Thomism the good of God and of man coincide: in the end, at the point at which creation reaches its goal and achieves success, there is no opposition (I had almost written, no difference) between the theocentric and the anthropocentric.

But instead of that last word it would be better to write "humanism", for man is not the centre of anything. All things find their term in God. So says the *Summa Theologica* in forceful, clear-cut Latin which is at once weakened by translation:

> Per sacrificia repræsentabatur ordinatio mentis in Deum. Ad rectam autem ordinationem mentis in Deum pertinet quod omnia quæ homo habet, recognoscat a Deo tanquam a primo principio, et ordinet in Deum tanquam in ultimum finem. . . . Et ideo in oblatione sacrificiorum protestabatur homo quod Deus esset primum principium creationis rerum, et ultimum finis ad quem essent omnia referenda. . . . Pertinet ad rectam ordinationem mentis in Deum, ut mens humana non recognoscat alium primum auctorem rerum nisi solum Deum, neque in aliquo alio finem suum constituat. (Ia IIae, q. 102, a. 3.)

> Sacrifice puts before our eyes the directing of the mind to God. . . . For the proper directing of the mind to God man must recognize that the goods which he possesses come to him from God as first principle, and he must relate them to God as the last end. . . . And that is why man in offering sacrifices avowed that God was the first principle of the world's creation and the last end to whom all must be related. . . . For the intelligence to be properly related to God, it must recognize no other original author but God and place its last end in Him alone.

The moral law which governs our human actions, pushed to the point of encounter with God and to the religious recognition of the Creator's rights, is fulfilled in a complete adoration which wins us perfect happiness. But during sacrifice all man's effort bears upon the creature, and in particular on that victim creature which is the *sign* and symbol of our personal religion. For we have no leverage over God. *Pure act without mixture of potency*, He has no need of our action upon Him; it is in fact altogether impossible. It is on ourselves that we act when we adore God; because to adore Him is to relate ourselves to Him. It is to tell Him that He is the last end of the universe. And at once in adoring God faithfully, that is in reality, we bring about in ourselves the realization of our own end. To *tell* God efficaciously that He is our end, that is to adore him as God, is to *do* our duty in achieving our destiny and to obey our moral law.

We must recognize that in the history of religions and liturgies sacrifice appears rather as a ritual ceremony and a gesture of adoration than as an act of the moral life. But this opposition is superficial, at least in the religion *in spirit and in truth*.

The word *communion*, which also belongs to this analysis of the idea of a return to God and union with Him, and which has so important a place in the theology of sacrifice, is used in two different and cognate senses. It may signify the actual encounter of the victim or oblation with God at the hour when He receives men's sacrifices. At this moment the accepted victim is at once united to God, and this is *the communion of the victim with God*, who accepts it, sanctifies it and in some sort, by making it His own, makes it divine. It may, then, if God and the form of the rite allow, be given back to men as the pledge or incarnation of the divine favours with which it is henceforth fully charged; and men, receiving it in their turn, usually by consuming it, will also be united to their Creator: it is now *the communion of man with the victim* and, by it, with God.

The French School has splendidly exploited the first sense, applying it to the Resurrection and Ascension of Jesus, when the Father, receiving the Incarnate Son at His right hand, "in His bosom", communicates to Him "His divine splendour and glory", and so enters "into communion with His Son as victim". (Lepin, *L'Idée du Sacrifice de la Messe*, 1926, p. 472.) The Epistle to the Hebrews not only suggests but demands this doctrine absolutely.

But ordinary Christian language has looked rather to the second sense of the word, applying it above all to eucharistic communion. Thus it is said that the Sacrifice of Calvary did not carry with it communion, that this is reserved for the Mass-Sacrifice. But we may regret this hasty mode of speech, which leaves the resplendent aspect of the Christian Paschal Mystery, Christ's entry in Heaven, too much in the shade.

The ancient Hebrew word *Alliance*, translated *Testament* in the Vulgate's Latin, combined these two senses. In the great Jewish sacrifices, there were successively the communion of the victim with God when the High Priest entered the Holy of Holies with the blood of bulls and goats, and the communion of Israel with God, by the sprinkling of this blood upon the people by the High Priest at the entrance: *ut sancta societate inhæreamus Deo*.

CHAPTER FIVE: THE TRUE IDEA (continued): THE RETURN IN TWO STAGES

THUS the interior religion, which the external rite figures symbolically in visible forms and engenders invisibly in the soul, consists in the complete offering of the creature returning to God as his end by a deliberate movement. Humanity in this sacred hour abandons itself to Him who alone can assure its perfect happiness and guarantee it against all illusions; *quasi suæ creationis principio, quasi suæ operationis auctori, quasi suæ beatitudinis fini*.* To achieve the conquest of its being and its destiny it casts itself upon Him who, by filling it completely, gives it the power to be its real self. At once and in a single movement it recognizes all the rights of God and bows before His transcendence: it adores and prays. And at the moment when these two beings meet and embrace, God's glory and love are satisfied and also man's restlessness and insufficiency.

In fine, sacrifice is the entire movement of our created nature. This makes us personified tendencies, subsisting relations to God; it demands our attainment of Him like the flight of the arrow to the mark.† Sacrifice consists in translating the direction of this living shaft into appropriate symbolic gestures and in giving impetus to the inward drive by the very expression of it in outward form. It is oblation in act, the creature giving itself and reaching God in a great impact in which our deepest needs are satisfied.

* S. Thomas, *Summa contra Gentiles*, lib. III, cap. 120.

† One of the great stumbling-blocks of Thomist metaphysics in the eyes of its opponents is its attribution of a special *entity* to relations. This shocks in proportion to the amount of nominalist and Cartesian prejudice one brings to metaphysics ; on the other hand as one's conception of reality becomes more spiritual and less spatial, one is less disinclined to admit that *order* can be a reality of a kind which is not *identical* with the ordered things. (P. Rousselot, *Métaphysique thomiste et Critique de la connaissance*, in *Revue Néo-Scolastique*, Nov., 1910).

[S. Thomas holds that the substance of creatures is not the same as their relation of creatures to God, as against the Scotists and others.—Tr.]

Man may give the impression of offering only his material riches, but by their mediation he is really offering himself. We might say that his goods do the journey in advance and that he sends them on embassy to the God whom he is himself to meet. The oblation is the symbolic image of the soul's complete surrender: *in manus tuas commendo spiritum meum.* Thus there is nothing to be surprised at if the victim so offered to God and accepted by Him becomes something wholly divine, and can then act as a sacrament, travelling back over its course, and bringing us by communion the pledge of heavenly blessing and protection.

But meantime our interior life of religion is that of a being in full movement, whose metaphysical parabola is not yet achieved because it has not yet attained the aim envisaged. And this drive, when we analyse it into its component concepts, falls into two stages or, if you will, two elementary and complementary movements, destined to fuse in the end, but logically distinguishable. On the one hand we tend toward our end and with the help of God we shall reach it; and this side of our mystery is the cause of our happiness, the source of a burning exultation, the fullness of which is translated by positive terms such as life and joy. On the other hand, we have not yet arrived, and we have not the right to stop on our way nor to tie ourselves to our present state which, without being bad (how could the road to God be bad?) is yet not perfect good.

There is the same complication when instead of considering the subjective side, our own activity, we consider the external object which for the moment absorbs us in delight. This object, in so far as it is a being and a means to attain to God, is an instrument for our happiness, and we must cling to it as a stage which heralds the final goal. But, in so far as it is a particular being and a halt on our way, to tie ourselves to it as if it were the last end would be the very rejection of that end, which alone can really satisfy us. Thus the object is also an obstacle or at least a danger.

This provisional opposition between means and end would not exist for a being which was completely achieved

D

and in full possession of its true self. It does not exist for
God, because He sees all beings in their tendencies and their
relations to Himself. He sees them all in movement and in
movement to Him; they serve as pure exaltation of His
glory: *benedicite, omnia opera Domini, Domino.*

But in us a conflict between resting-place and journeying
is always possible. When we stop on the road which leads to
God we always risk not reaching Him. Man, by coming to a
stop through weariness, boredom or pride, can create a fac-
titious opposition between the place where he now is and
that to which he goes, holding himself back for the joys
which he actually experiences, the first-fruits only of final
happiness.

To be safe from this danger we should need to have
finished our journey, to have seen God and all else in God,
to have given up abstractions for intuitive vision, freedom of
choice for perfect possession. And we are still travelling.
Cessation of movement is never impossible for a free
creature whose property is precisely not to reach the end
with a single bound but to have the power to pick and
choose. The abstractive power which is our definition allows
us to consider the particular good in isolation, and makes us
realise that to carry it onwards to God—itself and ourselves
with it—means recognizing that this object and the attachment which we feel for it are only partial joys. Thus in the
gift of ourselves to God abstraction brings into play a provisional though real renouncement.

And so, to repeat, in rational creatures, capable of
analysing and distinguishing and in free creatures,
capable of choice and preference, this duality is essential to their natures so long as they have not attained their
end.

We now realize that there are two sides to our religion
It is a fulfilment and an end, because in it we meet God: but
it demands detachment and effort, because we must always
be passing beyond ourselves and beyond the whole created
order.

Thus the gesture of sacrifice, even without mentioning

sin, may be broken into two elementary movements corresponding to the complexity of our nature. Man gives himself to God, the Perfect Good, and that is the positive and peaceful aspect of prayer, like the final result of sacrifice itself. But man is still journeying. To attain his end, he must be continually leaving the place where he had halted, giving up his state of rest, passing on beyond the ground already won, the provisional, temporary goal.

Undoubtedly this is no final renunciation. The direction of man's onward drive reveals his goal. The object which he offers and seems to be abandoning is itself going to its end in God. To return it to the Creator for whom it was made is not to lose it nor in the end to renounce it. It is to save it and ourselves along with it.

But abstraction can differentiate between these points of view; and our nature, defined by this power of abstraction, will suffer from the apparent conflict if its generosity is not proportionate to its undertaking, if it meets disaster by an exclusive choice where it had only to distinguish. We shall soon see that sin makes this possibility an actual fact.

Meantime S. Thomas is more than justified in saying that sacrifice so understood, reduced to its essential *schema*, is really an institution of the natural law. A creature cannot but adopt this fundamental attitude in regard to its Creator. In the absence of all supernatural religion, positive or revealed, under the law of grace or in the state of innocence, man would have had to perform this sacrificial gesture, which, in principle, is not a consequence of sin. It is simply humanism, humanism face to face with God.*

But we can also picture a more perfect state in which man,

---

* The thesis which connects sacrifice with the natural law is enough to separate Thomism from Jansenism for ever, in spite of verbal similarities which deceived Pascal. At Port Royal religion seems to be connected with sin at its very origin ; it is certainly practised in the framework of sin. But for the Scholastics, the Oratory and Saint-Sulpice, it begins at the creation and, like sacrifice itself, is previous to sin. For this central thesis see IIa IIae, q. 85, a. 1.—Cf. Bremond, *Ecole française*, pp. 359, sq.: "The teaching of de Condren rests on the fact of creation not, like the teaching of Port Royal, on the dogma of the Fall."

raised in advance by God to the furthest limits of his completed nature and perhaps beyond them, has already crossed
the intermediate stages which separate him from his end.
At this extreme, sacrifice would be completely unified; far
from seeming an abdication and a renunciation, even provisional, it would be only the joyful and glorious ratifying of
a conquest already won.

Then we should realize how sacrifice, far from being a
grievous waste, is in reality the best guarantee against suffering in this rigorously simple metaphysic. Suffering arises in
soul or body when there is a discrepancy between our desire
and the means to it, between our future end and our present
state. Now the completion of the sacrifice would bring us
with a bound to the limit of our essential tendencies. It
would jump the stages: it would swallow up distances and
delays, it would appease and satisfy our inmost longings, it
would solve the great problem of our spiritual life. In our
present state of sin we cannot picture this total coincidence
of means and end; but we have still the right to build the
theory of it. And we have even the duty to do so if we would
understand sacrifice as it is to-day; it is the wreckage of an older
religious *schema*, in which it finds its full explanation, just as
the remains in the Forum or at Pompeii are unintelligible to
us unless we call up the image of those lost monuments to
which they once belonged. Christ gives us a marvellously
delicate hint of this idea when he speaks of the mother who
no longer remembers her sufferings after child-birth, because the end has been attained, because a man is born into
the world, because she has a son (John xvi, 21). Let us suppose (a vanished dream) that we could join together *in
momento, in ictu oculi* the struggle and its issue, means and
end; the grief, which is the tension between that which is
and that which ought to be, would exist no longer. To-day,
when we have brought some undertaking to successful issue,
we try to forget the labour which it has cost us, like the
mother in the Gospel, and sometimes we achieve it; we are
even happy to have suffered! But we can imagine a state in
which we should be happy to suffer, or rather simply to act,

because the action, telescoped with its result, would not have been suffering at all.*

The existence of this limitation shows us also that the two aspects of sacrifice, as our analysis has revealed them to us, are not of equal value. Only the final stage is of true obligation and desired for its own sake. A previous renunciation is a means and its application can be left to circumstances or even to free choice. We must all reach God, but our ways of doing so can be different; we shall not all have to go through the same preliminary movements.

When the author of Genesis describes the first man's state and the conditions of obedience imposed on him, he makes Adam's happiness depend upon the observance of a positive commandment. This is a lesson to be borne in mind. Religion, as man's act, carries with it a certain freedom in the use of means; this element of hazard represents the creature's collaboration in the successful issue of creation, and underlines the relative and changeable character of our existence. In a supernatural religion like that of Eden, an intervention on God's part fixes the course which must be followed. But in principle it could have been different, replaced by other ordinances, and, on man's part, by other offerings.

Thus, thanks to this singular power of abstraction which enables us to scheme new worlds and bring back to mind

---

* This is not the state which the theologians call that of nature or of pure nature in which man would have lived on earth had he not been raised to the supernatural order, a state which would have involved struggle and so provisional suffering. Nor is it the supernatural state of innocence, to which the first man was originally raised (and from which for the moment we abstract so as not to complicate analysis). It is the natural state carried to its complete fulfilment, when, with all the possible results accomplished, the rigid laws which had to be obeyed for their success are seen the better in the light of it. We can gain a distant and also an enhanced picture of it by considering how far grace transfigures suffering in the saints who are almost at the term of their supernatural development. It seems that in them grief has changed its meaning and becomes joy : *desiderio desideravi*, said the Master ; and His disciples : . . . *mori lucrum* . . . *pati pro te*. Do they not see grief and its fruits as part of a single scheme, and the two aspects, positive and negative, on the same level?   Cf. Ozanam, speaking of S. Francis of Assisi, in *Poètes Franciscains en Italie*, 6th ed., Lecoffre, 1882, p. 72 : " One thing alone fetters human liberty, and that is fear ; and since all fear reduces to the fear of suffering, nothing now hinders him who has made a joy and a glory out of suffering, freed from all bondage and all trivial preoccupations. Francis lived in the contemplation of the eternal ideas, in the habit of devotion which raises every faculty of man, in a familiar commerce with the whole creation. . . ."

the Earthly Paradise, that vision of the ideal sacrifice is revealed to us which we need in order to explain and justify our own. Our essential and fundamental attitude in regard to God can be broken into two movements, the first expressing drive and effort and even a renunciation, provisional, apparent only, but at present keenly felt—the second an apotheosis, a magnificent conclusion, the satisfying of all our legitimate desires. The first movement must be renunciation to show thereby that we would not make our prey an object which is good but not the perfect good. But this negation has as its other side a positive gesture, an adhesion to Being, in which we realize our end by yielding ourselves wholly to Him who grants us by meeting and embracing Him to be in Him our own true selves. To recognize the rights of God, to make an apparent renunciation of ourselves, is to attain our end and to achieve ourselves. Between the two sides of this mystery, the obverse and the reverse, let us leave the thickness of a little finger, a narrow line seen by the power of abstraction, to leave space for human liberty and give it room to choose its destiny.

CHAPTER SIX: THE GREATEST
SACRIFICE (the result of sin)

THIS discrepancy has made sin possible. The first man should have seen in the sacrifice claimed by God, a sacrifice of praise and adoration, an avowal of his own condition as a creature, mentally distinguishable from the blessedness, the metaphysical completion, which this avowal would have won for him—but he clung to a partial good separated from the total one and substituted for it; straightway he tried in effect to deny his God. A free creature, intoxicated by his own beauty, he did not see fit to offer the homage of reasonable and sane humility to which his own nature prompted

him; he thought to find a contradiction between God's glory
and his happiness.

From this moment sin exacerbated an opposition which
was originally apparent only, turning it into real conflict. It
changed an abstract distinction into a concrete fracture.
Sacrifice becomes more than ever necessary, because it now
represents not only the rights of God but the only chance
offered to humanity henceforth to regain its vanished
happiness. But it will be as it were broken into two pieces,
and we shall feel keenly their painful separation. In the end
it will always be the great impact of encounter with God, the
apotheosis of our whole trembling nature throwing itself
upon Him who satisfies and satiates it. For sin has not
created the essential metaphysic of sacrifice with its two
sides, positive and negative, which we have already seen.
But it has produced a formidable development of the first
phase, that of apparent abdication. It has transformed it into
a genuine, though still provisional, abdication, and we have
now to justify its importance and to prove it necessary. Our
collaboration in the great work of our destiny will now be the
occasion of keen suffering, willingly accepted and even welcomed. Whence comes this great change, this scandal of
suffering and death?

To fathom that dark abyss it will be best to go down to its
depths in successive stages.

The particular goods which were given to us as means to
lead us to God have taken advantage of us and bewitched us
These creatures have attached us to themselves, not in so far
as good, as the work of God, but as creatures and as partial
goods. Instead of supporting ourselves upon them and passing beyond them to our end, we must now begin by breaking
with them, putting ourselves straight, and only when this
wrench has taken place can we make headway. This is the
medicinal aspect of sacrifice in its beginnings, salutary but
already grievous. The poets of human emotion have even
dared to hymn this bitter remedy which fortifies and
ennobles us, closing our deep-seated wounds and
giving us spiritual health. Musset has taken up this

great theme, at once biblical, stoic and romantic, in immortal lines:

> *Les moissons pour mûrir ont besoin de rosée. . . .*
> *Et nul ne se connaît tant qu'il n'a pas suffert. . . .* *

Naturally, for we must reclaim ourselves to know ourselves. *Melior est conditio possidentis*, says the world's wisdom. And, since sin, it is partial and created good as such that possesses us; against all justice it lords it over us. This error—normal and harmless in the brutes—may be considered a habit inveterate in our flesh which sin has brought us. This is philosophically a hypothesis, and theologically a thesis, which has nothing absurd about it, and, as we have just shown, nothing in it which is opposed to humanism. In any case such is our starting-place in the moral life, our first condition. The act of sacrifice must therefore start by breaking free from these undue and loathsome bonds. These attachments which it pains us to cast off are graven as it were on our psychology; our first instinct is always to fasten ourselves upon a creature as to our last end, as if no higher riches could be gained through it and beyond it, as if we were condemned to nothing better than these unripe fruits. The shattering thing is that we are delighted with them, proud of this metaphysic which is proper only to the beasts.

A bird in the hand, we say, is worth two in the bush. But we must really *have* this thing—this wretched shadow as it proves to be. And we do not really possess being till we relate it to its causes. As the mystics say, "We have in our hearts a void which the whole of creation could not fill. It can be filled only by God, who is our beginning and our end. The possession of God fills this void and makes us happy; the privation of God leaves us in this void and makes us miserable."† Yet it is this *nothing* to which we have obstinately clung.

The renunciation of this void, or rather this insufficiency,

---

* Alfred de Musset.—*Nuit d'Octobre.*
 † The opening words of Lallemant's *Doctrine spirituelle.*

this incompletion, will indeed be at first very bitter for us, for it will break those hidden fibres within us which, though only sin has woven them, are in our hearts and our very flesh.

But this is no reason for shrinking from this surgical operation, which will free us from an unjust bondage and bring us back to life.

We must press this dismal analysis to a further stage. We are now far removed from our end, from which sin has violently torn us. That coincidence of action and its results, in which we had thought to find the essence of our happiness, is now a vanished dream. The means, good in themselves, which God has put at our disposal so that we might reach Him, seem to us only instruments of torture, since they force long trials upon us without visible result; they have changed their meaning for us; and death, the summary of them all, is now a thing of dread. We see well enough what it costs us; we do not see what it brings to us. We see the view this side of that gloomy tunnel; we do not see the fertile plains of eternity which lie beyond it.

Christian dogma adds also that God has substituted for our natural end a supernatural one—and that this is still imposed upon us, a thing at once gratuitous, obligatory and magnificent. Consequently it is always troubling us in secret, ennobling our dreams, like a mysterious and irresistible call from unknown lands which send us their perfumes and beckon to us, but do not send their fruits, while we ourselves have neither oars nor sails to reach them. This is that indefinite enlarging of our essential needs which Lamartine took for the memory of a heaven from which we fell. True, we have never climbed there, but this heaven has come down to us to fill our hunger, the aching void which "diseases" us in the full and literal meaning of the word: *irrequietum cor nostrum*. We have the idea and the desire of a happiness, a knowledge, an immortality, which surpass our human possibilities. Only the supernatural order which could have bestowed them on us at the beginning can restore them now, and this hope stirs us to the depths.

Thus it is that humanity suffers from lack of those good things to which it feels itself destined, from which it realizes itself so far removed; and we see that the separation between means and end becomes still greater. The tragedy is pushed to the maximum intensity, and suffering pierces like a blade through our flesh and above all through our souls, homesick for a blessedness which is greater than anything that they have known, but which now and always summons them. We face the exigencies of *the greatest sacrifice*.

Our original elevation to the supernatural state, an extension of our nature in its height and depth, would have dispensed us from this waiting; we should have possessed our end without really passing through suffering at all. That was God's first dream. But sin by entering into the world has brought with it grief and death, its offspring. They will dog the steps of our religious life and cast a lurid light over our religious actions. Offering our life to God in Eden would have been a prayer, a thing supremely sweet; to-day this encounter is called the world over by the name of death. We must not smile then when the Old Testament tells us that after Adam's fall creation, subject to man before, turned henceforth against him and caused him suffering. Nature's course has changed. But on the other hand the supernatural is still, thank God, a summons and a programme. This encounter with God, in which, as S. Thomas has shown us, sacrifice essentially consists, can take place only in the lofty intimacies of the Trinity. We should never reach it unless God intervened. Buoyed by the hope of this grace, this new, gratuitous, unheard of gift, man must follow his path, the path to the supreme and final *rendez-vous*. But how long this path will be, since it is to lead us to such distant heights! The discrepancy between end and means has immeasurably widened. We can foresee a way of sorrows.

In short, there is disorder in the world. Well then, to accept this disorder and its consequences is already to bow before the order which sacrifice must finally establish for eternity by reuniting us with God. To suffer loyally the illogicalities of injustice is to recognize the logic of the truth.

Willingly to endure the consequences of error is to recognize that it is error; and to recognize it is to take the road of right again already.

Such is the other meaning of sacrificial sorrow; it endures the *penalties* or the chastisement of sin.

Is this enough? Or must we drink deeper of this cup?

Our eyes and lips are scarcely at its brink. We must go further and drain it to the bottom. We must have no fear. The final scene, we know, is radiant. Infinite love invites us to this bitter draught.

So far it has been only a question of going back over a wrong road and starting fair again. We were tied down and we freed ourselves; that is the medicinal side to it. But also we had moved away from the end and we resigned ourselves to the special effort needed for returning in the right direction; that is punishment.

We are men, free and reasonable beings, capable of love and hate. And we have become sinners. Sin is not only a disease and an error; it is also a fault. It is an act of perverse will, and, as such, it causes harm. It impoverishes the kingdom of love. A man who truly loves would try to balance this great loss.

We cannot create being and make God a present of it. But the course of history, the unfolding of being, is both an occasion for God's glory and in God's just order a source of happiness for us. Could we not, without diminishing God's glory, renounce these legitimate joys, to make up somehow for our forbidden pleasures and the harm that they have done God's love? Then in our human relative way we should be telling the Creator that we love him as much as we had failed to love Him in the past.

This strange crisis takes place within ourselves. There is no question of dimming the splendour of creation. But we must express to God with the only means at our disposal our will to please and love Him now at last.

Sacrifice at this stage is the contrary of sin, and, like sin, a violent and twisted attitude, provisional and altogether relative to our own impotence. Sin has tried to wrong justice and God, but without really harming them. Sacrifice tries to limit the splendour of creation without really lessening it. We alone suffer. God will not misunderstand the true meaning of our gesture of destruction. Behind this disorder the grand ordering of love's reparation is concealed. And then God will be satisfied, not to see us suffer, but to see that we would love as much as we have hated, would compensate for our undue love of His creation by renouncing the legitimate pleasure which we take in it for the Creator's will. One negative is cancelling another.

It is provisional only, for it is the work of man and the result of sin. It is also only the first act of the great sacrificial drama which will always end in a positive apotheosis. God will have the final word, and love will triumph.

But meantime we must tell God our sorrow; we, who have loved creatures in His place, now offer to His love the pleasure which they cause us.

Here we touch the very depths of human nature. If suffering is valuable for us, a ransom and redemption, this shows that we are not Gods but sinners. If the history of all great religions is written in that style, if we cannot live in love for long unless we suffer, this proves that we have found the root of all these problems which make us what we are, the very definition of our being.

CHAPTER SEVEN: THE PLACE OF IMMOLATION IN SACRIFICE

FOR all these reasons, bound up together in the framework of a single mystery, sacrifice has acquired a very painful sense for us; and that is why we are tempted to define it in the first place by the immolations which it nowadays requires of us. Our whole mental structure too is built about this new conception ; exercise has become painfull effort ; method has put on the appearance of constraint and discipline; the heirarchy of values seems a mortification, and the complete giving of ourselves to God a sacrifice in the ordinary popular meaning of the word, that is a costly and unpleasant business, since the return to God to-day means death.*

It is true that this grief and this death can still be offered to God in homage; not that He sets store by them for their own sakes, for they have no absolute value in His eyes—but because the good will which we show in submitting to them and in offering them is in His eyes the final proof of our renunciation of the sin which caused them.

This is probably the true sense (and a most realistic one) of that teaching of S. Bernard's which people have some-times tried to use to wrench from Catholicism its vigorous integration of all our humanity, all our humanism, in the mystery of the suffering and dying, the crucified and blood-stained Christ: *non mors, sed voluntas placuit ipsius morientis*. In the context given to it by the uncompromising Cistercian, the doctor and mystic who founded Clairvaux and who made all the Middle Ages weep with a compassionate love, the phrase means simply that the Passion of His Son gave God no pleasure. The Father could rejoice only in the love with which His Son had delivered Himself to death. But that does not mean that the blood shed by Christ was useless, nor that only the dispositions of His soul were profitable for salva-tion.† We must believe and maintain on the other hand that His inner life of religion and the salvation which it won for us were bodied forth in His sufferings and death and found in them the blood and tears without which there is now no true sacrifice on earth. The other view forgets, under pretext of preaching a religion of the spirit, that Christianity

* "Death is . . . something which we take for something else." Léon Bloy, quoted by Pierre Termier, *Léon Bloy*, Paris-Mamers, 1921, p. 22.

† S. Bernard, letter 190 to Innocent II, entitled by the editors *Tractatus de erroribus Abelardi;* see Migne *P.L.*, t. 182, col. 1053, sq. In chapter VIII (Migne, col. 1070) S. Bernard is answering an objection of Abelard's, who was astonished that God should have ransomed the sin of the first man by one still greater, deicide. But, says S. Bernard, it is not the death of Christ which pleased God but the voluntary offering which He made in dying; thus in the first part of this celebrated phrase the death of Christ is considered from the side of the executioners and as such it is obviously horrible in God's eyes. Yet God made use of it, *non delectatus quidem sed tamen bene usus*. But considered from the side of Christ His death is the cause of our salvation. That is the sense of the whole chapter, thus summed up (? by the editors) ; "Why did Christ adopt so painful and toilsome a means of saving us, since His will or commandment alone would have sufficed?"

is also a religion of realism and of truth. Would it not renew Docetic errors in our statement of the Passion? When we suffer and die, we have such great need to think, to know for certain, that Christ too suffered and died, and that this passion served some purpose. And we repeat in our own way the cry of S. Ignatius of Antioch to the men of Tralles; "If Jesus Christ suffered only in appearance why am I in chains? Why do I long to fight the beasts? Is it for nothing that I am to die?"* Our sacrifice is love—or repentance—incarnate.

It breaks the unjust bonds which we ourselves had forged. But God is not the author of the grief which this rupture causes us. We were originally responsible for breaking a line of splendid development, for stopping a magnificent movement which God had designed as a continuous whole. The Almighty, the Creator of our mortal bodies, could boast in Holy Scripture, that He has not made death.† His vision was of a rational animal, raised to the supernatural and, thanks to this, reaching at a bound the threshold of the Beatific Vision, jumping the stage of the great dark tunnel and its agony in the attainment of immortality. Who then has spoilt this lovely thing, this first project of God's love, and broken up the smooth ascent?

And when, in the sequel of the mystery which we see foreshadowed, the Son of God is delivered into the hands of His enemies, we must not say that it is His Father who is putting Him to death. Preachers say so in terms of would-be eloquence. But S. Thomas felt it right to explain S. Paul's *proprio Filio suo non pepercit Deus*‡ in terms far more cautious and subtle only in appearance.

But it is too soon to speak of the sacrifice of the Son of God. It is sufficient for the moment to have understood the sacrifices of mankind and to know why these great religious

---

* S. Ignatius of Antioch.—*Ad Trall.*, X.
† " God did not make death,
    And He feels no joy at the loss of the living,
    He has created all things for life. . .
    God created men for immortality,
    And He has made him to the image of His own nature.
    It is by the envy of the devil that sin has come into the world." (*Sap.*, II, 23-24.)
‡ IIIa, q. 47, a. 3 on *Rom.*, viii, 32.

gestures, charged with making our inner dispositions incarnate in the sight of God, make their appearance everywhere, in the high places of Canaan as in the sacred woods of the Gauls, in Aulis as on Garizim—and in the form of great suffering followed by great joy. It is a grief which precedes an apotheosis, a loss which issues in a gain, a destruction on which a mighty edifice is reared, a rupture which seals a pact, a stripping which heralds a splendid and beneficent alliance, a death which leads to life. In this road with its two stages we see in symbolic image the inevitable workings of man's nature. It is a two-act tragedy: first sorrowful renunciation, then dazzling joy, the journey's end in God. A time of anguish, striving and destruction is followed by one of glory and apotheosis.

One and the same object, the victim, takes part in both these successive moments which are only apparently opposed to one another. The same oblation serves in turn the gesture of breaking with creatures and that of fastening on God. It will be immolated then before it is offered. It will suffer before it is accepted. It will pass by way of death to meet the source of life.

This great transaction would have been simpler in the state of nature; and in the cool of the Earthly Paradise it would have been reduced almost to a unity by the reduction of these two stages into one. But even in this glorious state of things sacrifice, like the human nature which it expresses and completes, carried with it potentially, in its immanent metaphysic, the dichotomy now so obvious and inevitable. In any case we see God's plan condemned to a detestable delay which splits the movement of our religious life into two parts which seem at enmity with one another: first, a symbol of death as a negation of that dire negation, sin; then, in the wake of our victim which has found the right way again for itself and us thanks to this previous immolation, we taste God's peace when He welcomes and transfigures us.

Sorrow is not useless. The gesture of sacrifice as sinful man performs it represents a moral value in the intention and spiritual effort behind the gift it offers—and also, since sin, it

is necessarily a sorrowful affair. It has a price, and the price
is costly. This combination of the ideas of pain and value is
behind the metaphysics of asceticism and makes Christian
mortification legitimate, obligatory and in the end a thing of
sweetness. In fine, the Christian order, since sin, necessarily
contains *disorder*, provisional but obligatory and beneficial;
sacrifice, namely, and the spirit of sacrifice. Humanity has
always felt in secret this law of the fruitfulness of sorrow.
Christ realized it in His person; and, through Him, the
Christian joins in this constructive programme and profits
by it.

The liberty which is left man to choose to some extent the
road which is to lead him to his end has very easily given him
the impression that the value of his sorrowful sacrifice
depends upon his generosity. And he has not been wholly
wrong in this. To reach God is of obligation; the time which
we take for the journey at once raises problems of *more* and
less, which will form in Christian spirituality the sphere of
the venial sins which we must shun and the virtues which we
are advised to practise. Man puts into sacrifice something of
his own personal value; it has varying degrees of splendour,
for his gesture, though obligatory as regards the end in
view, is optional, indeterminate, as regards the means. The
undertaking springs from generosity as well as justice. It
involves an act directing creation to its end by impelling it
towards God, an effort for the development of being which
is itself of obligation, but in which nevertheless a greater or
less degree of good intention may be shown. So in
Christianity particular acts of perfection will be optional,
but charity, which is perfection itself, will be obligatory, at
least by way of tendency or of direction. In fine, in the
psychology of sacrifice there is an internal dynamism which
can never be translated wholly into obligation: man gives
that he may have, but he gives more than he feels obliged to
give in order that he may have yet more. And what God asks
of us is this *more*, in which is shown both our generosity and
love and our willingness to help in the betterment of a
creation which itself is good. S. Augustine and S. Thomas

saw all this: *Omne opus quod agitur, ut inhæreamus Deo*. In his phrase which points to an obligatory goal we see also willing effort.

The modern sense of the word *sacrifice* with its implication of generosity seems to be based on this psychology. We do not say that a man who does his duty or pays his debts is making a sacrifice. That does not seem to start until we willingly give something of our own to forward the betterment, moral or physical, of this unsatisfactory world.

When these deep thoughts are weakened and obscured in feeble minds, the picture of exchange and mart results. For in ancient religions these delicate shades of moral meaning were translated only by the number, great or small, of victims offered to obtain the help of heaven. Man thought himself in this a buyer making terms. Sometimes he acted as a generous partner; sometimes he claimed heaven's favour on the cheap. Crude and deplorable conceptions these, but with yet an earnest or remnant of the truth! Man, we have seen, takes part as God's collaborator in the successful issue of creation; this good will is especially declared in the beginning of his sacrifice, when he sets his course for heaven by provisional renunciations which are partly optional, for the choice of means is left to his initiative.

The spirit of sacrifice, without which the Church would long ago have died, brings into history an element of liberty, the very antipodes of the systems of the lawyers, the politicians and the economists. The appearance of new forms of asceticism, such as those which new religious Orders presuppose and exercise, at once causes fluctuations of an unpredictable kind on the market of spiritual values, which throw the Church into a holy ferment and stir men's souls profoundly. This is not anarchy, but free generosity in the service of an order which is itself of obligation. Love takes a hand, and the author of the "Imitation" shows us that love's interventions are not reducible to Minerva's foresight. Yet there is the life of the Church and its *raison d'être*. "What is wanting to the sufferings of Christ in my own flesh, I fill up for His body, which is the Church." (Col., i, 24).

E

We know to-day that Christ has bought us, or rather bought us back, for it is a ransom which He has so freely paid And although we must not look for a vendor in this unila teral comparison, His blood has truly been the price of ou salvation.

Before the time of the perfect redemption of mankinc there were at least proofs of good will in the sacrifices of th ancient world: men give that they may have; they struggl towards a goal and believe that they attain it. Among th pyres where the flame has consumed the offered victims among the heaps of ashes which mark the place of ruinec altars, may not our eyes be already lifted to Calvary for the solution? But for the present we must keep in check thi holy and legitimate impatience.

CHAPTER EIGHT: THE TRUE
IDEA (concluded): THE SIGN

IF we would fully grasp the essence of sacrifice a fina effort of understanding is imposed on us. In this fina definitive stage S. Augustine will still be our guide: *tu duca tu signore e tu maestro*.

So far we have tried almost throughout to treat sacrifice a an absolute reality, as if its *raison d'être* and its total value were contained within itself. When we spoke of the victim' return to God we seemed to suppose that it went heaven wards for reasons of its own and to find the solution of it own inner problem. That was over-simplifying; sacrifice is really far more complex, and it is time to complete the analysis and to reveal the fullness of its meaning.

The metaphysic of sacrifice which we have tried tc describe is realized by and through a symbolic liturgy. This has often been referred to already, but only now is it tc present itself to us as one of the essential elements of this great business. An object which meets with God and gains its end is not necessarily a sacrifice. That implies a whole apparatus of rites, focusing on a chosen representative victim round which and in which the action plays. For it is a great play, in the highest sense of the word, a great mystical play, whose unvarying rules, inherited from previous ages, are now required in tradition's name for the very issue of the undertaking. There are inevitable rubrics the breaking of which makes the whole project fail. This is a ceremony with symbolic and effective gestures each of which has its peculiar meaning. It is a rite with magical or infallible effects. To sum up in a single word in the language of S. Augustine and of Christianity, it is a *sign*.

Perhaps because of his Platonist education but above all thanks to the religious sensibilities of his subtle and affectionate soul, in such active communion with the deepest longings of humanity, S. Augustine had seen clearly that sacrifice is an institution on two planes, one above the other, or, as he said, "the sensible sign of an invisible reality."* The liturgical apparatus and what one might venture to call the theatrical *mise en scène* are only the efficacious expression of another and a real tragedy which takes place in men's souls. There are as it were two sacrifices, the ritual sacrifice of which the victim is the subject, and another, the sacrifice of souls, which is realized invisibly, the first symbolizing and signifying the second so as to engender it and at the same time give it outward form.

Our modern manuals have not completely forgotten this analysis, but do not draw out all its value. The reader does not see how sacrifice, like sacrament, is an efficacious sign, that is a visible symbol carrying in it the hidden reality that it represents. The sacrament comes from heaven to earth to bring us in a visible rite the grace which God has laid in it. Making the same journey in the opposite direction but in kindred forms, sacrifice raises itself from earth to heaven to

---

* Sacrificium visibile invisibilis sacrificii sacramentum, id est sacrum signum est. *The visible sacrifice is the sacred symbol, the sacramental sign of our invisible religion.* De Civitate Dei, lib. X, cap. 5. Cf. de Trinitate, IV, cap. 4 (Migne, *P. L.*, t. 42, col. 901). The definition is taken over by S. Thomas, IIa, IIae, q. 85, a. 2 ; IIIa ., q. 22, a 2 ; and implied by Trent (Sess. XXII, cap. 1).

bring the Creator the religion and adoration, the love and
fear, of men. These human gestures would be unintelligible
without the inner worship which they are trying to declare
just as religious experience would lose all its force if it
rejected the incarnation given to it in the colour and movement of these liturgies. Thus the visible is explained by the
invisible, and a theory of sacrifice which did not accept and
include this double value would be built in vain; above all it
is vain to look for a self-sufficiency in the mere ritual taken in
isolation. To give the sacrificial gesture an absolute value
would be to begin by committing an error in logic and above
all in metaphysics. The visible sacrifice then is first of all the
sign of an invisible reality.

When the Council of Trent in its twenty-second Session
(ch. 1) summarized this rich and balanced teaching of S.
Thomas on the sacrifice of the Mass in a period worthy of
Cicero himself (pointing our separated brethren back is, as
it may prove, to the steps of the Eucharistic altar) it inserted
the following parenthesis: *ut dilectæ sponsæ suæ Ecclesiæ
visibile, sicut natura humana exigit, relinqueret sacrificium*—a
fine phrase steeped in humanism both in matter and manner,
but only the stamping with a conciliar seal of a long tradition
traceable through the ages in the Fathers and Doctors as well
as the Scholastics. Among both Greeks and Latins the
equilibrium and harmony of the visible and the invisible in
religious rites is a pulpit commonplace and an alphabet of
sacrificial theory. The latter carries with it something
absolute in value, a metaphysic which we have already tried
to reconstruct, and an external representation of the unseen
reality. We must not confuse this visible image of an invisible sentiment which explains it and is illustrated by it
with the movement of soul of which it is the outward form.
Nevertheless we must not separate it from the inner life
without which it would be unintelligible. We must keep both
the relation and the difference between the elements; there
lies the secret of their meaning and the entrance to the
mystery. In the eyes of S. Augustine, who sums up all his
predecessors, the visible sacrifice is in the first place the sign

of an invisible reality within our souls. Clearly it is this inner religion which we have tried to rediscover and define. Now it is time to understand why it is clothed in symbols and figures, why it is incarnate in a victim, a representative.

* * *

What then is a *sign* in the religious sense of the word? S. Augustine, who seems to have been interested in this question all his life, has left us a weighty reply in the famous opening pages of the *De Doctrina Christiana*. He distinguishes two sorts of reality, those which have their explanation and *raison d'être* in themselves and those whose sole purpose is to mark or indicate something other than themselves; and these are signs.

It is easy to show that the use of signs is a peculiarity of man. The movements of the brutes, which we can hardly call gestures, never have a bearing beyond the mere muscular effect and no further goal than their immediate result. Since they never exceed their physical value, they never signify in the proper sense. Human gestures on the other hand often have a meaning far beyond their purely animal value, because they aim at a further one behind it in the invisible or spiritual world; they have a significance. This tremendous transition has its roots in our nature itself, composed as it is of body and spirit, with a perpetual interaction of bodily and spiritual forces working for common ends. The flesh animated by the spirit lends it its elements, and the spirit enriches the animal frame in which it is incarnate with its own higher tendencies. Man, living in both worlds at once, is accustomed to pass continually from one to the other and to pool their riches in a single act; and because he is much more accustomed to the handling of physical values than to communion with spiritual realities he regularly turns to the former for help when he would rise to the level of the latter. The visible becomes a sign of the invisible; the higher is supported by the lower. Thus by man's will (as by God's in sacrament and miracle) a bodily gesture carries with it spiritual value.

Angels do not use signs because the simplicity of their nature does not require or permit such language or such action. All their powers are exhausted upon the spiritual world to which they entirely belong, and the realities which they produce have never any value but themselves. This no doubt shows a superiority, but one which causes men no envy, for our joy lies in the play of symbol, in the use of line and imagery, in the rhythm of poetry, and in the spectacle afforded us by our whole life, the life of our own flesh, the vehicle and sanctuary of spirit. I speak, and the sound which strikes the air contains an idea. I move my arms to make gestures, and these are patterns quickened by my emotions. My poor animal body is wholly transfigured by the invisible whose tabernacle it is, while at the same time the body feels almost its creator.

God Himself, who is pure spirit, makes no signs, except for us. He has no personal use for them; His thought has no need of gesture in order to create, and His Almighty Word has sung His glory eternally in an invisible silence. But we, living both in the natural and in the supernatural orders, see certain divine interventions as signs, because we have to class them at the same time in both of these two worlds; their unity was broken by our sin. The supernatural omnipotence of God in its extreme effects pierces through nature's hard shell which the sin of the first man had, as it were, withdrawn from the divine control; and this violent and transitory irruption of an invisible force into the visible world is a sign for us because belonging in our eyes to each of these two different worlds: it is a miracle which makes us say: *digitus Dei est hic.*

But in principle miracle, by reason of this very duality, is less perfect than creation or (a fortiori) charity, which—like the angels—are values pure and simple. The Son of God, who saw His Father, had no need of signs in order to recognize Him everywhere: *ego autem sciebam quia semper me audis.* It is for the sake of us sinners that He works wonders: *sed propter populum, qui circumstat, dixi: ut credant quia tu me misisti.* (John, xi, 42).

Our double nature explains too why God has given us the sacraments as visible signs of His invisible grace. And for the same reason man has invented sacrifices, which are the visible signs of his invisible religion.

The Fathers of the Church had a keen awareness of these deep realities of which our unconscious Cartesianism has long deprived us: "If you had no body," said S. John Chrysostom, "God would have granted you merely invisible gifts, but because your soul is united to a body He gives you understanding of His teaching through the things of sense."

And S. Augustine, to whom we must always come back: "How profitable are the suggestions of symbolism for kindling and feeding the fire of our love; they move and enflame us more than if we possessed the realities themselves without veils or images. It is a fact that an idea suggested by an allegory moves and charms us more than if we hear it in its proper terms."*

But the richest of our texts on this subject is perhaps the splendid passage of the *Summa Contra Gentiles* (bk. III, ch. XIX) in which the greatest of philosophers sums up the whole patristic tradition in a few decisive phrases. These lines will always serve to defend Catholic sacramentalism and our respect for the flesh against all the pride of disincarnate thought: "It is not surprising that the heretics who denied that God is the author of our bodies attacked bodily signs of adoration offered to Him. They show in this that they have forgotten their own humanity, since they no longer see how sensible expression is necessary for the thought and love within us. Yet it is a fact of experience that the gestures of the body serve to excite our thought and love. Clearly then it is proper to make use of bodily things for the raising of our souls to God."

* * *

Signs bear all the marks of our status as rational animals: like our flesh, they belong by their matter to the world of sense which provides their visible elements; but also like the

* Texts collected by Thomassin, *de Incarnatione Verbi*, book X, cap. 2.

concept of our intelligence, which is a seizing of mutable being made static for our intellects, signs tie down the bodily values which they employ in fixed and rigid form. They are then called rites, and their smallest rubrics are unchangeable and sacred. Sacrificial liturgies always have their source in the dim and distant past; they are an ancestral heritage; and the meticulous care with which they are protected in their actual use makes the past survive as something fixed and hieratic in the present and the future. Thus signs have the power to stabilize the flux of things; we might say that on this earth where everything else is fluid only signs do not change—in fact, they have their value precisely in this unchangingness. The smallest error in the performance of these ceremonies would destroy their validity, just as the smallest confusion in the use of words produces misunderstanding. Signs put eternal elements into human things, and it is in relation to them above all that the theories of Melchior de Vogué and the wonderful words of Barrès about the *dead who speak* deserve to be remembered. In any case, here is the signature of rational animals, in this gesture formed to their measure and in their peculiar style by the conceptual intelligence, which uses sensation to nourish reason with flesh and blood and the abstract idea to give spiritual value to the body.

Clearly this interpenetration of processes and this unique achievement are possible only because reason and desire are behind the signs, explaining and legitimatizing by the presence of their immaterial wealth this extraordinary employment of the body in a region utterly beyond its scope. We do invisible work with visible tools simply because we are souls in flesh, flesh informed by spirit. For what is man? A great imaginer, but a thinker also. An animal, certainly: but also an intelligence and a conceptual intelligence. The meeting of concept and image gives birth to the symbol and to the sign.

This is indeed a marvel. While the animal, wholly engrossed by its prey, is so surrendered to sensation that it never goes beyond it, man, armed with his concept, has the splendid power of putting the greater into the less, using the lower world of sense to fix his hold on spiritual realities. It is his joy and triumph to clothe his idea with the image which has been its origin; it is his peace and his delight, when he thinks of the spiritual world, to steep himself again in the material element made clear and limpid for him by his power of reason.

It would be a mistake then to suppose that signs, taken in all their richness, are inferior to things whose value does not go beyond themselves. To repeat S. Augustine's examples, a mere piece of wood or stone, or a mere animal, are not equal in worth to that wood which Moses threw upon the bitter waters to sweeten them, or that stone on which Jacob laid his head, or that animal which Abraham immolated in the place of Isaac. For these Biblical symbols were filled with the spiritual value which they represented over and above their own material worth. They were at the same time themselves and more than themselves.

What makes us say so often that signs are inferior to realities is that we start by emptying them of all spiritual content. Thus the word becomes inferior to the idea, the image to the thing, the symbol to the being for which it stands, a false and narrow theory which makes our nature deny its complex unity, prescinding from the soul, as if our body were our body or even a body at all without its soul. The truth is that our souls dwell in our flesh and to possess the one is to have the other also. True, there are such things as vain words, empty gestures and barren forms; for man can lie and quench the spirit. But the word, considered as a sign, is a being composed of the idea which it translates and the syllables in which it is expressed. And gestures are not only a waving of the hands or arms but emotions and desires which have taken body to gain outward form; conversely they are muscles become intelligible.

So the sign is a visible envelope which contains an invisible reality; and like the human *compositum*, of which it is both offspring and extension, it is formed by the union of two sorts of value. The sign is not a mere envelope, an empty

gesture, a symbol pure and simple. Whatever may be ou
usual habits of thinking and speaking, we should be con
demned in advance to a complete misunderstanding o
sacrifice in general and of the Sacrifice of the Mass in par
ticular if we considered the sign as having an existence of it
own and independent of its spiritual value. We must find
place for this in our definition. Similarly an attempt t
exhaust the concept of miracle by defining it simply as
suspension of the laws of nature, leaving out of account it
spiritual message, would be to ruin in advance all apolo
getics based on signs from heaven.

If only the rich complexity of the rational animal car
explain this incarnation of ideas in images, the unique co
incidence of these two levels is possible only through the co
operation of the created world outside, of which our humar
nature is the final term and masterpiece. The world seem
built in spirals, as the ancients thought, and its organizatior
like its movement passes on its various levels through th
same rising stages, so that comparisons may easily be mad
between them and reminders of lower orders found to per
sist in higher ones. It is not idle then to underline thes
relations and make use of them as symbols: the lion's migh
is something purely animal, but it does evoke the thought o
the king's might which is something both physical anc
reasonable; and so the lion is the king of animals and th
Emperor of Austria and the Count of Flanders are powerfu
like the lion on their arms.

This use of images and symbols results in harnessing th
forces of emotion and sensibility, which the abstractiv
reason does not itself possess, for the penetration of spiritua
realities. Straightway our whole being is profoundly engaged
in the movement which draws it to its end in communior
with the entire creation: without proving false to the end
which is spiritual, it brings it the homage of its original o
basic values, which are of the flesh.

The sign must therefore bear an external resemblance to
the invisible value which it contains. Nevertheless symbols
by dint of sheer use, can become purely conventional, n

onger representing what they signify. Man's will and reason preserve in them a meaning which is no longer apparent outwardly to eyes and ears; these, as S. Augustine said (repeated by all our manuals), are artificial signs. It is probable that the choice of words was originally based upon an imitative resemblance which the centuries have overlaid and made unrecognizable. Nowadays we are condemned to learn languages and dictionaries by heart: in the beginning, before the invention of writing and the civilizations of developed speech, antediluvian man expressed when he spoke the very impact of the object, so to speak, upon his flesh. What seems to prove it is that even to-day, thank God, words still have semantic force: they are alive and moving because the intelligence with which they are still impregnated is always charging them with its own subtle purposes, flavouring and modifying them. Words would have no life if the intelligence behind the signs of language were not alive. An empty sign would be a dead one.

Now comes the all-important question: which of these two values in the sign is responsible for the existence of the other? Does the visible engender the invisible or *vice versa?* Do gestures without intelligence come first, or unexpressed ideas?

Form emerges from the potency of matter, say the Scholastics; and, at the other end of the scale, it is the sacrament which causes grace. It seems then that it is the visible element that gives birth to the invisible. In the action itself this is true: gesture engenders the sentiments which it expresses, the word conveys the idea, the sacrament contains grace and produces it *ex opere operato.*

But this remarkable influence of the visible on the invisible is possible only if the invisible has first its own existence, separate and absolute. If the word is intelligent, it is because there is intelligence in the world; and the sacrament which produces grace does not create it, for it was already in existence. So we shall see that the Mass, which is a true sacrifice because it contains the sacrifice of the Cross and is its sign, does not *make* the sacrifice of the Cross, which exists without it. Miracles which are signs in nature of the presence of the supernatural in the world only exist because the supernatural already does so.

In fine, there is reciprocal causality between the elements, though in differing ways.* Ontologically spiritual values can exist apart from the realities in which they are incarnate; but the sign, by incarnating them, makes them present; it does not create them, but it contains or produces them and in that sense causes them. I express my ideas to gain possession of them; but if they were not mine already, I could not speak of them. I make gestures to rouse my emotions; but if I had not been already moved, I should not make gestures. I offer sacrifice to nourish my religious life; but if I had no religion, I should not offer sacrifice.

So we come back at last to the great mystery of sacrifice which has given us such food for thought. Considering it in the victim which is its final point, we can see more clearly now how the latter is a sign or symbol. In this host I body forth my whole religion; the same mystic journey must be made by both of them. I offer it as the offering of myself; I immolate it because I feel the need and impulse of self-

---

* This theory of reciprocal causality, as it is called, is treated by scholastic chiefly in cosmology in connection with the "ultimate disposition" which is both caused and causer in substantial transformation. (Cf. for example, John of Saint Thomas, *Phil. Nat.*, Bk. II, q. 1, a. 7, referring to *Ver.* q. 28, a. 7 and 8 ; *In IV Sent.*, Dist. 17, q. 1, a. 4, quæstiuncula Ia; and q. 2, a. 5, qa. 3.) It appears also in psychology in connection with free acts (cf. Garrigou-Lagrange, *Dieu*, p. 635, 3rd ed.) and in theology in connection with justification. The very act which gives u grace can be accomplished only in a state of grace : cf. Ia IIae, q. 109, a. 7. c. and ad 1; q. 112, a. 2; and *Dict. de Théol, Cathol.* Vacant, art., *Grâce*, col. 1631 Applications of the same law can be made in dealing with the problems of the genesis of faith, the formation of hypotheses and the origin of ideas (where the imag acts as dispositive cause and the active intellect as efficient cause of the idea). This theory of causal reciprocity, which is both thoroughly traditional and thoroughly alive to-day, deserves more study and wider use.

Applied to the Sacraments would it not serve to end the depressing controversy about the physical or moral causality of the sacramental signs? For at least three centuries Dominicans and Jesuits have faced one another at this point of the theological front behind the same impregnable defences. Neither side make progress. Does the sacrament produce grace by the physical and immediate power of its matter and form over supernatural values, or morally, because as the gestur of Christ renewed by the mystic Spouse it is an occasion for God's generosity But why should not both these propositions be true, the one included in the othe like the soul in the body? If the sign is really composed of soul and body and produces its effect only by this union, why should not the Sacraments, sign deriving from the Hypostatic Union, produce their effects because they are the very omnipotence of the Incarnate Son which certain members of His mystical Body are qualified to draw upon by the renewing of His acts?

immolation. It makes its way to God as my representative and then, I hope, I am myself accepted. It has translated all the aspects of my religion, both my sorrow for my sins and my triumphant acclamation of God's mercy. In its ashes or its mangled limbs it contains the feeble effort of my religion, is its expression and its offspring; is in fact, its sign: *invisibilis sacrificii seu religionis visibile signum.*

And when soon after it returns to me, in communicating with it I shall communicate with the favours with which God has filled it, for now it is their expression also and the sign of them. When I put the cup to my lips and take food into my mouth I shall have through this symbol the visible image and effective sign of the heavenly alliance or reconciliation, the certainty that I also have reached God.

Such is the unique value of this host or this sacrifice, springing from the deepest laws of our humanity and from the very essence of a rational animal. For in sacrifice also there is soul and body, the first invisible, the second visible, both existing only in and for each other. The victim is not simply a part of me or of my possessions; it does not only take my place; it is not just my substitute. Far beyond all this, it represents me in the word's fullest sense, it carries my religion in itself, it has its value; and it is soon to have the value of God's mercy to me. It incarnates spiritual values, which surpass it, but which it contains. In it our history is made and our fate decided. It becomes in the end like an ambassador who carries with him the desires and destinies of a whole people. To venture upon a still richer word, fully verified in Christ alone, we could call our victim a sort of head or chief who draws all his clients with him in his ascent to God. But this expression, used of false or incomplete religions, does them too much honour. Among Jews and pagans the victim is certainly a sign and nothing more—and possibly inefficacious. But that suffices to explain their hopes, and to herald or to figure a more perfect sacrifice which shall be definitive.

CONCLUSION

In this long drawn out analysis we have examined one by one all the definitions of sacrifice which we have found in S. Augustine and S. Thomas, and we have claimed to find in them the inarticulate longings of humanity as well as an explanation of God's institutions. It seems desirable to find some formula by way of final synthesis. Latin words perhaps serve to harmonize the teachings of the two great Doctors with less danger of misunderstanding them. Let us try to build a sentence with all the words italicized taken from these sources. *Sacrificium visibile [invisibilis sacrificii sacramentum, id est] sacrum signum est,* in quo [sub alicujus hostiæ speciebus], homo, *in honorem proprie Deo debitum* et in ordinem *ad illum finem boni quo veraciter beatus esse possit, exhibet* quod a peccato se avertat (immolatio) et *spiritum suum in Deum ferat* (oblatio), ut, divina acceptatione intercedente, *sancta societate inhæreat Deo* per victimæ jam consecratæ participationem seu communionem.

Sacrifice is a sensible sign (or rite) in which under the symbols (or species) of a victim, man, to pay his dues to God and so to realize his end, bears witness that he renounces sin which is his evil (immolation), and that he turns to God who is his good (oblation)—hoping that the divine acceptance, sanctifying his offering, will win for him the heavenly alliance at which he aims and that the victim will bring him by communion the guarantee of it.

The words which merely reinforce the meaning and could be omitted without injuring the sense have been put in brackets. Sacrifice is thus the gesture symbolizing man's return to God, in which he expresses his desire and will for union with the Creator. This internal movement and external action presuppose that an intelligent adoring creature refuses to make itself its final end. In the state of sin this renouncing becomes a purifying in suffering and expiation, which the gesture represents and at the same time realizes. Then it is for God to welcome this return, to sanctify the victim by His acceptance. The victim can now come down again to men to be the sacrament of their communion.

More simply, sacrifice is the expressive, and, if possible, efficacious, sign of the deliberate and suppliant return of man to God, who receives him. That is why there is *action* in sacrifice, as S. Thomas constantly repeats. Something is changed. There is movement, activity, a great stirring of mankind towards its Master, turning deliberately heavenwards to reach the end without delay. Creation finds success, fulfils itself. Before sacrifice there was nothing achieved. After sacrifice order has appeared. Man has recognized God —*adoration;* has given himself to Him—*love and homage;* he has respected God's eternal rights—*religion and reparation;* the disquiet which is our very definition has been now appeased—*requiescamus in Te.*

Oblation and immolation in an actual ceremony seem to be opposed like joy and grief, or means and end. But if the first signifies our drive towards God and our meeting with Him, and the second the detachment from ourselves and creatures which, since sin, is painful for us, then it is clear that in principle the movement towards the Creator and the renunciation of our sinful or imperfect attachments are only the obverse and reverse, the positive and negative sides of a single undertaking, our restoration (namely) to right order, our adhesion to our proper end by the legitimate employment of the proper means. In the unfolding of a liturgy immolation and oblation may often be distinct and may often alternate bewilderingly, but their hidden mystery remains the same.

Such is the cycle, human and divine, which the ancient religions represented by so many rites, where always are found the same obstinate desires of attaining God.

Note on the History and Use of the word "Sacrament"

The semantic history of the word "sacramentum" has not been completely explored despite the labours of specialists at

Louvain presided over by M. de Backer and P. de Ghellinck.*

At least we know that the word existed in classical Latin, or more exactly in that of the law-courts and in the official language of the army. In each case it had a religious sense, referring to the caution money deposited in the temples by litigants or the oath taken by young recruits to the republic's eagles.

We know also that the word had nothing corresponding etymologically in Greek or Hebrew. It is a genuinely Roman word, which does not become Christian until the Church begins to speak the Roman language in Africa with Tertullian or earlier in pre-Vulgate Latin.

We do not yet know why this word was chosen for the Vulgate to translate the Septuagint's μυστήριον. But its success was great and rapid; it is one of the most used words in the religious language of the Latin Fathers. Those who are familiar with the Breviary are well aware of this and sometimes disconcerted by the many ramifications of meaning which this convenient word is made to bear.

But a conclusion does emerge: there is a *sacramentum* when a visible reality possesses an invisible value letting the eyes of faith see more and further than the eyes of flesh. We now realize why the word was chosen to translate the Greek μυστήριον, provided that the word is not thought of in the Catechism's sense of mystery, *a truth to be believed*, but in that of a *reality*, or *truth*, hidden beneath a sensible exterior. There is mystery when a great religious value hides its power and stimulus beneath an outward gesture or historic fact or image or (in short) a sign of any kind. Thus the Presentation of Jesus in the Temple and the Adoration of the Magi are mysteries or sacraments, because beneath the passing of events visible to the eyes of unbelievers as well as believers immense spiritual wealth lies hidden, seen by believers only.

* Cf. Elie de Backer, *Sacramentum* "The word and the idea represented by it in the works of Tertullian," in *Recueil des Conferences d'Histoire et de Philologie de l'Université de Louvain*, fasc. 30, xx-392 p., Louvain, 1911. J. de Ghellinck, S.J., E. de Backer, J. Poukens, S.J., G. Lebacqz, S.J., *Pour l'Histoire du mot "Sacramentum,"* I, les Anténicéens, in *Spicilegium Sacrum Lovaniense*, fasc. 3, ix-392 p., Louvain, 1924.

We must not understand this double value in the modernst sense, in which the symbol can be empty or without real relation with the truth, which it is impotent to grasp. In the true Christian sacrament, on the other hand, there is a very close connection between the invisible and the visible; the former reveals and demonstrates the latter (to the eyes of faith) and often it will contain it, for it is its sign.

Tertullian was justified in using *sacramentum* to refer to baptism, influenced perhaps by the *sacramentum militiæ*, with which he wanted to compare it But he was beginning to particularize the meaning of the term by applying it specifically to a ritual. This restricted meaning was to win the day. *Sacramentum* bears henceforth a ritualistic sense: it is applied especially to initiations. By its means a list of sanctifying rites—signs conferring *gratiæ primæ*—tends to take shape.

S. Augustine seems to have returned to the word's original extension. For him any sacred sign is a *sacrament* whatever its implication or its mode of efficacy. The list becomes indefinitely large again.

Scholasticism was to return, this time definitively, to Tertullian's views and, with a further and final restricting of the meaning, to apply the word only to rites conferring grace instituted by Our Lord: hence the seven sacraments of the New Law.

But the traditional insertion of the specific difference *of the New Law*, which is still in use, gives us the right to go on using *sacrament* as a generic term; and this is requisite for our present study, keeping as it does in general rather to the Augustinian terminology.

There is a sacramental sign or sacrament whenever a religious reality exists both visibly and invisibly, with a relation of causality or at least of significance between the elements, the one falling under the senses, the other unseen by eyes of flesh.

When man makes a religious gesture with his body or a visible object, to rouse or express or realize or finally to incarnate his interior religion, there is a sign. That is why

F

we have said with S. Augustine that sacrifice is a sign, o
rather a sacrament, since for him the two terms are practicall
synonymous: *Sacramentum, id est sacrum signum.*

Thus for S. Augustine *sacramentum* can exist in both
directions, from earth to heaven, the direction of sacrifice
from heaven to earth, the direction of sacrament in the
scholastic sense.

The Eucharist is a *sacramentum* in both directions, if we
consider it from the beginning to the end of the liturgica
movement which provides us with it: in the beginning it is
the *sacramentum* of the adoration of heaven by earth, unti
our oblations are accepted by God; from the moment when
God gives us our Eucharist for communion, it is the
sacramentum which heaven gives to earth, the *sacramentum*
in the Scholastic sense, which precisely distinguishes the
Eucharist-sacrifice from the Eucharist-sacrament.

But there is another possible distinction in the meaning of
the word. Does *Sacramentum* refer at the same time to the
visible and the invisible elements of the mystery, in the case
of the Eucharist, for example, both to the species of bread
and wine and the Body of Christ with the grace which it
brings—or to the visible element considered in relation to
the invisible? The language of Christianity took some time to
decide. For S. Augustine and the whole of Latin antiquity
deriving from him the second alternative seems the truer:
when the Latin Fathers speak of the *sacramentum panis er
vini*, they are not denying the real presence of the Body of
Christ, still less transubstantiation. It is enough that the
species remain visible for them to be able to speak of the
sacramentum panis et vini. But they also recognized, in
another sense, the sacramentum *corporis et sanguinis:* the
sacrament of bread and wine, which is the sacrament OF the
Body and OF the Blood.

But the modern language of Christianity has chosen long
ago the first alternative, and we sing to-day, thinking of the
invisible in the visible; ADOREMUS *in æternum Sanctissimum
Sacramentum . . . Tantum ergo Sacramentum* VENEREMUR
cernui.

The precise language of the Schools has suppressed these hesitations, distinguishing the *sacramentum-et-non-res*, i.e., the "empty" Sacrament pure and simple; the *sacramentum-et-res* contained in or under the former and produced by it; and lastly *res-et-non-sacramentum* or the effect of strictly invisible grace. Nowadays, when these valuable distinctions are so seldom used, the reader must find the proper sense of "sacrament" or *sacramentum* from the context.

BOOK TWO: THE SACRIFICE OF THE SON OF GOD

PART ONE: THE MYSTERY OF THE INCARNATION

INTRODUCTION

Carmen Christo tanquam Deo

IN the year 111 or 113 of our era an important Roman administrator whose name adds lustre to the history of Latin literature, Pliny the Younger, wrote to the Emperor Trajan from the distant province of Asia of which he was in charge the first official report known to us of Christians and Christianity. This good pagan was vaguely trying to pierce through the mists of antiquity in which his eyes were held to the secret of the new religion which was that morning the subject of his official interest. *I have interrogated these strange people*, he records; *my verdict has been on the whole fairly favourable to them: they are an ephemeral religious sect which will easily be brought to a proper state of mind. Their originality consists in engaging themselves by an oath to practise virtue and in celebrating Christ as a God:* CARMEN CHRISTO QUASI DEO DICERE.*

It would not be possible to give a better sketch of the infant church in a couple of lines; and taken along with another reflexion, still earlier in date, of another Roman Governor, Portius Festus, related in the Acts of the Apostles† (the accuracy of which was emphasized recently by P. Rousselot), these stray phrases of administrative correspondence contain the whole *essence of Christianity*‡ in its earliest days. If the spiritual blindness of these imperial functionaries made them poor prophets, they do at least excel in the art of accurate and rapid definition. A single glance had clearly shown them the oddity of adoring so recent a founder with the words: *You were dead, but you are alive; you are a man like ourselves, and you are also God in person.*

But, leaving Portius Festus and the younger Pliny, can we

---

* C. Plinii Secundi Minoris *Epistularum liber* X, 96. Kirch, *Enchiridion*, No. 24.
† Act., xxv, 19.
‡ Rousselot, *Christus, La Religion Chrétienne, ad init.* Paris, Beauchesne.

find in the souls of the first believers the first impulse carrying the Faith in this singular direction? Our holy and virile love of knowledge is never wholly satisfied until it reaches real origins. The author of Genesis had found the secret of human curiosity, when he saw fit to tell the mystery of what happened *in the beginning*. But how did Christian dogma come to birth on the bank of Jordan, when Jesus received the baptism of John, in the room at Nazareth where Mary heard God's word, in the intelligences of the first disciples and in Mary's own pure soul? Before the Epistle to the Philippians and the Fourth Gospel's Prologue how did men express that Hypostatic Union which is the *meeting of two natures unconfusedly in a single person?* Those were the terms in which the Council of Chalcedon in the fifth century, drawing its inspiration from S. Leo's letter, was to formulate our belief for all time in the eternal divinity of the historic Founder. But what was the first impulse which set in motion this great stream of thought?

In scrutinizing our oldest Christological texts with the reverent care which is their due we are trying to find the earliest attitudes of mind of those who, in the words of Péguy, "were the first Christians of Christianity, the inaugurators, the authors of it under God, the creators of it all along with Him. . . . They built the house for others, for all others, therefore for ourselves . . . these old saints, the first of all old saints, those of the earliest days. . . . Now that it is made, it is not so bad after all . . . and they made it for us. We work on what exists. But when they worked, it was not so. . . . They began Christian living. We have only followed them, and that is quite different. They inaugurated the Kingdom of God upon earth, the initiators of it all."*

It is the shock of this original initiation which we would grapple with, seizing the first movements of Christian thought and feeling.

Why must we first have philosophical introductions to our earliest texts before we set ourselves to read them?

---

* Ch. Péguy, *le Mystère de la charité de Jeanne d'Arc*, édition des Cahiers de la quinzaine, pp. 203 sq.

Because it is vital to the issue and even to the understanding of our own intentions. For these must first show us what the question is and how we are to find the answer. Only then can we return with profit to the Holy Scriptures of our earliest witnesses.

*   *   *

We shall first place the following analyses and the method which inspires them under the patronage of an acknowledged master by briefly recalling the conclusions so patiently worked out by P. de Régnon in his *Etudes de théologie positive sur la Sainte Trinité*. He showed that this theology contains a double strand for the excellent reason that, since Trinitarian dogma distinguishes between Three Persons and a single Nature, we can expound the mystery either by beginning with the Trinity of Persons, subsequently affirming their unity of nature—and that is the way followed for preference by Greek theology—or by starting from the unity of Nature, subsequently affirming it as subsisting in Three Persons—and that is the way followed by the whole of Latin theology since the condemnation of Arianism and since S. Augustine. Thus the same single road, the same single dogma, is explored in both directions throughout the history of the tradition to the great satisfaction of our minds, which feel the need to approach so formidable a mystery in both directions, one after the other. But we must recognize that a choice between the two carries with it—throughout catechetical instruction, apologetics and religious metaphysics—mental attitudes, habits of thought and language, theologies, in fact, which do not substitute for one another. Our two hands although so much alike are not interchangeable, precisely because one is the right and the other the left; but they join well enough in the position of prayer, when they are content to meet in the unity of adoration, foregoing competition. From Thebes to Athens and from Athens to Thebes, said Aristotle, the road is the same, but travelling on it in one direction is not the same as travelling on it in the other.* So with these two theologies of a single dogma.

* Th. de Régnon, S.J. *Etudes de Théologie positive sur la Sainte Trinité*, 4 vols., Retaux. Vol. 1, p. 263.

P. de Régnon has developed their history magnificently, giving our minds the fullest joy and satisfaction, but also perhaps giving us humility in face of these overmastering mysteries, which after all our efforts still remain above us.

But the dogma of the Incarnation also is expressed through the concepts of nature and person, claiming that in a unity of person there are found two natures.*

If the principles laid down by P. de Régnon are sound, it will be possible also to traverse a single road in two opposite directions in considering the mystery of the Incarnation.

One method will move from the duality of the natures to the unity of the Person, the other from the unity of the

* Since these pages aim not at expounding the mystery of the Incarnation but at grouping the texts of scripture which reveal it to us, it will be sufficient here to sum up the doctrine of the Catholic Church in scholastic form for the benefit of readers unfamiliar with manuals of theology.

When we press the noble concept of nature, essence or substance to its limits (according to the Scotists) or beyond them (according to the Thomists) we reach, through the pressure of metaphysical experience and by abstraction, the concept of person, *suppositum* or hypostasis. The three terms nature, essence and substance may be considered synonyms, because although they do not refer to the same idea they refer to or embrace the same reality, the substantial fundament of being, that which makes a being what it is beneath the changing, indeterminate flux of accidents. So too the three names person, *suppositum* and hypostasis, in spite of their very diverse etymologies, are really synonymous expressions—though with the proviso that the term person is valid only of hypostases whose nature is reasonable and free.

In brief, when we are faced with a substance completed in its essence, concrete and individual, the human mind can realize that this nature still lacks a final metaphysical note in order to possess a personality, so as to be not only *what* is called Peter but also *he who* is so called. In this supreme note, this fine point of being, lies the impossibility of referring Peter considered in his constitutive principles, in his material and formal causes, to any other being, even God; and on the other hand the possibility of attributing to him the whole nature that he is and all its accidents. Personality in the scholastic sense is thus neither the field of psychological experience nor moral responsibility, but metaphysical autonomy in the substantial order. A person, by reason of his perfection, cannot be followed by a genitive which names his essence : he is *sui juris*, as the scholastics put it, understanding by that the final and ontological right of the substance to belong metaphysically to nothing but itself.

With us a person always has a single nature and one of his own order ; but the Person of the Word, since the Incarnation, has two natures: one of His own divine order, common to Him with the Father and the Holy Spirit, and another, which is also His own, but yet is ours, belonging to our order, not to His, the human nature which the eternal Son took or assumed in the Virgin Mary's womb when she conceived her blessed fruit.

In speaking thus, that is in starting from the concept of nature and exhausting it (if one is a Scotist) or surpassing it (if one is a Thomist), we have followed the present order of Latin theological exposition ; it is the most convenient for teaching purposes. But is it what we might call the instinctive order of the human mind? Doesn't our intelligence, left to its natural movement, consider the person first and affirm its nature afterwards, and isn't this the order of reality? It is possible and even probable; the following pages will study this problem of logic in the history of the dogma of the Incarnation.

Person to the duality of the natures, with inevitable logical consequences on either hand for all later exposition. If the existence of these two theologies in the history of the Christological tradition has not been clearly pointed out, it is, we believe, because the first way, passing from the natures to the Person, or more exactly from the human nature to the divine Person (for the inalienable divine nature causes no more difficulty when once the divine Person of Christ has been admitted), because this first way was immediately displaced in apostolic and even scriptural times by the second, which prevailed in the Fathers up to the time at least of S. Augustine. And when under the influence of the latter and the pressure of the Latin spirit the custom returned of speaking of the Sacred Humanity of Christ before referring to the Person, this was the language of the scholastic dialectic and did not influence ordinary catechesis and the general outline of theology, in which the Trinity and the Word were still treated first of all, and only afterwards the Incarnation of the Son of God. That movement of thought, from the Person to the nature was already found in S. John's Prologue, and perhaps it was that of S. Paul and of the Gospels. The definitions of Chalcedon,* the charter

* Here is an attempt to translate the Council of Chalcedon's definition: "Following the holy Fathers we all teach formally and unanimously that it is necessary to profess one and the same Son, Our Lord Jesus Christ, at the same time perfect in Divinity and perfect in humanity, true God and true Man, always the same, composed of a rational soul and a body, consubstantial with the Father according to His Divinity, and consubstantial with ourselves according to His humanity, in all things like us, except for sin; both engendered by the Father before all ages according to His Divinity, and remaining always the same, in these last times for us and for our salvation [engendered] according to His humanity of Mary the Virgin-Mother of God; one and the same Christ the Son, the Lord, the only Son, whom we acknowledge to be in two natures, *without confusion, without transformation, without division, without separation,* although this union has taken nothing from the difference between the natures, but rather the two natures have kept their proper characters the more for being joined in one person or hypostasis. He is not shared or divided into two persons, but He is one sole and same only-begotten Son, God the Word, Jesus Christ. Thus the Prophets had spoken of Him in times past; thus our Lord Jesus Christ has taught us; thus we have handed on our fathers' faith."

In a classical passage of *Christus* P. Rousselot has shown the peculiar and outstanding religious value of Chalcedon's definition: "Is it not the whole joy and grandeur of Christianity that the *same* should be at once my brother and my God, etc. . . ? " (*Christus*, La Religion Chrétienne, section II, para. 2). But perhaps a magnificent passage of Mgr. Duchesne's on the same subject (In *Eglises Séparées*, Fontemoing, 1905, p. 39) is not so well known; it is true that he is considering Ephesus (431) rather than Chalcedon (451); "Jesus Christ is indeed God with us.

of our dogma, used that style and gave the Christian mind its cast of thought.

But however soon the first standpoint was abandoned, it had time to live and we may say, without levity, to be baptized. We hope to show that the apostles—Peter, James and John and the rest—when first they met their Master and heard His words, were in fact obliged to believe in Him in such a way. From this time onwards it left traces upon the writings of the apostles even when the other way had filled its place; this it is that may inspire certain passages which seem to us obscure and difficult because we persist in reading into them explanations which were not designed for them. And in any case this first trustful glance which the Apostles cast upon their Master gave place only gradually to other ways of thought and language: hence those rather awkward passages which we hesitate to use because we take for insufficiency what is only a venerable archaism; hence above all those that can be read in both ways, because they mark transition, not by a weakening of the idea or minimizing of doctrine, but on the contrary by the obstinate determination to preserve the truth in both these ways at once. Thus from whichever side we approach them, they can teach us the same truth—like paintings which are always looking at the visitor by whatever door he comes into the gallery. Hence, too, to sum up in advance, all those verses of the New Testament which are true of the human nature as well as the Divine through their unity in the Person of the Son, to which the author in the end refers them. For we must notice here already the peculiar force of those theologies as they react on one another.

From the classical standpoint of S. John's Prologue we

The Christian touches Him directly in a physical though mysterious union under the sacramental veils of the Eucharist. By this body and blood he makes contact with God. . . . To the poor labourer of the Delta, the unknown worker at the port of Pharos [the theology of Saint] Cyril [and the Councils] gives power to touch God in this world, without ecstasy, without extraordinary ascesis, and to gain assurance by this contact, issuing as it does in a mystical relationship, of solid pledges of a world to come."

What is so deplorable is that we are in agreement with all Greek Orthodoxy on the truths defined at Chalcedon, and yet are separated from it. How can one agree upon so searching and formidable a text and not agree upon the rest? . . . What a mystery is human misunderstanding!

think of and name the Person before affirming its human nature. Our glance falls first on the pre-existing Word, and since we can see it with our minds without bringing in human nature, we have acquired the habit, an excellent one for clarity of thought, of speaking of the Word, that is, of the Person, before the Incarnation, abstracting from the human nature which it was to have. And when we go on to speak of the latter, we can speak of it "precisive" as of a thing, a "principium quo", abstracting from the Person which we know already, the "principium quod." Consider-ing, then, the human nature only, we refer to it only those texts in which its human characteristics are affirmed, since we know that it is the human nature of the Eternal Word and our faith in Christ's Divinity is already certain.

But let us think of it in the other way, of a human nature subsisting in a divine Person instead of a divine Person who has a human nature. The fixing of abstractive thought upon the nature will expose us to greater dangers: in the first place our minds do not readily regard a concrete nature first and a person afterwards, because this intellectual attitude is no instinctive;* again a nature normally belongs to a person of its own order of reality. To speak without precautions of the human nature of our Lord before knowing who He is at once implies that He is only man, and thus denies in advance the Christianity which one is trying to expound. Hence the necessity for those who take this standpoint of anticipating what comes after, of seeing in the human nature all that shows it to be God's human nature and even all that proves it to be the human nature of the Son of God. Thus it may

* It is however the custom of Latin theology in teaching the mystery of the Trinity. We speak regularly in our catechisms and sermons of God existing in three Persons, that is of a divine nature subsisting in three hypostases. But the Nicene Creed, familiar to us at Mass in its translation from the Greek, was written in the other style; the Father has a Son and a Spirit in the unity of substance or nature; and our Latin way of thinking and speaking was not imposed on us until this Creed had finally secured belief in the Trinity against heretical interpretation. And in spite of it mediæval theologians, misunderstanding their own Latin tongue, tried to hypostatize the unity of nature independently of the three Persons; so strong is the temptation not to think of nature without person. Hence the queer error of a divine quaternity condemned by the Fourth Lateran Council of 1215 in very careful terms, the wording of which, less lyrical than that of Nicea, shows how many intellectual and literary precautions are required in Latin when the divine nature comes before the Persons.

easily be said—and in no Monophysite sense—that this human nature is divine and even that it is filial. For it is the human nature of somebody—and this somebody is the Son of God: and how should not the person put his mark upon his nature and somehow reveal himself by means of it? If, then, as we hope to show, the way which leads from the nature to the person was the way in which the faith was first explored, it has left traces behind it even when the other way, that of our regular exposition of the faith, had won the field. The habit will remain for long of speaking of the divine characteristics of Christ's human nature, translating, that is, into our own language the created privileges of His Humanity, the visible proofs of the Divinity of our Lord's Person. And the texts again for long after (as P. de Régnon incidentally remarks) "spoke of Christ, so to say, *en bloc*, seeming not sufficiently to distinguish between God and man. Thus there are texts which are not easy to explain. Isn't it that the Fathers of the first centuries, Tertullian, Irenæus, Hilary, understood the intimacy of the Hypostatic Union better than ourselves? By the Incarnation the sacred Humanity is so much moulded upon the Word that in Christ the human virtues have taken the very form of the Word's personal perfections, so that Christ says the same thing, utters the same expressions both as Word and man."*

But when the Monophysites had abused this language, Latin theology abandoned the adjective *divine* in reference to the characters of the human nature, the tangible proof of the divinity of Person. Now that this is no longer to be feared, at least among theologians,† there is perhaps no danger in saying that many of our Christological texts, nearly all those which speak of the relations of Jesus with His Father, are true twice over in two different meanings: they are true of the human nature when they express its filial religion wholly bent upon the Father, but it is bent on Him in so pre-eminent a way that Faith discovers through this

---

* De Régnon, *op. cit.*, Vol. III, pp. 180–181, on "Pater major me est" and "in ipso inhabitat omnis plenitudo divinitatis corporaliter."

† For many of the faithful, insufficiently instructed, show signs of it in their devotions.

sacred Humanity the second and eternal meaning, that of the relations of the Second Person with the First. That is what Scholasticism constantly affirms when it says that the *missions* are in the order of the *processions*—in other words that the former are temporal effects which are in conformity with the eternal Trinitarian relations. This means in Christology that the created human nature of the Son sent into the world is filial, not only because it belongs metaphysically to the Son in virtue of the Hypostatic Union, but also because, being that of the Son, it is wholly bent naturally and supernaturally upon God, as the nature of a loving son upon the person of his father. The divine interior of Jesus, say the mystics, understanding by this Christ's human nature, is conformed to the mystery of the eternal Word. If the Father created human nature in general in His image, much more has the Son taken hypostatically a human nature in His own image, in which the human virtues of charity and of religion are modelled on the eternal relation binding the Second Person with the First.

These things seem subtle to our modern attitude of mind which looks first at the eternal Person; and that is why we too readily abandon teaching them and using them. Yet these truths ought to be simpler to think and utter in the way in which men first made contact with the human and historic nature of the Word Incarnate.

*   *   *

Three stages seem distinguishable in the transition from the first way to the second: one, that of the first acceptance of Christ's divinity, in which He appeared as a human nature, or, one might even say, as a man, finding his completion in a divine Person; a second, in which Christ declared His divine Person by means of the "signs" (an eminently Johannine word) which it impressed upon His human nature; a third, the final intellectual attitude, that of the Prologue of the Fourth Gospel, in which the pre-existing word, that is the divine Person, is spoken of before His Incarnation and His historic human nature.

To three sections devoted to the study of these three concepts, distinct from one another and yet identical, we must add a fourth to give S. Paul's theology its proper place and to show the vast importance of his contribution.

It should be noted that the purpose of these pages is not just to catalogue once more the contents of the New Testament revelation and the teaching which Jesus gave about Himself. This task has often been renewed, always successfully, whenever heresies or negations have forced theologians to deeper study; in these latter days, for example, after the crisis of Modernism, we have all read the admirable analyses of PP. Lebreton, de Grandmaison and Lagrange and of M. Lepin. The present enquiry bears upon this teaching's *form*. Our aim is to pursue the origins of Christian thinking, its first intellectual moments. What was its course towards faith in the divinity of Christ? What door led it to this mystery? Here it is less a question of metaphysics than of logic, but it is always truth that we are seeking. Is it nothing then, even when we possess a doctrine as a sacred treasure, to know its point of insertion into human minds, to seize in some sort upon its very entrance within our ken, still in full process of movement, to recognize the direction which it takes, the character of its activity? In any case this is indispensable for a full understanding of our earliest texts; they mean nothing if we consider them just as hard lumps of evidence, for they are also *sources*, that is, witnesses of origins. For example, if we believe to-day in the hypostatic union of two natures on the firm foundation of Chalcedon, is it of no interest to discover what ferment of thought this now sacrosanct and precise creed, once a divine challenge, originally roused, when it produced that crisis in the history of the world which brought us truth and life? Must not the mystery of Christ be continually renewed for the Christian intelligence so that, with nothing added or taken away, it is always taking fuller hold on it? Otherwise the exactest dogmatic formulas, instead of being, as the Church would have them, the marriage garments of the truth, would end in our dried-up hearts and frozen intellects, through the very

verbal security which they offer lazymindedness, like wind-
ing-sheets of royal catacombs in which dead gods sleep.*

CHAPTER ONE: THE HUMAN NATURE
OF THE DIVINE PERSON

WHEN first Peter, James, Andrew and John met Jesus
of Nazareth by the waterside they knew Him only
as a man; and they continued for the time being to attribute
to Him a human personality like their own, although a
powerful and attractive one: *filius fabri.*† How could they
think in other intellectual categories since they had not yet
faith? We too easily forget that the name of Jesus, which for
us is the name of the Incarnate Word, was at that time for
the Saviour's compatriots the name of a man like themselves:
Jesus propheta a Nazareth.‡ The two syllables at which
to-day every knee bows in heaven and on earth referred
simply to an individual considered as a member of humanity.
And the first glance of admiration cast upon the young
Rabbi by those who had so recently felt his equals was not
a substitution in their minds of God for man, but a recognition that a merely ordinary view of Him did not account
for what the son of Mary really was. Their judgment in His

---

* "*This summit of Truth, as it is expressed in Scripture*, in the words of Jesus, in
those of S. John and S. Paul, certainly *surpasses* in richness the finest systematic
formulas . . . [S. John and S. Paul], in their inspired language, surpass the
precision of theology, which tries to give rational versions of their supernatural
contemplation, rather like trying to describe a polygon inside a perfect circle. . . .
*Above and below the theological precision of a S. Thomas there are two very different
forms of unarticulated knowledge: the full faith of the church, and the theological
residue which is all that the poorer sort of theologian can preserve.* These two forms
of knowledge are hardly more alike than Pure Act, superior to all determination,
and prime matter, inferior to all determination. . . . The Church declares
divine Faith far superior to any theological system however perfect ; let us not
confuse this exalted faith with what is far inferior to the theology of a S. Thomas—
the very mediocre doctrinal residue with which the smallest minds content themselves. We have an exact test of a theologian's worth if we can see whether, in a
great body of teaching such as that of S. Thomas, he has seized not only upon the
material side which is accessible to everyone on a first reading in the literal meaning
of the words, but also the highest principles which inspire the doctrinal synthesis
and really make it a work of the first importance." P. Garrigou-Lagrange, O.P.
in *La Vie Spirituelle* for July, 1924, pp. [272–273].

† *Mt.*, xiii, 55.

‡ *Mt.*, xxi, 11 ; *Act*, x, 38, etc. . .

regard demanded an expansion; they had to raise and deepen the very respectful view of Him which intimacy had already given them, and to admit that this man somehow completed His being by personal relations with God of an unheard of kind for which precise expression was not yet available. The transitional names, Son of Man, Prophet, perhaps at first even the title of Messiah, still placed Jesus of Nazareth as very definitely of the human family. But if he began by being taken as a man, *habitu inventus ut homo*,* it was soon seen clearly enough that the mystery of Him ended in divinity. How wonderful and loving must have been those first astonished glances in which faith found its earliest expression, which were the inauguration, the real origins of Christianity! It would be a great mistake to picture this movement of thought as the complete substitution of an altogether new idea for one now entirely rejected, a transubstantiation of humanity into divinity. It was something far better: an increase in value of a previous judgment, preserving all the solid realities of human friendship to which the disciples had first become attached. How far we are here from that scene at the end of "Tobias" which the Rembrandt in the Louvre revives for us, the Archangel's vigorous leap into the skies and the triumphant sweep of his celestial robe! Here a man, a fellow-traveller, suddenly changes into a dweller in Paradise, and putting off the appearance under which his immateriality had previously been veiled, declares himself to be what he really is, God's spiritual envoy, an essentially invisible visitor from heaven. So perhaps the imaginations of children picture the revelation of the Son of God and of Christian dogma at their catechism classes. But there is not a word in the Gospels to encourage such ideas, which would at once issue in Docetic heresies and so later in Apollinarism or Monophysitism. There is no trace in our sources of Docetism; that did not appear until the next generation when the last direct witnesses of the life of Jesus had disappeared; and then this deadly and seductive error was checked at once by the Apostolic Fathers, who on

* *Phil.*, ii., 7.

certain occasions cried out in horror or wept with rage when they encountered it. In the New Testament we touch the full, solid, obstinate, historical reality of Jesus of Nazareth, historical not only in the modern sense of documented, but in a material and corporeal sense, for we find here that human reality of His from which the whole movement of Christianity and all Catholic dogma take their origin. We are in the presence first of all of a man, and, without denying anything of this concrete experience, faith adds that this man is the Son of God, giving this ancient biblical and Messianic expression its full sense, its absolute and Christian significance. Such a movement or travail of thought imposed on the minds of the disciples would be described to-day in peripatetic terms as the raising of their minds from the human nature to the Divine Personality; Jesus of Nazareth, who seemed before a mere human companion, must complete His lovable and mysterious being in Divinity.

Such a formula, which tries to seize upon those earliest glimpses of the truth, may seem deficient in dogmatic accuracy; the glimpses themselves in the early stages, when hearts had not been fully won, have seemed to some ambiguous. But there is no ground at any point for claiming a Docetic or Monophysite movement of thought at the birth of Christianity, which was in fact impossible. And the route which Christian thought naturally took, with *filius fabri* as its start and *filius Dei* as its end, is one in which the second term can replace the first only by keeping a place for it and recognizing that it is profoundly true: Jesus, the Son of God, is always the son of Mary.

Any novice in the school of Aristotle knows this route: it goes from a nature to a person,* and from a human nature to a Divine Person in the case before us.

* We hope that we shall not be reproached for inserting into a Scriptural account words such as "nature" and "person" which are not in the actual text. What does this matter if in fact this earliest Christian thought moves straight in the direction of Chalcedon's definitions? To read a text is not merely to repeat its written syllables but also to reveal the implication of its living reality. By constantly explaining the clear and convenient words "nature" and "person" by their earliest equivalents one could construct laborious phrases which would succeed by dint of continual precautions in avoiding heresy, v.g. "the son of man who is before us and speaks to us, born of a woman according to the flesh, is also born of

We have some difficulty in following it ourselves now that the Prologue of the Fourth Gospel has definitely put in the foreground of our idea of Christ the divine Personality. But Peter, James and Andrew had first seen the man, and only declared Him God when they had heard His words. Their faith in the divinity of the Saviour, in which the whole of Christianity is contained in germ, could not start straight away with "in principio erat Verbum". But, *this man is God, this man is the Son of God*, that was the familiar course of their thought, as was later that of the centurion on his way from Calvary. The first glance, then, bears on what we call the human nature. And while we consider it only after first affirming in our minds the person who is its subject (unless, we are using purely abstract language), the disciples on the other hand first reached the concrete human nature and the Divine Person only afterwards. However unpleasant the necessary mental readjustment, we shall never perhaps fully understand certain early texts unless we try at least to take up this position for a moment. We have difficulty in thinking of a human nature which could be the subject of a proposition without implying human personality. Strange though this logic may appear to us, it seems to have been primary in Christian experience. This was the earliest support of faith for those who morning and evening, as they walked and ate with Him, saw and heard *this man* who was *the Son of God* (Mt. xxvii, 54; Mk. xv, 39).

The earliest of all references to our Lord, before He gave testimony of Himself, made at the time by men inspired by the Holy Spirit, or those made later by men who had not heard Him, will therefore move from the human nature to the Divine Person, attributing the former to the latter. But as this is a mode of speech unfamiliar to the human mind the texts which take this standpoint seem unnatural to us.

God before all creation." But with a system of language of this sort either a mere reproduction would result of texts already known (and in that case why not simply buy a good edition of the New Testament?) or there would be a departure from the letter of the text in the attempt to interpret it and sum it up, which would be to renew without authority and with second-class materials the task which the Church is reproached for having done in the most universal and rigorously philosophical of languages.

Yet it is perfectly legitimate. Further, these verses and the mental attitude behind them are decisive in advance against Docetism. They start from a human reality which materially is not divine and they affirm it of the Son of God. This attitude, later overlaid by others, may have continued underground for a long time, and it is possible that certain later texts, read usually as moving in the opposite direction, from the Divine Person to the human nature, may be read also in the previous way and thus possess two complementary senses.

In any case the thought of the earliest disciples must normally have followed this direction, for they had known the man before knowing Him as God, and naturally they started from the first in order to declare the second. Our theologies still use this method when they study Christ's human nature in isolation. Then we speak of the sacred humanity of our Lord Jesus Christ or of the Son of God. But our expressions, stamped by centuries of teaching, are scholastic ones; by making concrete use of the general and universal term "humanity" we maintain the reality of Christ's human nature, and yet we disallow relentlessly any notion of a human person, we take from this sacred humanity all personality in its own order. The earliest witnesses passed through this stage of thought unarmed with our vocabulary. Remember that only yesterday they attributed to Christ a human person; thus they still speak of His humanity as if it were an independent being, but only in and by someone transcending it. So the word Christ, understood in the simple Jewish sense of Messiah, simply gave a picture of a divine human being; after the coming of the Faith the name had straightway to unite something which was of man and someone who was more than man. But for the time *something* was mentioned first in order to refer to *someone;** this attitude of mind produced some very valuable expressions, testimonies of the most primitive Christian language, which, like every living source, has a secret influence on later formulas, although it has vanished from the scene.

* It is a necessity of the human mind to be unable to admit the existence of a nature without conceiving of it in the concrete, that is in a *suppositum* or a hypostasis: *Contra Gentiles*, bk. 1, cap. 30 ; *Summa Theolog.*, 1a. p., q. 13, a. 1, ad. 2.

Here perhaps are some of these ancient traces of the first Christian vocabulary. Those which seem most representative are from the Gospel of the Infancy : *Quod enim in ea natum est, de Spiritu Sancto est* (Mt., i, 20). *Quod nascetur (ex te) Sanctum, vocabitur Filius Dei* (Lk., i, 35).

Quod nascetur ex te Sanctum. Although commentaries must not be built on too slender a foundation, we may admire the exactness of this *neuter*, so full of mysteries and lessons for us, which while unmistakably placing the child who is to be born among the human family, where it takes rank by reason of its nature, keeps the name of His Person in the masculine for the morrow—*vocabitur (quia erit) Filius Dei.**

In writing thus the Evangelist underlines that side of the mystery on which it was first revealed to us, which makes it at once so precious to our faith and hope: Jesus is born of the human race. The son of Adam in all but sin, the son of the patriarchs whose hopes He fulfils, He has that blood and nature of our own, of which we are so proud when we keep them pure as God would have them—which are so lamentably shameful when we profane God's gift.

So much for those who under the pretext of aggrandizing my Saviour would make Him vanish into an unsubstantial vision! So much for all the dreams of *gnosis* and the false shame of Docetism! Rather we could dare to reverse the passage in Genesis and say: *factus est Deus ad imaginem et similitudinem nostram.* But again we are making the name of the Person the subject of the phrase, according to our usual theological habit, when we were trying to keep in touch with the earliest Christianity whose thought moved the other way, showing in the realism of the Annunciation scene a chaste womb alive with a new fruit, a human fruit. The new life which pulsed in the Virgin's womb was a human life, but metaphysically, if we may so say, living by right of the Son of God: *juris Filii Dei.*

---

* The centurion at Calvary, when without previous instruction he tried to frame an act of Christian faith, gives a definite impression of using language in this sense : *vere hic homo Filius Dei erat. Mk.*, xv, 39 (and parall.).

Lord God, in spite of the tenderness of this mystery, or rather because of its tenderness and charm, let us remain calm and attentive, though so greatly stirred, before such realities. Our nature, this splendid and sorrowful human nature, is henceforward yours—a body informed by a soul begins to grow, and both we must call yours. . . . What draws us to you in this prelude of the Incarnation is your humility; but this humility seen from our side is an equality: *totus in nostris.* . . .

And when we, entering into ourselves, begin to live more fully the life of that nature which we now know so much better, we may think that you have trodden all the ways of man's experience, except for sin, which we tread all our lives.

Lord God, grant us not to be afraid of your humanity, never to substitute for your truth, by a false shame, any of those bastard heresies which your Church condemns. . . .

When this Church, remembering the *Lamma Sabacthani* of Calvary and the *In manus tuas*, the last utterances of the Saviour's mortal voice, invites us to think of the ancient verses of the prophet in his desolation as upon the lips and in the human heart of Christ, we must interpret these texts first and foremost only of Christ's human nature in the Messianic context from which our Christian piety has sprung, we must return as we chant the Psalms to the original standpoint of the Apostles as they first met Jesus.*

---

* The mystics whose daring knows no bounds have often recaptured this primitive vision of the mystery of the Incarnation by the sheer power of their contemplation. M. Olier, for example, had the courage to plumb the depths of this abyss :

"As man, our Saviour was a creature, and therefore nothing: so all that He was came to Him from without; He came from God . . . who had brought Him out from nothingness. . . . That was the source of the Son of God's humility, which made Him so humble, more humble than all mankind together, for having more light upon the nothingness of creatures than all men He was incomparably more cast down, humiliated and abased in His own eyes and before the majesty of His Father, with whose greatness He was so perfectly acquainted. He saw clearly that as a creature He was of Himself nothing just like the rest of men, and that His Father had drawn Him from the abyss of nothingness to make Him the depositary of all His wealth. Therefore He was perpetually annihilated before Him, avowing that He was nothing." (Jean-Jacques Olier, *Introduction à la Vie et aux Vertus Chrétiennes*, ch. V, de l'Humilité, section 3).

Apart from the word *nothing* applied to the creature, in the exaggerated style of the 17th century, this passage is rigorously orthodox, since it envisages only the human nature, but it is not in our usual style except perhaps when we are commenting upon our Lord's energetic expression, related by the Synoptics, when for the

It is not surprising that these same apostles in their first discourses in the Acts, when they had to preach the divinity of Jesus of Nazareth to people unprepared for it, fell back upon formulas analogous to those of the Gospel of the Infancy: *virum approbatum a Deo*, Acts, ii, 22. *Sanctum puerum tuum Jesum, quem unxisti (Domine)*, Acts, iv, 27. *Jesum a Nazareth: quomodo unxit eum Deus Spiritu Sancto . . . quoniam Deus erat cum illo*, Acts, x, 38.

To reinforce the dogmatic value of these texts, which seems rather meagre in their literal sense, we are anxious to explain that *puer* is equivalent to *filius*, etc. . . . This may be all very well. But the interpretation which we propose does not require such substitutions. If there is any impoverishment in these texts uttered and written to make their adherence to the new religion easy for those who were just now its enemies, to smooth the transition and deaden the shock (as S. Paul did with the Athenians of the Areopagus), it lies in the words *approbatum* and *unxisti*, which are more biblical than evangelical. But the words *vir* and *puer* are perfectly satisfactory: the Apostles are speaking of a man, a servant of God (though mentally taking from these terms referring to an individual nature their connatural hypostasis), a human being completed in a Personality which is divine. Here is that first glance of theirs again! When the glance is only feeble in its penetration, as with the disciples journeying to Emmaus, Jesus of Nazareth becomes nothing but a man: *de Jesu Nazareno, qui fuit vir propheta, potens in opere et sermone coram Deo et omni populo* (Lk., xxiv, 19).

Perhaps, too, that is the way to find a less rigid inter-

---

moment He abstracts from His divine mystery: *quid me dicis bonum? nemo bonus nisi solus Deus* (*Lk.*, xviii, 19, and parallels). Ordinarily we expound the mystery of Christ beginning with His Person; and the foundations of His humility seem to us then so rich and complex that we must be excused for expressing them here in the scholastic idiom: being the eternal Son and not the Father, Christ can adopt in His human nature an attitude of dependence (and so of humility) as regards the Father, a created participation in the movement of that eternal procession in which, while equal to the Father in nature, He is the term and not the principle. M. Olier was lost in admiration of that attitude (which is that of the discourse at the last supper, for example)—it is one of the main features of the French School's spirituality ; it is the religion itself of the Incarnate Word adoring His Father. The following section will show us how our Lord has given us this precise idea in the Gospels.

pretation of the very difficult verse in the heading of the Epistle to the Romans (i, 4). *Who* or *what* had this resurrection established in the power of the Son of God? Wasn't S. Paul suddenly going back to a mental attitude which was no longer habitual to him, but which had existed, in which first and foremost the sacred humanity was considered as raised to the grandeurs of the Sonship?*

Our Lord had clearly accepted this direction of thought in the two phrases of the Holy Eucharist's institution, when he had pronounced, taking His own humanity as starting-point, the definitive words: "This is my Body, this is my Blood." And still to-day when theologians are considering the principle of the Eucharistic presence they tell us that the Body and Blood of Jesus Christ are present *vi verborum*, and that the Person of the Word is present in virtue of the Hypostatic Union (Conc. Trid., sess. XIII, cap. 3), because the mystery starts with the Body and Blood, that is with the sacred Humanity, demanding the concomitance of the divine Person.†

Lastly, this direction of synoptic thought at its outset seems to be the only one which fits the texts in Matthew, Mark, Luke and the Acts which speak of the relations of Jesus with the Holy Spirit in a style not followed by S. John. He speaks only of the sending of the Spirit by Jesus, and these are the texts of the Fourth Gospel which establish the eternal processions: the Spirit proceeding from the Son as from the Father. In S. John there is never any question of an action of the Spirit upon the Son, because the Fourth Gospel is impregnated with the eternal relations of Person to Person, in which the Son is the Spirit's principle. But since the Synoptics envisage the human nature in the first place, they can say quite properly that it undergoes the Holy Spirit's action. Expressions such as *Jesus plenus Spiritu Sancto . . . agebatur a Spiritu* (Lk., iv, 1), are strictly true only of the human nature, and they recall the time when the name of

---

* We mention this passage with hesitation. But we shall have to return later to S. Paul's position.

† Cf. Dom Vonier, *A Key to the Doctrine of the Eucharist*, London, 1931, p. 111.

Jesus was only the name of a man pure and simple in the minds of the earthly compatriots of the Son of God.

Faith rose upwards then to the personal hypostatic divinity of its Founder from this groundwork of humanity. But the Jesus who was thus lifted to the skies did not lose in the minds of His own His attachment to our poor earth, upon which authentic Christianity to-day and always bases its historical, full-blooded, realism: *ecce homo*, our Christ is a man, the Son of God is a man. "Jesus Christ, the descendant of David, the Son of Mary, was really born, He ate and drank, He really suffered under Pontius Pilate, was really crucified. . . . If He suffered only in appearance, as some faithless men pretend, who themselves are alive only in appearance, why then am I in chains? Why do I long to fight with the beasts? Is it for nothing that I am to die?" So spoke the venerable bishop of Antioch, Ignatius, writing to the men of Tralles (IX, X,) and going to his martyrdom under Trajan, *Christo quasi homini carmen dicens*, Pliny the Younger being governor of Bithynia.

*   *   *

Long after the time of S. Ignatius, when the last Fathers were about to write the symbol of faith in the Incarnation at Chalcedon, and so to put an end to Christological heresies, we find S. Augustine choosing to take up this almost forgotten primitive conception:* "*homo quem Dei Sapientia gestabat*," he chooses to say to designate Christ; and the term *man* under his pen often replaces the word *humanitas* which we should have preferred to put (texts collected by Portalié under *Augustin* in *Vacant-Mangenot*, vol. I, col. 2364).† But at Hippo this is a scholastic approach: S. Augustine is beginning a method of instruction which the whole of Latin theology is to follow and which consists, especially in the case of the Trinity, in referring to the nature before the person.

---

* One which the Nestorians in the East and the whole Antiochene school must have made suspect by preaching a human hypostasis.

† The Roman Breviary in the second nocturn of Good Friday quotes a passage from S. Augustine in the same style : *homine quem (filius) gerebat.*

For in spite of external resemblances between the primitive style and S. Augustine's, there is the same difference as between a thirteenth-century Gothic cathedral, born of the uncompromising faith of our fathers and the technical preoccupations of mediæval architects, which now suffers from the rough handling of the centuries, between this and a cathedral in imitation ogival style, conceived in the study of a Viollet-le-Duc, built without passion, correct, impeccable and almost historyless.

In the Gospel the historical vision of the human nature subsisting in a divine Person is a concrete everyday experience charged with palpitating life. In S. Augustine and among ourselves it is a method which facilitates the difficult exposition of the truths of the faith and in particular the study of the sacred humanity of God's Son.

But what do these shades of meaning matter so long as the same love binds us together around Jesus of Nazareth, around this man who is the Son of God? Christian piety still exploits every day the charm of the disciples' first experiences; our devotion always lives in the atmosphere of the Gospel spring and of the dawn of dogma. The inner life of the Church has not thrown to waste any of the freshness of the first fruits. Always there exists a most faithful and tender, a most virile and realistic devotion to the sacred humanity of the Saviour.

This devotion, particularly in relation to the Passion of Jesus, to the agony in the Garden and at Golgotha, is one of the traditional characteristics of orthodox mysticism. The greatest speculative thinkers, the most severely abstractive theologians, if they would remain Catholics, never lose sight of the suffering Body which died for our salvation, and the perceptible historical details of the human soul and human life in which the mystery of our Redemption was performed.

And the Church in every century feels the same respectful emotion, the same tender adoration in presence of the body and soul of the Saviour: from this perceptible contact with the Word of God she derives the same sense of her own supernatural power: founded as she is to lead men of flesh and blood to heaven, she teaches them to respect and to purify their flesh and blood at the holy source whence faith first sprang in the presence of the sacred humanity of Jesus Christ.

Hence in the liturgy those realistic verses which do not move us so much now that Latin has become a dead language, but which, properly translated and understood, are the poetic echo of a bold familiarity with the Saviour's abasement, of a realization of it in the concrete:

Vagit infans inter arcta conditus præsepia:	He cried, a child in His narrow manger:
Membra pannis involuta Virgo Mater alligat,	The Virgin Mother binds His limbs with swaddling-bands,
Et Dei manus pedesque stricta cingit fascia.	The hands and feet of God are tightly swathed.

Hence in the history of devotion those apparent innovations which in reality are carrying on that same movement inaugurated in the Gospel in honour of Him who then was seen and heard. In every generation this salutary return to the realities of the Incarnation will always prevent the Church from falling into bigotry, puritanism, or a dissolving symbolism. Our religion is not cloudy or fluid, but has the solidity and resistance of a fact; when necessary it is frankly realistic. It speaks to man of man, because its God was a man. It knows the needs and griefs of bodies as well as of souls, because its Founder, who was the purest and highest of intelligences, had a body in which lived His genius, His love and His Divinity. It would be easy to show in the Fathers and beneath their formulas, which always seem to us a little stiff and distant, this attachment to the spirit of Christianity which we are here trying to emphasize in one of its essential features. It must be enough to observe how the Doctors rose up of old when the crisis was upon them; it broke out in the Platonist and idealistic East when Emperors imperfectly converted to the sturdy ways of the new religion wished to proscribe as childish or idolatrous the holy images consecrated to picture to the senses the lineaments of the Saviour and His Saints. To save the Crucifix, the supreme token of the sacred Humanity, the whole of true Christianity was up in arms.

In the Middle Ages the worship of the Saviour, not only abstractly and in mere theology—not only the worship of the mystery of the Redemption but also of the suffering Body, of its redeeming griefs, its wounds and disfigurements, its anguishes and loving affections—all this stirred the hearts of our fathers to give birth to the iconography of Europe; Emile Mâle and others have told us of this miracle.

Modern times, people say, are less simple-minded. They are no less realistic. The meditation of the Passion and of the whole mortal life of Jesus remains the great stimulus of our faith, the Way of the Cross one of our great devotions, the crucifix in its nakedness, regal and sorrowful at once, the sign in which the Christian still recognizes his Saviour.

Devotion to the Sacred Heart, so modern and so ardent, so popular, too, despite its mystical and aristocratic origins, is only the latest effort to reach the Word of God through these holy, corporeal realities in which the love which saved us was made manifest.

It would be almost as difficult to break down Catholicism itself as to take from it the body, the blood and the heart of Jesus, or to forbid Christians those prayers which cause us no astonishment now that the folly of the Cross is familiar to us, but which would have seemed fantastic to the good people of the ancient world, to Plato or to Cicero:

Corpus Christi, salva me:	Body of Christ, save me;
Sanguis Christi, inebria me;	Blood of Christ, inebriate me:
Aqua lateris Christi, lava me;	Water from the side of Christ, wash me:
O bone Jesu, intra tua vulnera absconde me.	O good Jesus, within your wounds hide me.

From this spontaneous movement towards the humanity of God comes also in the Church, in all Christianity, its astonishing respect for the humanity of men, and of all men. From contact with the Master born of our flesh we have learned to put a higher price upon the grief-stricken nature which is ours and was His: a legitimate humanism is the normal conclusion of the joy which humble creation at the close of the day of miracle uttered through a woman's lips acclaiming the Saviour above the voices of the crowd: "Beatus venter qui te portavit, beata ubera quæ suxisti. Blessed is the womb that bare Thee and the breasts which Thou didst suck."

CHAPTER TWO: THE DIVINE PERSON IN THE HUMAN NATURE

FROM the time when Jesus opened His lips to preach of Himself, the movement of thought from the human nature to the Divine Person was condemned to disappear. Expressions beginning with "I" can only envisage the person in the first place. Yet the faithful hearers of Christ in Judaea and Galilee did not take at once to the order of ideas in S. John's Prologue, in our catechisms and our theology, where we consider first of all the pre-existing Word apart from humanity and only afterwards the taking of a body and a soul like our own. He who speaks to us in the Synoptics and throughout the Fourth Gospel does so in virtue of what He sees in His human mind: it is the human and temporal speech of the eternal Word which His disciples hear and the witness of a human soul knowing and realizing that it is the Son of God's.* We declare who we are, but we know it by

* When we think of Jesus and His human consciousness we too often fall into Monophysitism (or at least Apollinarism). We take it for the consciousness of God, as it is in the hypostatic order, but in the psychological order this is false (by reason of the distinction of the natures which, as Chalcedon says, are not confused). We must therefore begin with a human consciousness and allow to it such powerful religious experiences (in the language of to-day), or rather, to use the proper theological and Christian language which alone is really acceptable, a beatific Vision of God of such a kind, that He knows that He is the Son of God. Or if we wish to distinguish the senses of "He" (which are identical metaphysically, or

what we have. We speak of being someone, being a person—
principium quod: but we speak of possessing a nature—
principium quo. Now it is through the *principium quo* that the
principium quod is named. The conclusion follows that Jesus
who is the Son of God sees and experiences this in His
human nature. The latter obviously bears within itself that
by which it is human nature, as we have seen in the previous
chapter, and also that by which it is the human nature of the
Son of God, that is, in brief, that by which it is human
nature *reduplicative ut sic* and also that by which it is divine
human nature, not in the Monophysite sense of divine nature
humanized, but in that of Chalcedon, the human nature of
Him who is God, with all the powers, privileges and rights
which this hypostatic ownership involves for it. Those
familiar with the field must pardon this insistence; accuracy
here is so important for an intelligent reading of the Fathers
in the time before Monophysitism, but above all to help us
to understand what our Lord says of himself in the Synoptics
and especially in S. John. If the starting-point already
explained has been clearly perceived and the reasons why it
is the starting-point, we realize why our Lord had no need
to underline His human nature; it was the first object of all
thought in His regard, and moreover, as S. John repeated
with emotion in his old age (I John, i, 2), this humanity was
seen and touched; He ate and drank (Mt., xi, 19) and slept
(Mt., viii, 24), and was to suffer and to die. But Jesus had to
teach that this historical reality was the human nature of the
eternal Son; and, to say this, He did not declare for a start
like the Prologue of the Fourth Gospel, "In the beginning
was the Word, and the Word was made flesh," but rather,
"look, see, touch, and you will have proof of what I know
and of what I say, that I am in this human nature God's
own Son."

A whole series of consequences follows from such an
attitude. While this nature is substantially human first and

rather hypostatically, but distinguishable psychologically according to the distinction of natures), His human intelligence knows that His Person is the Son of
God, and that this glorious inner life, which is in Him and unfolds itself according
to the laws of human psychology, is the human life of the Son of God.

last, the divinity claimed by Jesus, by this exigent "I" who is revealing Himself, will be that of the person. Theology, soon to be sanctioned by the Councils, will draw this conclusion, and it is inevitable.

Meantime the intelligence of Jesus shows us, as He speaks to us, this hypostatic Divinity through the human nature which bears the proofs of it, in the sense explained above in which it is divine, that is for God and of God: let us add, since we also know the name of the person, in the sense in which it is filial, that is of the Son and for the Son.

And as a result the order and arrangement of the ideas revealed in the Gospel are not quite the same as those which we have adopted in our manuals for purposes of exposition. We approach the mystery from the side of the eternal Person, and at once go on to say that this divine Person took a nature like our own. In that brief phrase we enclose all the essentials of the mystery and even of the metaphysics of the Incarnate Word. We are all the more attached to this ontology in that two subtle heresies lie in wait for us at the outset between which (as between the two Detroits) the bark of Peter and of S. Leo must pass on its voyage to Chalcedon: on the left bank, Nestorianism, dividing Christ into two hypostases; on the right bank, Monophysitism, contracting the two natures into one, once divine only and remaining divine, but now also incarnate.* We must prevent

* It would be, unfortunately, an illusion to take these heresies with remote names for dead and buried errors. They are only too much alive, not merely because there are still strange dispersed Christian communities, so we are told, in the mountains of Persia calling themselves Nestorians; not only because our brothers the Armenians and the Copts, the Abyssinians and the Jacobites, schismatics from the Greek Church before becoming so for the Church universal, still obstinately maintain their fidelity to the ancient Monophysitism of Eutyches in a highly developed state of civilization, but because among ourselves many badly instructed Catholics have their view of Christ influenced by unprecise, vague and dangerous ideas where perhaps the shadows of Nestorianism and especially Monophysitism are predominant. They do not know the names of the heresiarchs, but they still yield to the eternal temptations of their religious halfheartedness when they are faced with Jesus. And what was at Alexandria and Antioch in the fifth century only a metaphysical intoxication survives in these modern minds as an unhealthy fog.

Monophysitism is the regular temptation of pious but ignorant people. The Christ whom they adore and to whom they pray, is, as they say, *the good Father*. And they understand by that—God making more or less a semblance of being man to put Himself within our reach. They do not refuse Him a body, like the Docetists: this too crude form of heresy has definitely disappeared. But this body is only the historic vesture of God, who is thus visible and lives among us with all what might be called the application to Christ of the idea of communicating containers. Faced by such subtle enemies we cannot avoid laying down at the outset a metaphysical definition of Christ as a single person in two unconfused natures. And it is only after having thus safeguarded orthodoxy that we can return to the concrete history and psychology of Jesus of Nazareth, to the sacred humanity as an object of historical experience. We can then see without running any risk how far this nature has undergone the influence of the person, and, behind the person, the influence of this single and consubstantial divine nature, common to the Father, the Son and the Holy Spirit.

Then and then only the theology of the Schools, taking over one of those superb expressions which fell from the pen of the great Unknown who hid his glory under the name of Dionysius the Areopagite, then this theology builds its magnificent doctrine of "theandric" operations which fills the whole second part of the treatise of the Incarnation; in the human nature of the Saviour, now clearly distinguished from His divine nature, every faculty, every operation, is in some way divino-human, or theandric (S. Thomas said as well or even better *congruens Deo, Deo decibilis*, worthy of God),* because all these powers and actions admitted to the

His love and intelligence; and this love and this intelligence are the eternal love, the infinite intelligence of Him who bends towards His creatures in their borrowed garments. God became incarnate. But the idea of the Incarnation does not mean a substantive to these heedless spirits; it only brings before their eyes an adjective. Devotions which the Church does not watch carefully always end by fading into this gloomy and unsubstantial heresy which renews the mere theophanies of the Old Testament under a Christian guise. All the realism of Christianity has then evaporated. It is a religion without force or originality. Unfortunately it is widely spread in a diffuse form in pious writers and it is hard to diagnose and to expel, like a subtle microbe.

Nestorianism is the temptation of vigorous thinkers who would remain Christians, but at little cost. When they speak of the Saviour, they do not call Him the good Father or the Sacred Heart but *the Christ*. And they understand by the name a historical personage before whom they bow as the highest human personality who has honoured our poor earth. This great man Christ speaks to them simply in the name of the God with whom the Church identifies Him. She therefore adores Him. But they do not adore Him. They too return to the Old Testament, not to see God come down on Sinai, but to sée Christ, the new Moses, go up to it. The Christ of Eutyches was the supreme theophany; that of Nestorius is the greatest of the prophets and, in the language of to-day, the most perfect representative of the religious ideal in the history of humanity. But these respectful and distinguished formulas are as unsatisfactory in the ears of the Church as the pious phrases of unwitting Monophysites.

* III^{a}p, q. 19, a. 1.

feast of union carry in and upon themselves the mark or sign of the eternal ownership. And for the expression of this truth the famous phrase in the letter of S. Leo the Great to Flavian of Constantinople passes from doctor to doctor, from Council to Council, and to-day from manual to manual: *agit utraque forma quod proprium est cum alterius communione, Verbo operante quod verbi est, et carne exsequente quod carnis est,** in which are affirmed at the same time the influence of the divine Person on the human nature, and the distinction, union and co-operation of the two natures which combine to produce these unique results without the least confusion with one another. In sum there are in the sacred humanity of Christ visible signs of the divinity of person; we find the consequences of it everywhere.†

* Denz.—B., 144.

† We may try to make more precise, even dare to put in tabular form this admirable "theandric" *compositum*. The manuals provide all the elements for the following scholastic classification :

Operations of	the Divinity	Strictly and absolutely divine, common to the Father, the Son and the Holy Spirit, in which the humanity of Christ does not co-operate.	for example, the creation of the world.
	the humanity	1. Those sometimes called divine in a wide sense by ancient authors, because they manifest the divinity : now called theandric in the strict sense. These are the operations of the human nature under the direction and influence of the Word, making the Word known.	*Examples :* the resurrection of Lazarus.
		2. Those for which the ancients reserved the word "human" in the strict sense: which some modern authors call theandric in the broad sense. These are the operations of the human nature which do not manifest the Word, but which, by reason of the Hypostatic Union, are like the others under the direction and influence of the Word.	The sleeping in the boat, the fast in the wilderness.

This classification has been made according to the relations between the natures in which the influence of the first upon the second is exercised without any inter-mingling. It does not give the visual impression of the Hypostatic Union as a union within a single Person, and applied to this without discrimination it would produce Nestorianism, the division into two hypostases condemned by the Church.

Further, the lower part of the table has the drawback of seeming to make an absolute separation between two sorts of human operations, between which there does not in fact exist any well-marked frontier; for we pass insensibly from one to the other down a sliding scale, according as Christ is described in the Gospels as revealing more or less of His hidden mystery. Some of His actions reveal nothing,

This truth which for us is a conclusion was in the Gospel an initial discovery, and the Saviour made these privileges of His humanity the basis for His preaching of His person. It was by communicating to us the lights which His created and finite intelligence itself possessed that He revealed to us the eternal secrets of the Trinity.

So then the divinity and eternity of the Son are demanded by the psychology of Jesus, by the vision which He possessed in His human nature of the Father and of His eternal and

others only His Messiahship, others His holiness and some His Divinity. Of these last signs the most perfect, though to us invisible, is the knowledge which He has of the Father and of His own eternal filiation : *nemo novit Patrem nisi.* . . . The other, more visible, signs such as the miracles authenticate this latter. In fine, there are not three but only two sorts of operation in Christ, the divine or eternal and the human or historic, that is theandric. But the table has the advantage of providing an exact setting for most of our enquiries about Christ's activity. Let us take the problem of the kinds of knowledge in the Word :

Kinds of knowledge in the Word	Divine, eternal, infinite knowledge, common to the Father the Son and the Holy Ghost.	*Mediæval Subdivisions.* Knowledge of pure intelligence. (*Scientia media*) Knowledge of infinite vision.	
	Human knowledge of the created and finite intelligence with its double character.	1. Perfect and divine in the theandric sense because its perfection is a consequence and a sign of the Hypostatic Union. 2. Limited, that is not infinite, because that of a human intelligence.	Knowledge of intuitive vision. Infused knowledge. Acquired knowledge.

Finally this scheme makes it possible to bring out the following point generally left unexplained by the authors: the strictly divine knowledge or activity which collaborates in the theandric activities belongs wholly to the three Persons of the Trinity; it is the infinite Trinitarian energy, common to the Father, the Son and the Holy Spirit. It can be attributed indifferently to the First, Second or Third Person. Theology, at least since S. Leo the Great, attributes it to the Word, for example the famous phrase *agit utraque forma*, etc. . . . But the Incarnate Son, speaking with His human lips, attributes this action in the first place to the Father (John, v, 17, 19, 21, and especially 30) and then, dependently, to Himself ; and thus through His humanity He reveals at the same time both His divinity and the eternal relation which unites Him personally with the Father and constitutes Him as the Son. The theologians, who finish the treatise on the Trinity before they begin that on the Incarnation, leave this relation on one side and, to make things clear and straightforward, attribute the *agit utraque forma* to the Person of the Word This is a scholastic position useful and necessary for theological instruction, a position also characteristic of the Latins, who always bring out clearly the distinction of natures, so dear to our need of clarity. But the Saviour, whose teaching always had in view the relations of Person to Person, saw this activity in the first place in the Person of the Father. Indeed His whole message might be summed up (almost all these words are in S. John) "the action or mark of God (that is, of the Father) upon my human nature is such that I am the eternal Son." He lived in this world a created mystery parallel to the uncreated and eternal mystery of His relations with the Father.

personal relations with Him.* Instead of *psychology* we
might say equally the rights, privileges, and powers of
Jesus, provided that we mean the rights, privileges and
powers of the human nature. We must take the historic
reality, bearing the *signs* (a great Johannine word) of the
divine ownership, and start from that. That, we might even
say, is the fundamental mystery of the entire Gospel, of the
four Gospels, of the *Confiteor tibi, Pater* of Matthew and
Luke, for example, but above all of the Gospel of S. John,
the key and secret of it. "My human nature," Jesus seems
always to be saying, "is such that I am eternally the Son of
God." This is an apologetic attitude, and the Fourth Gospel
does in fact insist upon the disputations of the Saviour with
the Pharisees, underlining the proofs and signs, repeating
the arguments and what we might call the formal logic of
Jesus's message.

All the words of the Saviour in which His relations with
God are in question thus have at least two senses: a created
analogical sense referring to the human nature in so far as it
is that of God and of the Son; and an uncreated eternal sense,
true only of the Person.

Two or three expressions of a more marked kind will unite
these two parts of a self-same composition, written in two
different keys, but always harmonized. For example, the
verb *to send* which is so common in S. Paul and S. John:
"God has sent His Son, God has sent me." The difference
between these two dogmatically equivalent expressions must
be noted: "The Word was made flesh—God has sent me:
Verbum caro factum est—Misit (or *dedit*) *Deus Filium suum.*"

The Word was made flesh is true only of the divine Person.

But *God has sent me*, if we consider the accusative *me*, is
true in the first place of the human nature in that it is
the human nature of the Word. The expression could have
been applied as well to this human nature simply as human
nature. Jesus need have been only a prophet and the son of a

* This is the logical order for revelation and apologetics: the psychology of
Jesus proves that He is God. But the ontological order is the reverse : the divinity
of Jesus demands that He should have this psychology, this vision of the Father and
of Himself.

H

prophet to say of Himself, like Isaias and Jeremias, "God has has sent me." This mouth, this tongue, this thought which directs their words, this body and soul, were sent and given to you in the historic order at the day of my birth and of my appearance in your midst. The Father is the author of this vocation: "He has made of me a sharp arrow, he has hidden me in his quiver."* From all eternity He thought of this historical reality which comes to you. He loved it in His predestination of it before the world's foundation:

> Before forming you in your mother's womb I knew you,
> And before you came forth from her I consecrated you.
> I have made you a prophet of the nations.†

This weak sense of *misit me* is obviously insufficient for the declarations of Jesus which make more far-reaching claims; but although surpassed or absorbed in these deeper significances it retains a certain value, easing the transition from the Messianic theology of yesterday to the Christian dogma which is being born to-day.

In this new dogma *God has sent me* is true above all of the human nature of Jesus in so far as it belongs to the Son and to the eternal Son of God, *juris filii Dei*. The mystery of this psychological and moral consciousness, the vision of God which this created intelligence enjoys, the knowledge which it has of the Father, the rights and privileges of this soul, the unique powers of this flesh, are possible only because this nature is the nature of the Son. He lives in a human way the replica of a previous mystery, without which the historic mystery would not exist. The marvels of Galilee and Judaea are possible only because God had an eternal Son.

"I leave you the task of working it out for yourselves," Jesus seems to say (a very common attitude of the Saviour in the Synoptics and S. John), "the visible facts of which you are the witnesses are possible only because I am eternally the Son of God."

And then *misit me* and *sic Deus dilexit* take on a supreme sense, so great a significance that in revealing to us at this

---

* *Is.*, xlix, 2.   † *Jer.*, i, 5.

deeper level the eternal mysteries of the relations between the Father and the Son they gain as their final meaning: the First Person is eternally the principle of the Second. Theology is justified in this conclusion: such a *mission*, it tells us, implies *procession*. Yet *sending* may be used in the proper sense only of the Incarnate Son. When we turn our gaze to eternity, only one verb is admissible, to *engender*—only that envisages the Person only. *Sending* presupposes that the Person possesses a historical nature, but it reveals through this nature the mystery of the eternal Person.

A word with a still more remarkable explanation is the verb *to descend*, as in the *descendit de cœlis* which found its way into the Nicene Creed. There could be no question here of the divine nature, which, as the Catechism teaches, is everywhere and has no ups and downs. If we must localize, we must leave it in heaven, as the Church sings with S. Thomas Aquinas:

*Nec Patris linquens dexteram.**

This time the word *descendere* is not true even of the human nature as such, which comes not from heaven but from the womb of the Blessed Virgin Mary; and this word is itself enough to show that Jesus is not a prophet like the ancient seers of Israel; they were sent by God, but they did not come down from heaven. So the word *descendere* must be understood of the human nature in so far as divine, that is in the Catholic sense, in so far as it is taken in possession by the Word; or, reversing the expression, of the Word in as much as it takes a human nature. But to give a precise meaning to this last phrase, as also to the word *descendere* uttered by a human mouth, we must remember that, since the Eternal Word is changeless, motionless and present everywhere, change and movement in the phrase *the Word in as much as it takes a human nature* refer wholly to the human nature in conformity with the general theory of the *missions;* and, let us repeat, as the nature as such comes from the womb of the Virgin, it comes down from heaven only in the sense that it belongs to the Word who has so condes-

* The Hymn *Verbum supernum prodiens* (Lauds of Corpus Christi).

cended. In this way the Incarnation seen from our earthly side appears to us under the splendid figure of God's coming down to us.* But this always brings us back to the assertion that the human nature sees and realizes itself as the human nature of the eternal Word.

*   *   *

With such truths as these to relate to men, what was the formal logic of the Evangelist? What method did he adopt to put into the third person what Jesus said of Himself in the first? It was possible simply to record the words of the Master, and this was done. The Gospels are full of discourses and λόγια. But it was also possible to report facts which would perhaps be still more precious for the oral instruction of coming generations.

We ask once for all to be excused for turning for preference to the texts of S. John. As a fact the critique of the Fourth Gospel is moving more and more towards Christian traditional solutions. We owe this advance to that of psychology in general and religious psychology in particular. Knowing more of our own souls, we are better able to understand the soul of this great ancient who at the end of the first century traced for all time the characters of the soul of Jesus and the definitive formulas of Christian dogma.

Who at that date could have succeeded in the hazardous task of beginning over again the work of the Synoptics without copying them, except a surviving witness who knew the events which they related from independent evidence? In eighteen centuries of intelligent Christianity no one has dared to make a serious attempt of this kind, because no one has been able to boast that he has *seen* and *heard*. He alone had the calm courage for it. His work differs so much from

---

* On the meaning to be given to *descendere* as applied to the Incarnation see IIIa p., q. 57, a. 2. resp. ad. 2. S. Thomas clearly distinguishes the descent to Hell, which is a local movement of the human nature of Christ, from the great descent of the Incarnation *descendit de cœlis*, which belongs to the Person in so far as taking the human nature but is not a local movement. And he opposes it to the Ascension. The descent of the Incarnation is true of the divine Person in virtue of the human nature. And the Ascension is a right of the human nature in virtue of the divine Person. But for our purpose these two different mysteries reach the same conclusion : Jesus reveals His divinity to us through the human nature.

that of his predecessors with its determination to teach us something which they had not said, or to do it in a way other than that already used by them. And yet the Jesus of S. John is added to the Jesus of the Synoptics like a figure in high relief covering another, similar but less deeply cut. The setting is different, but the subject is identical. If Jesus spoke the *Confiteor tibi, Pater* of Matthew and Luke, it is natural that He should have spoken sometime or other the Johannine discourses; for how could a soul who once let fall such secrets fail to live habitually with so sublime a vision? A mystic who was a mystic only for five minutes would be a strange phenomenon; modern psychology on the contrary would consider the continuance of the supernatural state the normal thing.

Why have not the Synoptics shown in greater detail the divine heights on which the Master lived? But consider the psychology of these humble scribes, preoccupied with the task of instruction, writing for the crowd of the simple faithful, and realize that their aim was first of all to record facts of dazzling import without in fact dazzling the reader's mind. And then at the end of this first century you will find it quite natural that someone should arise to take up this tremendous historical subject once more in the light of his own memories and his own inner life.

He seems to have chosen to relate those events which had not been offered to the public from the start. His accounts too retain their note of intimacy down to the last miracle, the resurrection of Lazarus, which he shows us as performed in the secrecy of friendship, but in which he sees also the full flowering of hatred in the souls of the Pharisees, the final incident which precipitated the arrest, the trial and the death. All the biographers of the great explain human tragedies like this: all mark the course of events like this, showing hidden desires and deep-seated motives more accurately than writers who give briefer and more abstract explanations. The rapid sketch, the schema, the bulletin, are for the crowd. But a man who is acquainted with the intimate and secret details, who has leant upon the breast of the Founder that last evening, must have the sensitive pride proper to old men who themselves have seen and heard, who hear others tell the story and themselves gently, almost teasingly, complete the picture.

Add to this no light thing—the travail of a soul who has pondered these events, for sixty years perhaps, of religious and mystical experience. We do not realize so well and understand so clearly at the time the great events through which we live. It is poor psychology to make human memory a photographic plate locked in a darkroom drawer, for this noble faculty is supremely living (though not therefore unreliable), enshrined in intelligent flesh which every morning stirs its gathered stores to fresh activity, assessing its greatest moments at their proper worth; it is its function and its right to underline and stress decisive hours, distinguishing them from all those others that have passed, apparently so similar and so monotonous, upon the weaver's roll which, in the vision of the prophet, is man's life. For S. John fidelity to sacred memories meant discovering in the conversations of the past the words which summed up the whole life, the whole teaching, the very soul of Jesus. We can almost hear the old writer saying to his young readers:

You did not know the Saviour, you young people, because you were not born when He was living in our midst; and you feel some difficulty in making a picture of His moral and religious attitude, His extraordinary power, His commandingness, the penetrating force of His words, the claims of an intransigent doctrine which has yet stolen away your hearts as it stole ours. Until now we had Matthew, Mark and Luke with their respective qualities and their omissions; and these humble summaries, these rather restrained, not very colourful, pages have been enough until now for men of my generation, because we poured into their calm λόγια the emotions and memories of our youth and of our vocation.

But for you there is the risk that these little books may seem a trifle drab, and the figure of Jesus of Nazareth in these calm and accurate verses might—not become effaced or disappear—but lose its brilliance, like an old medal which wear and tear depreciates. Well, then, I am going to tell you how things happened and who Jesus was. I am going—not to over-draw characteristics—but to keep only the chief of them, leaving those less immediately useful on one side. There are too in my memories of the past words, gestures and looks of Jesus which I now understand much better than when I witnessed them: some vigorous emphasis of the Master's which had then passed unnoticed in our eyes, some strange and energetic declaration, some expression full of both light and mystery, the deep significance of which we had not realized. These things of old time, constantly renewed before the hidden eye of memory, have gained greater meaning; prayer, love, faith, the meditation of a lifetime, have helped me to understand them better. When I lived them for the first time I was only a boy, easily distracted, simply happy to be the privileged friend of a man whose name was on all men's lips. The time has come to underline the vital points in the teachings of Jesus "so that you may believe that Jesus is the Son of God, and that, believing, you may have life in His name."

The author of the Fourth Gospel begins then by pointing out with tender realism the historical characteristics of the Saviour's sacred humanity, of this body with all its nobility, its needs and its sufferings, of this soul with all its powers and interior states. And so by drawing out all the implications of humanity, by making them visible and tangible in Jesus, he closes the door once and for all to all theological shrinkings and misconceived religious tendencies. "The characteristics of the historical figure which emerge so clearly from the synoptic catechesis are not dimmed or attenuated in the Fourth Gospel, but on the contrary stand in still brighter light. It is not remarkable that the two great characteristics of the Jesus of the Synoptics, a singular tenderness and a sovereign authority, reappear exactly, but with greater force and emphasis, almost schematized, in the Fourth Gospel."[*] After reading S. John it is impossible to

_____

[*] Rousselot, *Christus*, La religion chrétienne, Le Nouveau Testament. Edit. princeps, pp. 742–743. Cf. Joseph Huby, *L'Evangile et les Evangiles*, Grasset, 1929, pp. 230, sq.

pretend that divinity diminished or modified in Jesus the essential constituents of human nature. The modern reader with a taste for clarity and contrast might reread the "spiritual" gospel in two columns, showing the proofs and signs of this double aspect of the Saviour's mystery.

Jesus comes from heaven: iii, 13, 31; vi, 38, 41.

But He comes also from Nazareth: i, 45-46.

He has no Father but God: *passim ubique*.

But He has also a Mother, a poor woman, though moving and impressive: ii, 1; xix, 25.

He is the Truth: xiv, 6.

But He groans and is troubled: xi, 33.

He is the Light: xii, 46; vi, 1, 12.

But He hides Himself: xii, 36.

He is the bread come down from heaven: vi, 50.

But He eats that of earth: iv, 31.

He gives to drink of the water springing up to eternal life: iv, 14.

But He thirsts for that of earth, drinks it from a well and drinks vinegar from a sponge: iv, 7; xix, 29.

From Him come grace, truth, the Spirit: i, 12, 14; xv, 26.

But from His body come forth blood and water: xix, 34.

He is the resurrection and the life: xi, 25.

But one day He dies: xix, 30.

Thus there are in Jesus of Nazareth two series of characteristics irreducible to a single explanation; and S. John, as a faithful witness, is determined to make these distinctions clear.

But at the same time—and this is his finest and most special method—the Evangelist shows how the Divinity is seen and proved through this real humanity. There are characteristics of humanity which serve as "signs," because the visible element, without being confused or mingled with the invisible, heralds it, reveals it, makes it visible, shows and demonstrates it. The author of the Fourth Gospel has been seized upon by this profound truth: in that sense and in that alone he is a symbolist (better a sacramentalist), because the choice and the character of the works done by Christ are in conformity, analogous with, His invisible mystery, and the human nature, created on the model of the eternal Personality, declares this last to our mortal eyes. The eyes of faith see through those of flesh.

How is this transition made?

First by giving literary currency to this concrete symbolism. By choosing carefully from the outset the most significant historical characteristics we can find as before two series of statements, this time parallel with one another :

Jesus feeds the crowd with loaves and fishes: vi, 11.	To prove that He is the living bread come down from heaven: vi, 35.
He gives sight to the man born blind: ix, 9.	To give, being Himself light, the light of the faith: ix, 39.
He restores the life of the body to Lazarus: xi, 39.	To show that He is Himself eternal life: xi, 35.

It is this marvellous coincidence that brings out the meaning of the adjective *divine* in S. John and above all in the whole patristic tradition which depends on him. The *human* in Jesus means the human characteristics which prove that He is man and which do not serve as symbols or sacraments to the divine truth later to be seen. The *divine* means those characteristics of the same human nature which can only be explained as privileges of the human nature of God's Son. They are still visible, historical, created, but they demand something invisible and *divine* to cause and explain the finite, human symbol. The divine then is not, as after Monophysitism and the Council of Chalcedon, the invisible and eternal itself, what is held in common with the Father and the Spirit, the eternal relations between them, but what in the visible is the consequence of the eternal.

This language has a long history in the Church, probably up to Chalcedon, just as the evangelical attitude to the Trinity is kept until Nicea. The latter, as P. de Régnon has well shown, gave the Church, so as to crush Arianism with a single word, the rule and habit of preaching the one God before preaching the Three Persons. In the same way S. Leo and Chalcedon, in order to stifle Monophysitism, had to reserve the adjective *divine* to the eternal operations of the Word, as studied in the treatise on the Trinity. This was a great gain for clearness of language and exactness of thought. But to read the early Fathers correctly and to understand S. John an earlier vocabulary must be learnt. In the Fourth Gospel, the resurrection of Lazarus, which has nothing of the eternal in it, is yet a divine action of the first order, for this action, although visible and created, taken in conjunction with the statements made by Jesus, proves that He is the eternal and uncreated Son of the invisible God.

But we must go further. Merely human facts and signs of divinity all lead in our Gospel to a single Person, that of the Son. For when Jesus speaks of His relations with the Father and straightway declares Himself, the writer who before was dualist and sacramentalist in method, gives us now a single text only for a single affirmation; Christ is not twice over Son of the Father, once in a symbolic sense and secondly in an invisible one. He is just the Son.

Previously two facts of different orders were juxtaposed so that one should serve the other as its introduction and its proof; we found two foods, two lights, two lives, those of the body and of the soul. Now on the other hand we have the relations of the Son to the Father which are always the same, though with different effects in the temporal and eternal orders—on the one side, subordination and mission, on the other, origin and procession. But we must see them in a single explanation itself expressed by one text only, for there is one Son.

Previously two parallel texts led to a unique mystery which the very parallelism helped us to discern, the mystery of the Person; now a single text, relating to the Person, puts us in presence of a double mystery, that of the two natures, which each in its fashion, by way of parallel but at different levels, realizes the relations between Son and Father.

All the religious wealth of Christianity, "that He who is my God should be my brother also", is within this final framework. From the merely literary point of view such a concordance is a masterpiece; and the Gospel of S. John would be the marvel of religious literature, if it were not the highest peak of revelation. This pen, which had to bring to unity divine and human orders, and then to make this unity live on these two different levels so that the same one word should be twice true—this pen did not falter for an instant, and never did it use the empty artifices of a forger or a sophist by the employment of a single badly chosen word. The garment which lets us see the spotless flesh of Christ is truly without fault or flaw. The splendid language of S. John, later to be the language of Christianity, shows no blots or fumblings.

The fumbling is sometimes on our side when we are faced with bold expressions which simply flow from a relentless logic, when, for example, we understand *Pater major me est* only of the human nature. The Greek Fathers, who were closer to the sources, never made that mistake. *Pater major me*, the relation of Person to Person, is true in eternity, where it means origin, and true in time, where it demands dependence and inferiority. It is always the same Son.*

But at this fine point of the Person which we have reached, the Evangelist has long ago ceased to use his own words, giving us instead those of Jesus which themselves must tell us the mystery of His filial relations. And we find ourselves at the end before the spectacle which held us at the start,

---

* C. P. de Régnon, *Etudes de Théologie positive sur la Sainte Trinité*, Vol. 3, pp. 166, sq.: texts collected from the Greek Fathers. It must be enough to quote S. Athanasius "The Son said that the Father is greater than He . . . because the Son is engendered by the Father " : and S. John Damascene: "When we say that the Father is greater than the Son . . . we understand these words only in the sense of a procession ; they mean that the Son is engendered from the Father, not the Father from the Son, and that the Father is naturally the principle of the Son."

The Latin interpretation, opposed to that of the Greeks, is summed up by S. Leo the Great in the *Letter to Flavain*, Ch. IV: "*Ego et Pater unum sumus* (John, x, 30) and *Pater major me est* (John, xiv, 28) cannot be said of the same nature . . . the humanity inferior to the Father comes from us, the divinity which He has equally with the Father comes from the Father."

S. Thomas, in the *Summa contra Gentiles*, bk. IV, Ch. VIII, while faithful to the Latin interpretation of *major me est*, is far more subtle generally in his reading of S. John.

before the witness of this consciousness, of this human intelligence, which sees, knows and declares itself as the historical and human consciousness of the Son of God.

So then, at the hour of departure, anticipating the inevitable logic of the mystery already so great and glorious and beatific—the mystery of His filial intuition of the Father—feeling at hand the last stage yet required to fulfil the Scriptures, to save us men and do the Father's will, this human soul utters its cry, the last cry of certitude and enthusiasm before the holy resignation of Gethsemane and Calvary: "*Clarifica me, tu Pater, apud temetipsum, claritate, quam habui priusquam mundus esset, apud te.* Give me, my Father, with yourself the glory which I have always had with you before the world's creation."* This does not mean as Monophysites, children and so many pious but shrinking souls suppose: "Give me, Father, the splendour which I enjoyed at your right hand before I came to men." This deformation of dogma is unacceptable at the tribunal of the Gospels and of Chalcedon. Christ would be longing to regain in heaven the glory and the happiness which He had left for our salvation, *propter nos et propter nostram salutem.* But the two natures are free from alteration or confusion. The Son of God did not leave the glory of the Father when He became incarnate; never having lost it, He has therefore no need to regain it. But now He must reproduce it for His second nature; and He says quite simply and more profoundly in the usual Johannine way: "Give to my human nature, which I have from my Mother, this fulfilment of blessedness which will not make it know any better who you are or who I am, but will join it to the glory of our divine, eternal nature. May its mystery, held back by the work of the Redemption, soon be accomplished and remain so always."

Here we must dare to seek a glimpse of this apotheosis, this dazzling illumination of the soul and body of Christ as He entered Paradise, either by trying to mark a difference in joy between successive stages of a vision which was always beatific (but more so than ever after the Ascension), or by

* *Jo.,* xvii, 5.

recalling that He remained *viator* like ourselves on earth until the day of Resurrection.*

Not having yet been glorified, not having been in heaven, not born there but taking its origin in the Virgin's womb, this glorious and holy nature does not yet know the glory of the Father to the full before the Resurrection. But it knows that it is its own, that the glory awaits it and belongs to it. It had the right to it; up to the present it has provisionally renounced it out of love for us, but it desires it and in a sense requires it. And, when it reaches heaven, a human consciousness sees for the first time *in full glory* what it is to be God's eternal Son.

The neuter has been used throughout to keep the human nature in view for the last time and not to touch as yet on the eternal. Péguy had contemplated the same spectacle less circumspectly, but his use of the masculine properly understood underlines the unity of Person, to which all, even the entry of the human nature into heaven, must be attributed:

His seat was waiting for Him at the Father's right hand,
He was the Crown Prince rising to the King.
An eternal kiss would bathe His spotless side. . . .
An eternal kiss from his Father would bathe His living
    wounds. . . .
The Father's kiss would be placed upon His forehead. . . .
Like a tired traveller at the end of his journey
        He saw His home.†

* A distinction between intuitive vision and the beatific vision is not unheard of in the Schools. But it does not seem acceptable to good Thomists; to conceive of a vision in the intelligence without *gaudium* in the will seems a very difficult position to maintain. We must therefore keep to the accustomed formulas : the Saviour's intuitive vision, which was already beatific on earth, did not prevent Him from being *viator* like ourselves and from leading, though without sin, the life which the sin of Adam brought upon us. Billot, drawing on S. Thomas, seems to have expressed this mystery with the greatest subtlety: Comprehensor Christus, respectu substantiæ beatitudinis quam habuit ab initio; viator respectu consummationis beatitudinis nondum adeptæ. . . . Esset sensus falsus si quis intelligeret quod solum corpus, et non anima, subjectum exstitit seu privationum seu operationum quæ in Christo viatore fuerunt. . . . Verus sensus est, quod omnes defectus omnesque conditiones ad statum viatoris pertinentes se tenebant radicaliter et causaliter, non ex parte animæ, sed ex parte carnis mortalis et passibilis in qua nobiscum communicavit. (Billot, *De Verbo Incarnato*, 5th Ed., 1912, p. 285. Cf. IIIa, p., q. 11, a. 2 ; q. 15, a. 10.)

† Ch. Péguy, *Le mystère de la charité de Jeanne d'Arc*, first edition of the *Cahiers*, pp. 114 sq. Péguy says also that Christ returns to heaven :

In this splendid lyric passage we have regretfully left out some verses which, though splendid perhaps, are capable of a Monophysite interpretation. But what do our literary regrets matter! It is not for the poets to relate these things; the Gospel is enough for us.

"I go, I come, I ascend," says the Saviour in S. John. And these deliberately precise expressions again recall to us the single mystery in the two natures and their marvellous parallels in the life of the Trinity; the Word is eternally in movement towards the Father by whom He is begotten: παρὰ τοῦ Πατρὸς . . . πρὸς τὸν Πατέρα, as the prologue of the Fourth Gospel is to tell us. The human nature of the Word from the first moment of its existence follows the same road, wholly directed towards the same Father. And it is now touching the goal: *nunc autem ad te venio*. The mystery of Christ, seen from the side of the Person, is absolutely unified.

Jesus of Nazareth! How near you are to us in spite of the nineteen centuries which separate us from the lake of Tiberias—or rather because of them, for leaving us time to think and pray, they let us gain in the light of the ancient Councils a better understanding of the Scriptures which tell us of you. Nothing has been left to reproduce your lineaments, medal, *graffito*, or even marble fragment: henceforth your human form belongs only to the history of art, not to that of documents, for these have not retained the picture of you. But what does it matter if we have your soul so close to ours! The civilization of your time and of your tiny country has disappeared beneath so many waves of invasion

He re-entered the house of His Father
and it is the poet's right so to speak, since he hears the same note sounding in the liturgy :
    Jesu qui viator in cœlum redis (Office of the Ascension)
    Reversus unde venerat (Office of Pentecost).
    But it must be remarked that the words re-enter, return, with the sense of going *back*, do not belong to the vocabulary of S. John, who speaks of ascending and not of re-ascending. It is not that the Saviour fears to repeat that He came from heaven as a Person and that He thus returns to it; He had often said *exivi a Patre*. But at this last hour He does not wish to give the impression of a final leave-taking, and He foresees and announces a return among us in the future ; *vado et venio ad vos* (John, xvi, 28). That is why He ascends rather than re-ascends, goes rather than goes away.

and through the gentle but inevitable pressure of hours, days, years and millenaries. The last comers to Palestine, the English, will probably complete the work of devastation by laying rails and making airfields. Again what does it matter! Anyhow the Holy Land has never been more than the goal of a crusade or pilgrimage; we never meant to live or die there; and you, the eternal Son of the Father, who created all things, will not reproach us for being modern and loving modern life. We realize, Jesus, that it is not necessary to know the pictures of Tissot or to have read Papini or thumbed Baedeker's "Palestine," or (dreadful thought) to have seen *Christus* at the cinema, that we may know you and feel you near us, as if it were only yesterday that you had left the Cenacle and said to us *Vado ad Patrem*.

We have the Gospel and the right to look deep into it, to bend over these ancient texts which are so old and so young, to find them coherent, logical, clear and compelling, in spite of the mystery or because of it. Through these sacred words, O Jesus, your soul lives always and this is the one thing necessary for us. Your soul, your inner life, your vision of God, your witness, your certainties, are all ours and for us. The progress which we make in every generation in the knowledge of ourselves far from separating you from our earth makes the place you hold more and more intelligible to us; though so high by the Father's side it is yet so close to us. Our successors, thanks to our prayers, will possess you still more, but *in eodem sensu, in eadem sententia*. They will deepen but they will not correct our faith. We ourselves have not corrected the faith of our fathers, we have not taken away an *iota* or an *apex*, and that is why in this morning of a distracted century you are so real, so close, so intimate to us, and why we abandon ourselves to your influence, your lordship, your possession, O Master, we the sons of your soul and of your thought, your sons according to the Spirit, O Jesus, our Founder and our Head!

CHAPTER THREE: THE ETERNAL PERSON

OUR faith, confirmed by travelling in the clear light along the far-off road of the first century, must achieve the object of its eager quest. And the Prologue of the Fourth Gospel welcomes it to give it rest, like the threshold of a flawless temple built upon a sacred mount. The very richness of the texts which we have put together makes us divine that a time would come when the Saviour's last reserves in the statement of His mystery would yield to the pressure of His doctrine's implicit fullness. Then a disciple inspired by the Holy Spirit would take his pen and write the definitive formulas for Christian thinking. S. John then must soon write his preface. He must bring us not a teaching different from that which was given in Galilee by the Son of God Himself, but a new distribution of concepts in an order which will give permanent satisfaction to our minds, greedy as they always are for clarity and logic.

For a third way of grouping the data of the same divine message was possible for dogmatic thought. This would consist in speaking first of the eternal and pre-existing Person, before any Incarnation, before any creation, and then showing it taking a human nature like ours in time and in historic fact. Such was the approach of the author of the Prologue whose genius sketched the permanent pattern of Christianity in short and decisive formulas, yet without modifying the primitive content of the Faith. With a few strokes of the pen he fixed the language of Christianity, traced the outline of all future theologies, and summed up the most prodigious of mysteries. Jesus had said: My human nature is such that I am the eternal Son of God. S. John reversed the phrase without dropping a word or adding a thought and said: *God had an eternal son who took human nature*.

Like all immortal and profound movements of thought, this has a very simple course: it goes from the pre-existing Person to the fact of the Incarnation, from the eternal Person to the historical nature:

The Word was God, and became man.

Here is our familiar idea of Christ, our usual approach to the Saviour, following the arrow shot by this little phrase of four Latin words: *Verbum caro factum est.* Such is the way in which we ordinarily think of Christ in our manuals, our sermons, our hymns and prayers. We can never insist too much on the dogmatic and theological importance of the Prologue. It is this that has definitively canonized the categories of Christian thought, arranged their order, imposed their grammar and vocabulary. The scheme of twenty centuries of theology is traced there: it consists in starting from eternity and from God and then contemplating in time the redemptive Incarnation, in which we find the principle of grace and, following from that, the sacraments. S. John then is not only the last prophet of Christian dogma, but also the first professor of Catholic theology and at the same time the author of our scholastic language. For nineteen hundred years, in academic or ecclesiastical chairs and in our catechisms we think of God and we preach Christ in that same order in which S. John once thought and spoke: *In principio erat Verbum, et Verbum caro factum est.* The eternal Word has taken a human nature, and Christ is the Son of God incarnate. *There are three persons in God, the Father, the Son and the Holy Spirit; and the Son became Man to save us.* First communicants of every country in the world stay their stammering faith upon this firm, concise and venerable proposition.

The marvel of marvels is that the fourth historian of Jesus, after finding this supreme formula, had the courage and the tenacity never to make use of it throughout a narrative in which he wished to be a simple witness, in which his purpose was to report things not as they were to be expressed henceforth by Christianity, but as they had been uttered by Him who had the right and the required experience to put them in a different way. S. John then gives us a lesson in fidelity to purpose when, after tracing his glorious Credo, he carefully refrains from writing the remainder of his Gospel in that style. From being the theologian of eternity he becomes

I

the historian of what he has seen himself on earth. Christ had not spoken in the language of the Prologue. So these pages written by the disciple "who bears witness" use another approach, which we have already studied, the most complex and suggestive one, giving a double sense to the texts, because the filial mystery of the unique Person was then realized simultaneously in both the natures. In the Prologue the natures succeed one another or rather the one existed when the other had still to come into existence. In the Gospel they are juxtaposed, the lower giving knowledge of the higher. But thanks to the Prologue the whole mystery, welded to the eternal Person, appears in the two natures with a complete exactness. This mystery is wholly turned towards the Father: πρὸς τόν θεόν. The Son always follows His eternal course, even in historic time. And this movement towards His Father which was His before the creation of the world He now begins anew in another nature, a human nature, this too all taut in the direction required and demanded by His Person. At once this sacred humanity of Christ reveals to us the infinite secrets of Trinitarian life, and grants us a share in it as adopted sons. And there is the whole of Christianity.

Reduced to this short proposition, the formidable dogma of Christianity seems so simple that it is fitting for us here to imitate the concision of the Fourth Gospel's Prologue, to be dumb in the presence of the Word made flesh and to adore in silence. There seems nothing further to be said.

CHAPTER FOUR: THE GLORY OF THE SON

BUT before the Prologue of the Fourth Gospel had been written someone whom we have scarcely even mentioned so far, a little man who towers over primitive Christianity, Paul of Tarsus, in his anxiety to find for his readers dogmatic formulas surpassing Jewish modes of thought, had already written two or three decisive pages, a few triumphant verses, on the mystery of the Incarnation. These texts are thirty or forty years earlier than those which we have just been studying; it is more than time to read and use them.*

It was better to start by showing that the witness of the Gospels is self-sufficient without the need of any outside buttressing. But the time has come to mark S. Paul's position, remembering that independence of which he always boasted and which he used as an argument to stress the absolute agreement of his teaching with that of the other Apostles.†

He had not been a witness of the earthly life of Christ, of that human nature which bore in it the signs of divinity without enjoying yet the rights and the glory which it could have claimed. The Jesus who appeared to Paul on the road to Damascus‡ was the risen Christ in whom the mystery had been fully accomplished and whose body and soul were at last in the state which the dignity of His person logically demanded. Thus the fragmentary and primarily historical vision of the Evangelists is replaced in the Apostle of the Gentiles by a unique vision in which the humanity of the Saviour is in harmony but not confounded with the divinity. And in view of the anthropomorphic restrictions of our intellectual powers and the poverty of our human vocabulary to express invisible things, the same words are called upon to formulate both the divinity of the Person and the glory of the human nature. For it is this glory of the Resurrection that fits the rights and requirements of the Person. Both are divine in different senses—the glory because it is the normal state of a human nature which is that of God, the Person because it is God absolutely from all eternity.

It is the doctrine of the Fourth Gospel but seen from the other side of the empty tomb. And the rearrangement of

* The most important are: *Colossians*, i, 15–20 ; ii, 3, 9, and above all *Philippians*, ii, 5–11, which is the very loftiest Christology. Other passages will be quoted in the course of this chapter. Cf. Lévesque, P.S.S., *Comment Saint Paul prouve la divinité de Jésus-Christ*, Beauchesne, 1918.
† *Gal.*, i, 11 ; ii, 10.
‡ *I Cor.*, xv, 8 et alibi.

doctrinal content does not modify the dogmatic whole. The
Saviour speaks in Judaea and Galilee before the Resurrection, and the Apostle writes after Easter day. The Gospel
says: the extraordinary, superhuman, divine signs and
characteristics of the human nature of Jesus are the proof
that despite His humiliations He is the Son of God and will
one day rise from the dead. And S. Paul teaches: the Resurrection and the glory of the Son are the proof that these
humiliations which you have known and loved were not in
conformity with His true rights and that the pitiable state
to which you have seen Him reduced was not that which He
might have claimed. Henceforth the divinity is transparent
through a humanity in conformity with it, and their respective mysteries become the single mystery of Glory. Such a
view of Christ and of the unity of His whole mystery would
run the risk of Monophysitism only if we could forget the
witness of the Gospels and if S. Paul had not also been
careful to sum up the human history of the Saviour in those
concrete features which are the Alpha and Omega of the
entire Redemption: the birth of Christ formed in a woman's
womb* and his death upon a cross under Pontius Pilate.
And the Apostle who declares that he had seen only
the risen Christ declares elsewhere that he knows only
Jesus crucified.† The course of dogma then is as clear and
precise as in the four Gospels, and faithful in advance to
Chalcedon. But with these precautions once taken, these
limits once marked, we must leave the Apostle free to follow
his own genius, or rather the Holy Spirit; instead of speaking
to us of the Word made flesh, he tells us of Christ seated at
the right hand of the Father. Christ is that unique being who
is born before all creation and established in the glory
which His eternal Sonship claims, but established only in
His human nature, because His strictly divine prerogatives
are without historical incident, without progress as without
eclipse. The human nature, on the other hand, has a mortal
history which Paul does not ignore, but which he does not
choose to dwell upon, not having been a witness of it. He

* *Gal.*, iv, 4.   * *I Cor.*, xv, 3, etc.   † *I Cor.*, ii, 2.

prefers to see it as it is to-day, in full glory, as it would always have been if the sin of man had not held back the fulfilment of the mystery of God's Son. This mystery, now accomplished, is henceforth worthy of its divine demands; and, since Christ is risen and His human nature glorified, we may give the eternal Son without hesitation the historical name of Christ, which is to-day resplendent in the heavens where He has been raised to His Person's royalty. Even the eternal Person can bear this name which is now a name of glory, *before which every knee bows in heaven, in the earth, and below the earth.*

Such is the powerful summary which contrasts with the statement of the mystery *in stages* which S. John's Prologue was later to provide; and this vision of unity leads to audacities of language which disconcert the reader who is not prepared to take S. Paul's own standpoint. The text of Philippians, for example, seems to imply that the Son of God was already called Christ in His eternal existence; and the mystery of humiliation and then of glorification of which the human nature was the subject is attributed (most legitimately) to the Son, but as if during the Passion the rights of God had suffered an infringement; which is of course also perfectly correct, but not in the sense that the divine nature had undergone *kenosis.**

Here we find again all the force of that original spring from which Christianity arose. S. Paul, inviting us to give the eternal Son the name of Christ even in His eternity, recalls to us that the mystery of the divinity was seen through the humanity, and that it is as Christ, that is as the incarnate Son, that the Son is given to us.

We should know nothing of the invisible mystery of the Trinity if we had not seen the historic and tangible humanity of Christ; and although S. Paul no longer needs to recall the miracles of His mortal life, since he has before him now the greatest of all the signs, the Resurrection itself, yet it is

---

* A technical theological expression from the Greek verb ἐκένωσεν used by S. Paul in *Philippians*, II, 7, in speaking of the abasements of Christ. The Vulgate has excellently translated " exinanivit", *He emptied Himself*, in the etymological sense of ἐκένωσεν.

through the glory of the humanity that he declares the eternal and infinite glory. Christ is glorified—therefore God lives.

Of course the Son of God has always been the Son; but if we consider His human nature, we must say that it has been truly glorified as is its due only since the Resurrection, and in that sense established in its complete being only from that moment. Through it then we may say that Christ has been established as the Son of God, meaning by that constituted in all His rights at that hour of final victory. That is certainly the sense of Romans, i, 4.

The long and the short of it is the unity of the Person— but of the Person seen through the human nature which, not having been at all times what it had the right to be, introduces into the mystery of the Son a history, variations, which eternity would not have involved. To-day, now that the mystery has been accomplished, the sacred humanity shares in the glory of God; and we, who know the humanity better than the divinity, can give the Son of God, even in His eternity, these historical titles which are henceforth exalted.

Such, it seems, is the intellectual framework which we must accept to understand the Christological texts in the Epistles of S. Paul. We must take careful note that this is not altogether the position of the Fourth Gospel's Prologue. That speaks of the Son before His Incarnation, and gives Him so far only His eternal titles. It envisages Him apart from humanity, performing the works of creation as the Father's Word. S. Paul had the boldness—which all Christian devotion continues unceasingly to imitate—to give Him the name of Christ and even the name of Jesus in this eternal State; *in ipso condita sunt universa et in ipso creata sunt;* but the Apostle is seeing the Trinitarian relations at a glance through the created temporal realities, and unhesitatingly, because the Resurrection has now accomplished their complete accord.*

---

* This short cut leads to some of the finest effects in the language of Christianity. The pre-existing Word comes to be called regularily by the name of Jesus: *Jesu, redemptor omnium.*—Quem *lucis ante originem.*—Parem paternæ gloriæ—Pater supremus edidit (Christmas hymn in the Roman Breviary).

In so speaking S. Paul clearly shows his chronological position between the Gospels and the Prologue. He still borrows from the Gospels the habit of naming the divine Person only through the human nature; but he already heralds, leads to and calls for the Prologue, since the things of eternity are continually attributed to Christ—to the Christ who, born as man the other day, has also infinite origin, an eternal birth, to which S. John is soon to consecrate a special preface.

All this being so, it is perhaps unfair to force S. Paul's expressions into dilemmas which had never crossed his mind. Some commentators ask, for example, whether the *primogenitus omnis creaturæ* of the Epistle to the Colossians, i, 15, is to be understood of the humanity or of the divinity of Christ. Must we translate: *first-born of all creation* or *first-born before all creation?* The answer is not to take either reading separately but both together. These magnificent titles given by S. Paul to Christ are the privileges of the human nature which betray its union with the divine nature within the unity of Person. The Son's priority over all creatures is a property of His sacred humanity, but it possesses that quality only because it is the humanity of the eternal Son. And thus there are rights belonging to Christ's human nature proving the eternal divinity of His Person. Why then forbid S. Paul to utter this fundamental dogma, this magnificent piece of theology, in the three powerful and inspired words: *primogenitus omnis creaturæ?* Is it his fault if our modern tongues have lost the secret of conciseness? So much the better for the Apostle and for ourselves if the Greek tongue which he employs allows him this significant ellipse. Why should he not mean both at once if in fact his attitude of mind allows him to grasp the same mystery simultaneously on its two different levels?

When he says of Christ *in ipso inhabitat omnis plenitudo divinitatis corporaliter* (Col., ii, 9), *ipso* is not the eternal Word of whom S. John is soon to say *omnia per ipsum facta sunt, et sine ipso, etc.* . . . It is the Incarnate Word, and we may translate "in Him the fullness of the Godhead dwells in a human body "—and perhaps even "in the body of this man dwells all the Godhead." This second version, which may be found between the lines of the first, would be a remembrance of that primitive view of Christ leading from the human nature to the divine Person, the text thus preserving for us precious traces of it. It would be like yesterday's perfume clinging to a vase which some vigorous plant makes fragrant each morning with new flowers from the self-same stock. So, if we treat this text respectfully and refrain from scribbling comments on its ancient margins, we may see perhaps beneath the thought which the Apostle is expressing another and still more ancient order of ideas—as when in Rome earlier structures are found beneath modern basilicas honouring the same God in the same place under the patronage of the same martyr. We may consider in the words *Christ Jesus* primarily the man; and from this angle the text of Colossians, if we handle it with infinite precautions like the writing on a papyrus which might crumble into dust, would provide a primitive sense differing from the previous one but harmonizing with it in its translation of the self-same dogma.

"Christ", says S. Paul elsewhere (II Cor.,viii, 9), "was rich [of right]; He became poor [in fact]." What riches are in question here? Human or eternal? Both, but more immediately human ones. This wealth of Christ is in the first place the abundance of created privileges to which He had the right in His humanity and which He renounced. But He had the right to them only because He is in His eternity the infinite owner to whom everything belongs.

Must we not approach the text of Philippians from the same point of view to draw out all its value? "Christus Jesus, qui, cum in forma Dei esset . . . semetipsum exinanivit formam servi accipiens . . . factus obediens usque ad mortem." (Phil., ii, 5-11).

The ordinary and cursory interpretation brings in the text at the end of a dogmatic course when it has become already the equivalent of the Fourth Gospel's Prologue. Although S. Paul expressly names "Christ Jesus" here, the regular exegesis takes the *Eternal Son* as subject of the phrase, and the text, or at least the opening of it, is understood as follows in the Prologue's style: "The eternal Son, although in a divine condition of existence, was not attached to this equality with God as to a prize; but He despoiled Himself of it so as to take (through the Incarnation) the condition of a slave, making Himself like men so that He was recognized as such in all His outward life; then He abased Himself (still more) becoming obedient even to death, the death of the cross. And therefore God has glorified Him, etc."

But may we not ask, why go so fast, why simplify so deep a text like this? Since S. Paul speaks of Christ and not of the Son, he ought still to be contemplating the Incarnate Word from his usual angle, seeing through His mystery the very mystery of God.

The Apostle is keeping to the ordinary ways of Gospel thought which hardly ever view the Word without the context of the Incarnation. And yet the proof for the Divinity of Christ and for the Word's pre-existence remains just as strong and perhaps stronger. For the glance of Paul still sees in Jesus, in the human nature of Christ, all the signs which it bears of His rights, privileges and powers, which make it the human nature of the Son of God. And so the thesis which the former version with an unnecessary impatience would read straightway in this decisive text is to be found concealed in it but ready to emerge: after such implications the pre-existence of the Person is inevitable. But why take away from this pre-existence, by too hasty an interpretation of the proofs on which it rests, the splendour and privileges, the vision of God and the divine powers of this marvellous human nature? Thus the thesis of S. Paul to the Philippians is exactly the position of Jesus in the Gospels with the glories of the accomplished Resurrection superadded.

The Epistle to the Philippians is therefore infinitely precious since, without uselessly anticipating by thirty years the Fourth Gospel's Prologue, it preached the mystery of Christ in such terms that this passage of S. John must one day inevitably follow it. Exact coincidence of ideas and words was not required. Was it even possible? Isn't S. Paul sufficient in himself? And wasn't the dogma of the Incarnation rich and magnificent enough to be considered twice, in two accounts differing in detail but with the same complete significance?

If this interpretation is correct, if the subject of the phrase in Philippians is *the Incarnate Son* and not *the Son*, our version is as follows: "Christ Jesus who was God did not cling as to a prize to the rights which this equality with God (personal, hypostatic) conferred (upon His human nature)—but He despoiled Himself (of His privileges) to take the state of a servant, this making Him like men in all things. Having thus become man like ourselves, He was humiliated and made obedient even to death, the death of the cross. And therefore God His Father has glorified Him (at the Resurrection and Ascension), and given Him this name which is above all names, since (to-day) at the name of Jesus every knee bows, in heaven, on earth and even in hell, and every tongue confesses that our Lord Jesus Christ has entered into His Father's glory."

According to this exegesis, which flows like clear spring water, the *forma servi* is not the human nature quite simply as in *Verbum caro factum est*, but the humiliated and pitiable human nature of our everyday experience; it is this miserable diurnal lot which came from sin and ends in death; *ipse enim quotidianus defectus corruptionis*, says S. Gregory in the Breviary,* *quid est aliud quam quædam prolixitas mortis?* A man who was God has lived the ordinary life of men, suffering their common death. That is the condescension which transported S. Paul, and which he offers the Philippians as an example. It must be carefully observed that he takes the mystery of Christ in its entirety, the Incarnation and the Redemption together, or rather the Redemption as including and presupposing the Incarnation. He does not stop at the stage where the learned and scholastic language of the Prologue stopped, in which the Incarnation

---

* *Brev. Rom.*, Commune unius Martyris, lect. VII.

is separately considered, prescinding from Calvary and the Cross, later made by theologians the subject of a special treatise. S. Paul goes at once to the heart of the mystery, and with a single glance, in a single phrase, takes it all in: "He who had the right not to die accepted death": once again it is the whole of Christianity.

This version would have the enormous advantage of providing at once a coherent, definitive and solidly grounded account of the mystery of the Redemption. Christ Jesus, who in virtue of His divine condition had the right as man to every sort of privilege, renounced it to take on Him the condition of a servant. We know why: we have been saved by this renunciation: *pro nobis*. . . . And this new approach to the mystery takes us beyond the limits of the present chapter. For here is the very source of the dogma of the Redemption which we shall soon be treating.*

* This exegesis would have the additional interest of avoiding absolutely the fantastic theory of a kenosis affecting the Divinity itself. The manuals speak of this heresy in connection with the sixteenth century Protestants. They show themselves in a very strong position in regard to this idea, yet at the same time not without a certain weakness. In a very strong position, because this vague and obscure theory of the Word abandoning His eternal glory for the time of His mortal life is wholly foreign to tradition; with a certain weakness, for if we begin by making the eternal Word the subject of ἐκένωσεν it is then rather awkward to deny some kenosis of His eternal glory. By attributing the phrase to the Incarnate Word we obviously escape the difficulty; it is Christ who is despoiled and humiliated, that is the Word in His human nature, which alone can really suffer such subjection.

Nevertheless the ordinary interpretation does not take this course and prefers to read, as we have said above: "Christ who is God was not attached to His equality with the Father [which He possessed in His divine nature] as to a prize, but He humbled Himself to take also [by the Incarnation] the state of servant, which made Him like men in all things. [Then] He was further humiliated and made obedient even to death, etc. . . ."

We must allow that the resemblances between the two versions are greater than the differences: perhaps there is not so much difference after all between the regular classical view of the commentators that the kenosis must be understood of the Incarnation and that according to which it must be understood of the voluntary humiliations of Christ in His incarnate life, that is of the Redemption.

Let us pause to think: why is it said that Incarnation is an act of humiliation, a kenosis, on the part of the Word? We cannot say that it is because it suppresses or suspends the infinite glory of the Son; that would be the Protestant theory which has been condemned. It is, we are told, because the Incarnation "veils" the glory of the eternal Word and makes Him appear no longer as God; that is to be the sense of *habitu inventus ut homo*. It is admitted at once that an Incarnation which did not "veil" the glory of the Son could not have been kenotic. And this is exactly what the second view holds. For an Incarnation in which the human nature of the Son of God with all the glory, splendour and privileges belonging to it by right would have been recognized as the nature of the Son of God, in which it would have enjoyed in fact all the consequent rights, would have been precisely what S. Paul sees it to be eventually after the Resurrection, when the kenosis is

It is above all in the Epistle to the Colossians and the Epistle to the Hebrews that the gathering force of S. Paul's irresistible teaching, like waves thundering among the rocks, carries his expression not beyond his thought but towards a new form which only S. John is perfectly to fix.

Once seen as part of this great movement, these two epistles, however different their aims, their literary characters, their method of approach, are witnesses to the power of an idea which has been working itself out from the beginning—the sap is rising still. Faithful to the regular approach "the author always reaches the Son of God

done away with. For no Christian would dare to say that Christ now glorified in heaven is humiliated and in a kenotic state. Yet He is always the Incarnate Word.

The word *veil* (*adumbrare*) appears as far back as S. Leo the Great's letter to the patriarch Flavian; *obumbrata majestatis suæ immensitate*. S. Thomas takes up the picture and the idea with perfect exactness: *in cruce latebat sola deitas* (in the Hymn *Adoro te devote* for the Corpus Christi Procession).

Have we not confused the verbs *to condescend* and *to humiliate oneself* in common speech and preaching? The Word, in becoming incarnate, deigns to descend, He condescends. But the Incarnation as such (that is, apart from the conditions of humility which the Redemption of our sins imposes), is this a humiliation? A down-coming, yes! But a humiliation? Only superiors can give themselves the pride (and the joy) of condescending. The Incarnation, like the Creation, is one of those magnificent acts in which God grandly condescends, interesting Himself in our poverty, but without losing any of His riches, without emptying Himself: to empty oneself is the etymological sense of ἐκένωσεν. *Deus non mutatur miseratione*, says S. Leo. Yet we must recognize that the Te Deum sings *non horruisti Virginis uterum*.

S. Paul perhaps would be much surprised at the alternatives which we offer him in our commentaries on these texts of his which have such wealth of meaning in them. We force him to dilemmas which have no significance except through the development of our theologies, that is through the distinctions of discursive concepts. But his own complex thought was of a depth which made these bifurcations quite unnecessary. Perhaps he does not choose between the two senses which we offer him but embraces both in one profound and all-inclusive vision in which one of the readings overlays and postulates the other. Take the first sense in its full force, with all its background and inevitable implications; delve into the mystery which it sets forth, develop it—the second meaning will emerge from it in a blaze of glory. Perhaps then it is not necessary to choose between these two readings of Philippians, because one presupposes and prepares the way for the other, just as the body of S. John's Gospel presupposes, prepares for and proves the theology already stated in the Prologue. We choose when there is opposition, divergence or at least alternative. We are not obliged to take a side when there is a seed developing, a natural implication of thought, a logically inevitable connection; we surrender ourselves to a living current of ideas certain that it will bring us safe to port. It is interesting to note particular points on one's way, to find the place which one has reached on the map; but the real traveller is always more interested in the goal of his journey than in the countryside along the route. And what does it matter to a man who thirsts for truth whether he drink from the source or the conduit provided that the water is still pure?

See Prat, S. J., *La Théologie de Saint Paul*, Vol. I, 1st ed., 1908, p. 438, note 1, for these opposed forms of exegesis. [Eng. Trans. 'The Theology of Saint Paul' (Burns, Oates and Washbourne), 1926].

through the human nature."* And this angle is the more
familiar to S. Paul in that he is thinking almost always as he
writes of Christ in His glorious body, of the Incarnate Son.
But from time to time his thought shifts suddenly towards
a pre-existence for which the book of Wisdom provided the
word and formula; his pen seems to tear the parchment as
if it tore a veil; and in spite not of himself but of his usual
style he writes words which he must have realized upon
reflection to have no longer strict application to the body of
the Saviour *born of a woman*.† This vision, a little dazzled,
charged with powerful emotions, the emotion of a Rabbi
knowing and using his old Bible, the emotion of a neophyte
using it for the glory of his Master who only lately passed
from sight, a Master so young and yet eternal, this vision is
clear for us and infinitely precious. Yes, it is indeed Christ
of whom he speaks, the historic Christ, *the head of the
Church*, *the first-born from the dead*.‡ But through the vision
of this humanity S. Paul sees Him "in whom all things
have been created,§ Him by whom God made the world".‖

Certainly the created soul of Christ did not yet exist *when
God laid the foundations of the earth*¶; but to-day, in the
fullness of its divine Resurrection it shares, as was its right,
in the glory which is the Creator's due; seated at His right
hand, it receives the praises due to Him *who has made the
world*. And again all Christianity is there at once in that
tremendous summary, which only S. John will have the
power to make us see more fully, so that this faith fixed
from the beginning, on the road to Damascus, on the journey
to Emmaus, at the empty tomb, at the Cenacle, in Galilee
and by the Jordan, may at last be expressed in formulas
which children can learn, theologians enunciate and
Councils solemnly define.

* Eug. Lévesque, op. cit., p. 28.
† *Gal.*, iv, 4.
‡ *Col.*, i, 18.
§ *Col.*, i, 16.
‖ *Hebr.*, i, 2.
¶ *Prov.*, viii, 29.

CONCLUSION

Through this tradition it is not only Christ who comes near to us, whose teaching and whose very soul we find in the Scriptures—thanks to Christ, we find the Father Himself; we can see and hear Him. Such is the power of Christianity and of the mystery of Jesus. "Philip, he who sees me sees the Father. Why do you ask to see the Father?" (John, xiv, 9). We realize at last the meaning of this strange-sounding saying which is yet so simple and satisfying in its profundity.

To see Christ is to enter with the eyes of the body and the gaze of the soul into relation with that glorious human nature of His which is the companion of our pilgrimage and claims our admiration and our friendship. It is to be the disciple of a man who belongs to time and place, and who exercises on the religious thought of the world, on human loves and longings, that gentle and sovereign influence in which all our hopes of eternity are fixed, but which is first of all an influence of history. We see Him, touch Him, hear Him, because He is of our flesh and blood, of our kingdom —the kingdom of humanity—and of our race, that of rational animals. He is an object of experience; and His figure, towering over the centuries at the highest point of man's religious life, is an eminently real, concrete figure. His thoughts are higher than ours, yet He thinks according to the laws of our minds; His loves are purer than ours, but He loves as men know how to love. Even those who refuse to bow before His divine titles will keep for Him none the less the privileges of genius and worth, of courage and loyalty, of faithfulness and heroic abnegation. He is a man who does honour to humanity.

But perhaps what we admire more to-day than His moral greatness in this supreme representative of our race is His inner vision of the things of God. Let us have our preferences, or rather His, on this; for the highest eminence of which this soul, so proud and yet so humble, ever really boasted, is that which lies in knowing God: "no one knows the Father except the Son and him to whom the Son wills to reveal Him"; that is in S. Matthew (xi, 27) and in S. Luke (x, 22) and belongs to the Galilean ministry. "Father, the world knows you not, but I have known you"; that is from S. John (xvii, 25) and dates from the last evening.

It is this knowledge of the Father which defines Jesus. To know, said Aristotle, is to be in some sort *the other*. And it is a profound Thomist doctrine (if indeed it is not the whole of Thomism) that to know is to seize upon, to possess Being, to make it one's own, and in a sense to become it. Jesus in S. John (xvii, 3) made eternal life to consist in the knowledge of God. And on the strength of this alone, without troubling ourselves with Aristotle, let us say simply that the knowledge which Jesus has of the Father and of Himself in relation to the Father is such that He realizes and knows Himself as the eternal Son of God. To know God thus He must be the only Son.

But at the same time the relation which unites the Father and the Son defines them so perfectly that if we know the one we know the other also.

But do we know the Son? Yes, for this magnificent human nature which we have just been contemplating, which is historic and visible, is wholly *filial*. Its hypostatic dependence upon the Son of God is not only a juridical title of ownership or metaphysical connection, even though the closest possible; for this nature, its psychological and moral life, its consciousness and thought, its inner vision, its loves and emotions, its desires and hidden activities, its whole being, are endowed with all the Son's requirements, privileges and rights which the status of His Personality involves. The nature has taken those characters which are proper to the human nature of the Son. And these created, visible things of time and history we can behold with our fleshly eyes which reveal this flesh to us, with our intelligences to which this intelligence is speaking, that it may reveal both Son and Father to us.

As we see them, the dispositions, feelings, states of Christ, and his whole inner life, a human life, all are turned upon the Father. What attitude would you expect this man, the object of our human experience, to take up towards God, Himself enjoying the experience of divinity, except that which His personality and name impose upon Him? He takes then in that human order which is our own, in the human nature which is His own, the course and direction which, in the bosom of the Trinity, is that of the eternal relation which defines Him. And we are actually to see with our bodily eyes what is this Son and, correlatively, what the Father is. We are to know God as we see this man. We have only to look at this human nature to see through its soul and body the invisible Father towards whom it is wholly bent.

So we always come back to this idea which is nothing but the Chalcedonian dogma defining the truth of the Gospels, that in Christ the human nature, which we see, so participates in the privileges and also, we now realize, in the "bent" of the Person, as to make the Person known to us. In Him all is filial. What more is needed for the understanding of S. John, S. Paul and all the other witnesses? His nature like His person is πρὸς τὸν θεόν, because the Son keeps in His humanity His eternal attitude, His single unvarying direction; the activity which was His from the beginning in the person of His Father He now performs in His finite and created nature, as S. Paul says, σωματικῶς.*

The authentic Christianity of Chalcedon, Nicea, S. John,

---

* Usually the proof of the divinity of Jesus based on "Philippe, qui videt me. . . ." bears directly upon the eternal consubstantiality of the Father and the Son which is found in the text. This is a Latin method, clear and demonstrative. But, as always, it seems to us more in conformity with the method followed by Jesus in His revelation of the mystery of the Incarnation to move from His human nature and its privileges to the divinity of His Person, and to show on the basis of this the relations between the Persons, concluding only after this to the unity of the divine nature. This is a longer but a finer proof because more psychological and more evangelical.

When Bossuet wrote the magnificent sentence, inspired by S. John's Prologue; "At length Jesus Christ begins to preach His gospel, to reveal the secrets which He saw from all eternity in the bosom of His Father" (*Discours sur l'Histoire Universelle*, Part II, ch. XIX, ad init.), the Dauphin's tutor is expressing himself in the manner of the Latins, who have no fear of the Monophysitism vanquished in 451 and jump the stages of their exposition. But Chalcedon would have dwelt more upon them, writing perhaps: "Jesus Christ begins to reveal the secrets which He saw in His human intelligence and had seen from all eternity in His Father's bosom." The verse in S. John allows one to choose between these forms of exposition, because it comprehends them both: "*Unigenitus, qui est in sinu Patris, ipse enarravit*"; that is, "the only Son, who is in the bosom of the Father, He it is who has manifested God." (John, i, 18.)

S. Paul, the Gospels, brings us then to a man of our own flesh and race whose body, soul and intellect let us touch God Himself. *Manus nostræ contrectaverunt de Verbo vitæ* (I John, i, 1). Modern men, with such a prodigious hope suddenly opening before our troubled minds, our restless religious longings, will feel their human hearts stirred above all by this consciousness of Christ which saw and realized itself as the human consciousness of the Son of God: "O Father, I am your Son!"

All generations as they have passed before the hill on which Christ preached and that on which He died have hailed the name of Him who thus fulfilled so utterly the most ardent hopes of earlier ages.

The true sons of Abraham and Israel have seen in Him the Messiah promised to their Fathers. The Greeks have adored Him as the clear, harmonious *Logos* who purified their minds from taint of error and gave reality at last to the dreams of the children of Attica, of the sons of Plato. The Orientals have cast themselves down before Him who triumphed over the labyrinth of the prophecies when He realized in His own person, as advocate of His own cause, the words of the ancient seers, convincing Jewish incredulity of error. The Middle Age has recognized Him as the perfect master of the whole interior life, Francis of Assisi as the Divine Lover of Poverty, Dominic and his Preachers as Incarnate Truth. Bossuet has woven periods like magnificent Gobelins upon His sovereign and royal majesty. For S. Ignatius, Jesus is the prince of all spiritual chivalry, and for the 17th century he is the perfect religious of His Father. De Bonald glorified Him for having known so perfectly the laws of order and society, and the Romantics loved Him because He alone had established love upon the earth.

But when we come in our turn to ask His secret of Him, furtively like Nicodemus or Zachæus, or in the full light of day like those Gentiles whom Philip once brought before his Master, what moves us most perhaps in His divine presence is that He is a man, the companion of our journey,

J

our own dear friend, *and that this man, one like ourselves, sees God.*

It is as man* that He was first heard, loved, discussed, accepted and admired, and this was as it should have been, for He was man and the masterpiece of God's creative hands. As Man He knew His Father and His own divinity and all the divine mysteries, contemplated in the beatific vision in which His human intellect was bathed.

In an hour when we are asking whether humanism is a possibility, when humanity is intoxicated with the hope of overpassing the bounds set so far to its qualities and powers, it is a joy and pride for a Catholic Christian to think that the man who gives most honour to mankind, who most consoles us with the thought of our humanity when we sink to animality and egotism, the man who raises us too above ourselves, is our Founder also, and not man only but our God. And then, inverting the words of Pliny the Younger, who was too attentive to these sacred novelties to be entirely uncomprehending, the song which rises to our lips is that which our humanism sings to the humanity of our God in the style of S. John's Prologue: *Deo tanquam homini carmen dicens:*

Memento rerum Conditor	*Remember, Creator of the world,*
Nostri quod olim corporis,	*That once being born among us*
Sacrata ab alvo Virginis	*From the sacred womb of a Virgin*
Nascendo, formam sumpseris.	*You took our flesh and blood.*

---

* "A man would go to the synagogue to hear of the Messiah who was to come and to listen to some wise Rabbi describing in learned detail the characteristic traits of the Redeemer; and then, tired by the long discourse, he would entertain himself by looking at his neighbour ; unknown to him, it was the Messiah who sat next to him. . . . A woman goes to draw water at the fountain; she finds there a stranger, who asks her to give him drink; they begin to talk of religion and she speaks to him of Christ. The stranger says: 'I am He' . . . Christ was there, could be passed in the street at any moment."

PART TWO: THE MYSTERY OF THE REDEMPTION or THE SACRIFICE OF THE CROSS

CHAPTER ONE: THE ONLY SON'S RETURN

IF anyone ought to have returned in His sacred humanity to God it is surely He who, being the eternal Son of the Father by His divinity, had as such never left the bosom of the Trinity where He is born eternally. This requirement of a return, obligatory for the whole creation, was a right for the human nature of Christ, created like our own but hypostatically united to the divine nature. The Word should have and could have brought His body and soul to the right hand of the Father from the first moment of the Incarnation in an immediate impact of joy and glory. In this unique sacrifice the departure and the return would have coincided. Every creature, issuing from God as from its efficient cause, returns to Him as to its final cause. The Son, in His body and soul, is the work of the Almighty's hands. He came forth from God only to find the goal in Him. Thus the Word in His humanity returned to the Father; and this was a sort of replica of that immeasurable activity in which in the bosom of the Trinity the divine life flows back from the Son to the Father. But because to-day the Son is made man this second return is henceforth a religion, a form of worship, a sacrifice.

Scotist theology has contemplated the spectacle of the religion which would have been the Word's on the hypothesis that there had been no sin to be redeemed. Without necessarily accepting the Franciscan view of the Incarnation's motives we may picture, pushing the theory of perfect sacrifice to its furthest point, what would have been in principle the personal cycle of the Word made flesh with the departure coincident with the return, the coming among us men followed by the eternal glory *in ictu oculi*, a sacrifice the more perfect in that it would have been without suffering, without immolation, without Calvary.

Such were the rights of the Son in His humanity, which at once merited all the glory due to the human nature of the Son of God. And thus too the Father's desires to receive the worship of His incarnate Son would have been best respected: the glory of the one would have been the other's happiness. But this was for the Scotists as it is for the Thomists nothing but a dream.

Nevertheless, in virtue of these principles, we may now take ourselves in thought to the culminating point of the historic mystery of Christ, to His Resurrection and Ascension, to His eternal dwelling at the Father's right hand, which shows us the triumph of right and the reward of justice. The spectacle of this final victory will make us understand better later on the bloody price of our Redemption.

Bossuet, in his early oratory, indulged the splendid luxury of orchestrating in this way the lyricism of the Epistle to the Hebrews. He saw Christ, our forerunner, enter within the veil, that is into heaven; and keeping in touch with the text of S. Paul, the preacher carries his youthful ebullition to the point of quoting the Apostle in the Greek so as to find in the original tongue the ancient doctrine of total sacrifice: "Christians, Jesus had not to shed blood to enter heaven; He was Himself from heaven, and heaven was due to Him by natural right: and yet He entered it by His blood; He did not ascend to heaven until after He had died on the cross: it was not then for Himself that He entered thus. We, we it was who had need of blood to enter heaven, because being sinners we were guilty of death; our blood was due to the rigour of divine vengeance, etc. . . ." Here the edition of Urbain and Lévesque adds a variant "justice (divine)". . . . For it was the time when the eloquence of the French Church hesitated between dogmatic precision and oratorical exuberance. But what does that matter here? Other splendid summaries follow: "Jesus had the natural right [to enter heaven] and the acquired right; He keeps the first right for Himself; He enters and dwells there eternally; the second right He transfers to us, etc. Hence the Apostle calls Him our forerunner, etc. . . ." And at the end "Courage then, my Sisters, let us follow this divine eagle who goes before us. Jesus Christ does not only fly before us; He takes us, lifts us, holds us up. *Expandit alas suas.* . . ."*

* Sermon for Ascension Day, Metz, 1653 or 1654.

Bossuet thus reminds us that the history of the Redemption, before becoming our mystery as the cause and reason of our salvation, was first of all the mystery of Jesus. The Passion, Crucifixion and Resurrection were not for Him only events of a mortal existence through which He had to pass, personally untouched by their results, which He did not require for Himself, a sorrowful but disinterested, almost indifferent, victim. In such a case His part would have been to undertake a redemption which was no direct concern of His. He would have been in a sense external to His work or at least to the consequences of His devotion to it, nothing but the instrumental cause of our salvation without being engaged in His own person in the divine tragedy.

In spite of the delicacy of the subject and the necessary precautions to be taken lest we make the Saviour merely a Son of Adam like ourselves—and on condition that we fully preserve the absolute innocence and limitless sanctity of Christ's humanity—we may say that such a rapid view of the mystery of the Redemption, although lying half unconsciously behind the ideas of many of the faithful, is inexact and incomplete. The mystery of Jesus, in the sense of Pascal and the tradition, that is the historic Redemption, is first of all His mystery and later ours. By passing through suffering to enter into glory Jesus solves, although by means which were not in principle obligatory for Him, a personal problem which He could not avoid, which He desired to end as soon as possible: that of rising to the Father, of finding the goal in Him, bringing to Him the worship of the Firstborn of creation. The grievous means which He chose were not needed by His innocence nor conformable to His holiness; but sacrifice, conceived as a return to God, was imposed upon Him.

To restrict the Sacrifice of Christ to the events which took place on Calvary, to pin it down to the account of His suffering and death, as a piety more compassionate than enlightened is wont to do, is to deprive the teaching of the Fourth Gospel and the Epistle to the Hebrews of all that splendid culminating vision of the entry to the eternal tabernacle; and, for our purposes, it is to compromise almost completely in advance our understanding of the Mass-Sacrifice.

This is the moment to recall our study of sacrifice in general. The history of religions showed us the oblation rising from earth to heaven, after an immolation, it is true, demanded by our sin, but when once accepted by God changing its master and owner and so its value and significance. Then it can act, in virtue of its consecrated state, as the beneficent bond between the Creator and His creatures.

Christ, who is for ever the Son, had no need to change his Master and still less to change his nature; but, accepting the life of us sinners though Himself without sin, He found Himself here below in a waiting state through which He was to move to the right hand and to the bosom of His Father. So in that sense a solemn welcome was possible for His return; and since He had voluntarily passed along our path, that is, the path of death, He must be exalted after His humiliation. This glorification is essential to His sacrifice. The apotheosis following upon an immolation, abolishing not the fact but the wastage of it, thus fulfils Christ's consecration as His Father's victim. He is a victim, because He is accepted after immolation; and the two mysteries of immolation and glorification, which are successive in time, in reality give birth to one another: the first demands the second, and the second is the retribution for the first. Christ, still claiming His personal rights which the Resurrection soon restores to Him, offered His sacrifice in the conditions which sin had laid upon Adam's children. But the end is the same always: the Father welcomes in a triumphal embrace His Christ, who is His glory, His love and His good pleasure. He is His Son eternally.

But meanwhile the preliminaries were those of our ordinary human lot. Jesus Christ suffered then the common life and common death of men; His mystery unfolded itself in a historic setting like that which sin imposes on ourselves.

Born in poverty at Bethlehem, He lived an unknown labourer at Nazareth. His ideas suffered from the contradictions of His adversaries as His feet from the stones of the highway. His tears or His blood had already flowed; Christian piety was later to gather up these precious drops in a series of mysteries, which, with the sorrows of the Virgin Mother, are the preliminaries or heralds of the supreme sacrifice. Then the day came, preceded by a night of betrayal, of scourging and of mockery. One Friday He was placed upon a cross. He, though without sin, died the death of sinners.

The mystery of Christ then had unfolded itself in time and He had known the passing of the hours. That was for our sakes. Jesus had taken part in our adventure; He had taken upon Him the forms of our protracted sacrifices, *formam servi accipiens;* and He had acted as if He had been only a servant, and a guilty servant. His sacrifice had therefore passed through those stages, those delays, which we have seen to be the results of sin, the principle of sorrow and death, undergone according to that scheme of things which Adam had inaugurated. Immolation had preceded union with God, because human logic had replaced the logic of God's Son.

In that sense, and only in that sense, *God had made Him sin*. We must heavily underline the true significance of this harsh saying of S. Paul's. Eloquence has no part to play at this decisive point. Scripture is enough. The Son has never ceased to be loved. He has never been cast off and cursed. When His sufferings were bitterest, in the midday agony on Calvary, He was still the object of the Father's good pleasure and lived Himself in full activity His life of filial devotion. But it was really the life and death of sinners that He underwent. That is the full meaning of *peccatum fecit*, that and nothing else. The rest is rhetoric.*

Throughout this sorrowful journey on which the sacrifices of mankind must linger He fulfilled His personal religion and destiny ever driving Him onwards to the Father; thus He

---

* ii *Cor.*, v. 21. See Prat, S. J., *Théologie de Saint Paul*, Vol. II, p. 294 (1st de., Beauchesne); and d'Alès, *Dictionnaire Jaugey-D'Alès*, under *Rédemption*, Col. 549. To M. Rivière, here as elsewhere, belongs the credit for recovering the true Christian tradition beneath the strange borrowings of French learning from Port Royal, Ypres, Louvain and perhaps more distant sources.

lived two mysteries at once, His own and ours, enfolding our religion in His own. He has then really brought to the Father, to whom He was Himself returning, all the sacrifice which men would have to offer to come back to God.

But His mystery is accomplished before ours, although so closely linked with it. At the moment when He gives back His soul to the Father eternity enclasps Him. For sacrifice is in the end union with God, an apotheosis in which the victim and the offerer finally regain all that they had seemed to lose.

So the Father receives His Son, embraces Him, exalts Him, glorifies Him in His risen body, in His soul delivered at last from the servitude of suffering and mortal flesh. It is the hour at which the rights and privileges of Christ are recognized or rather granted. The Resurrection and Ascension are the final respecting, accepting, accomplishing and ratifying of the Son's logic, and this is also the moment when the sacrifice of Christ is consummated in the eternal Holy of Holies, not built by man's hand.*

So speaks the author of the Epistle to the Hebrews. Far from arresting the history of Christ's sacrifice at the moment when Jesus dies for our sins on Calvary, fulfilling the Scriptures, he sees the great movement of religion and the mystery of salvation accomplished only in Heaven, because he realizes that, since sacrifice is in the end the meeting of the creature with the Creator, " ut sancta societate inhæreamus Deo," the rite gains its full effect only when God receives and accepts the victim, at once fulfilling its purpose, granting its destiny, ratifying its being, giving it its true life in Himself. The Incarnate Word, during His mortal life, did not possess His real rights, did not perfectly enjoy the true position of His human nature. What He allowed us to see was His resemblance with ourselves, but not, save very rarely as on Thabor, his filial existence. At the last He is in His place at God's right hand. Then there is finally fixed and established that movement of sacrifice and devotion which from the first moment of the Incarnation was driving the

* *Hebr.*, ix, 11-12.

sacred humanity towards the Father and made the whole life of Jesus Christ a glorious holocaust.

And in a certain sense Christ in His humanity was not recognized as the Son by His Father, that is did not receive from Him in his created flesh all the glory to which from the first He was entitled as the eternal Word until the hallowed times of Resurrection and Ascension. It was a sort of second enthronement of the Son upon this earth. Then the Father repeated to Him with all the meaning that the title now entailed:

"*Filius meus es tu.*"

That is that meeting of the two great Kings which the epistle to the Hebrews depicts, that installation at the right hand of majesty, that great address of welcome of which no palace heard the like:"To-day I have begotten Thee. . . Thou hast loved justice and hated iniquity; therefore, O God, Thy God hath anointed Thee with the oil of gladness above thy fellows."*

Jesus Himself, during His mortal life and at its end, spoke of this meeting to which He aspires with all the force of His being, using the two words *sanctified* and *glorified* and using them of Himself. The first of these terms belonged to the vocabulary of sacrifice, the second expressed magnificently the end to which men's efforts tended in all their costly immolations; sanctifying a victim, making it sacred, so that God may graciously accept it, is the complete summary of this great institution. Jesus, who knows and realizes Himself as the perfect victim pledged to the perfect glory of the Father, sees His approaching death as the means of His return to God. And of these two mysteries taken together, the raising upon a cross and the raising to heaven, He makes only one, His glorification. This will not be for Him, as for other victims, the source or cause of sanctifying, for He is holy from the beginning, He whom the Father has sanctified from His entrance into the world.† But it will be the proof and

* *Hebr.*, i, passim.
† *Jo.*, xi, 2.

ratifying of His primal sanctity, and *in that sense* He can still ask the Father to sanctify Him more,* that is glorify Him definitively and in perfection.† And this goal is that sought after of old and in vain by all the ancient sacrifices and now reached victoriously by the only Son.

CHAPTER TWO: THE SON'S RETURN AND ITS TWO STAGES

SO the Son of God in His humanity returns to His Father to bring Him in this movement all the religious force of His glorious created nature; and, at the same moment when the Father receives Him to His bosom in this truly human form, the supreme encounter in which religion finally consists exhausts at the same time all the rights and all the duties of the Son: all the duties, because He gives to God the perfect adoration due to Him; all the rights, because God grants Him at this moment all the splendid privileges due to the human nature of the only Son. Such, in the impact of sacrifice, are the mutual relations of creature and Creator.

But if this meeting has been delayed, if the religion of the Son towards His Father did not fully unfold at the moment when the Word took His place among creatures *ingrediens mundum* (an apotheosis which would be for Him the norm), it is because, not content with offering His own sacrifice, He has also offered ours, which obeys other laws than His.

That is why, before this time of glory, all takes place on earth in the mortal life of the Saviour as if He had like us to approach the Father by the winding path which sin had made. That is why His mystery is in two stages like our own, the mystery which the poets had sometimes accepted for their heroes, which the human race throughout the centuries

* *Jo.*, xviii, 19.
† *Jo.*, xii, 23 ; xvii, 1.

set forth in obedience to a hidden instinct in the sacred and prophetic scenes of ritual sacrifice. A victim played the part of the race itself. It moved symbolically through those stages which are imposed upon us: immolated first of all so that the loss of its use and of itself might cost us dear and cost itself dear indeed, it embodied that sorrow which brings expiation and satisfaction; it was the sign of our repentance. Then in a grand gesture, positive this time, it was offered to God for His acceptance and for His acceptance of the race presented to Him in its guise: this was the meeting with Him, always sought and never perfectly fulfilled, the hour of union. Then the victim could return to us in communion, as if it brought to us from above God's ratification, the hallowed olive-branch of peace with Him.

This is the highway—man's eternal way—which Christ followed, not liturgically like the victims of old, but in the reality of a mystery sufficient of itself; so that His death, instead of being a rite, was a fact, a happening. Instead of being first and foremost a sign, His sacred Passion took the place of symbols and suppressed them all. After the death of Jesus religion knew no immolation but His, and His was the last blood shed as holocaust. This victim was not the image of another sacrifice, inward and more perfect; rather all the liturgies of yesterday were as the figures of this historic suffering.

For Christ had accepted the law in which all the ancient sacrifices found their metaphysic and their explanation; thus He has expiated, satisfied, merited and made reparation according to the logical requirements which the levitical ceremonies were trying to fulfil in the religions of the past.

And because sacrifices since sin are essentially double-faced, partly negative and partly positive, the mystery of the Redemption, falling into two parts, shows these two traditional and complementary phases. Writers who have tried to distinguish here two streams of thought among theologians, confining the Greek Fathers to the one and claiming them as mystics, the Latins to the other and classing them as realists, have not grasped the full significance of the

Pauline texts and have failed no doubt to find the highway. The mystery of Christ is redemption, immolation, sorrow, suffering and death; it is also divinization, healing, victory, illumination, Resurrection and Ascension. But those are inseparable aspects, like two sides of a single strip of cloth. Sacrifice has always shown these facets. Since sin we cannot otherwise conceive of it; and it is just this duality which explains why the offering is cursed and blessed successively, a victim and sacrament at once. This conception came naturally to our forefathers who had so keen though so implicit sense of things divine and human. Shall we not now grasp these great laws? The scene would then light up for us. And we should see that the Mystery of Christ harmonizes—not immediately with Jewish sacrifices and still less with pagan ones and oriental myths—but with the metaphysic behind them which they reach at different levels, the drama behind them which their diverse rites were trying to perform. It is clear enough that the sacrifice of Christ is no liturgical representation; there are no rubrics here, no rituals, but a God-Man put to death and buried under Pontius Pilate, who rose on the third day.

Thus we see why the mystery of Christ is so like and so unlike the Jewish sacrifices. In each case there is shedding of blood and death and glory, but in very different conditions. The Epistle to the Hebrews saw these relationships in the clearest light, and ended with a *quanto magis* which placed the immolation of the goats and heifers far below the great sacrifice of Calvary. Christ gave His blood not to imitate levitical rites but to satisfy a deep-seated law which that of Moses had already tried to follow. It is not surprising then that there should be analogies between the liturgies of the Temple or the synagogue and the historic drama once performed on Golgotha. But, in spite of chronology, it is the Old Testament that depends for this similarity on the New and not conversely. That is what theology expresses, following S. Paul, by saying that the law is the figure or the shadow of Christian realities.

*   *   *

"It was necessary that Christ should suffer and so enter into His glory" (Luke, xxiv, 26). When the risen Saviour thus spoke, He was only taking up once again with renewed emphasis, in the light of events now come to pass, the constant teaching of His whole mortal life so often vouched for by the Gospels. "Remember what He said to you, while He was still in Galilee: 'It must be that the Son of Man be betrayed into the hands of sinners and crucified, and that He rise on the third day' " (Luke, xxiv, 6-7).

His inner mystery, that is the history of His relations with His Father and the prelude to His eternal destiny, had unfolded itself in that process which our previous study of mankind's religions has revealed to us; we have learned its necessity and explanation, its law and end: to die before living and in order to live, to suffer in order to gain, to immolate oneself in order to find God, in a word to sacrifice and to sacrifice self in order to regain it. This rigid system of relations with its two sides forming our inner tragedy by their interplay, this law traced upon our being, but carrying with it for ourselves exceptions, palliations, and diminutions, was verified in Jesus with an austere and grievous but triumphant accuracy. The Apostles in Galilee and Judæa, with their narrow views, spent their time trying to gain a derogation from it for their Master, that is for themselves. But the Scriptures, the will of the Father and of Jesus, were too strong for them. The mystery was accomplished with all the dreadful happenings of its first phase, Judas's betrayal, the hatred of the priests, the cowardice of Peter, the cruelty of the soldiers, the carrying of the Cross, the crucifixion, death, piercing with the lance, and burial—but also with the heavenly requital, the historic Easter morning on earth and the eternal morning of heaven, the vacant and vanquished tomb, the appearances of the Angels of the Resurrection, those of the Master Himself, and in Paradise the Father's summoning of the Son to His right hand, while heaven, earth and hell sing the glory of the risen Christ, His right of primogeniture and His universal sovereignty.

Here we find again all the traditional imagery, all the symbolic figures, in which the religious history of humanity inscribed its beliefs, desires and hopes, the two inevitable phases, first that of the immolation which, since sin, is laid upon us, but tracing still man's positive and final tendency, bodied forth by his oblation, and then the second, that of achievement in the presence of God who receives, accepts and consecrates, the hour of apotheosis.

The author of the Epistle to the Hebrews saw all this in imagery. He saw in vision the priest of the Old Law, with the blood of the victim already immolated, raising the veil of the Holy of Holies where he is face to face with the glory of Jahve, when man's worship meets decisively with God's acceptance. The priest is Christ, who, covered with the blood shed on Good Friday, entered the third day into the eternal tabernacle, where He was received at the right hand.

It goes without saying that this mystery, for which in its first stages our sin alone is responsible, must be considered only in Christ Himself. The executioners, the soldiers, Pilate and the Jews are nothing but lay figures. Christ has performed the sacrifice in His own person, has offered and immolated Himself. This generosity has solved in an instant problems otherwise insoluble, and of these one which has concerned us earlier receives not the least an admirable explanation. "Where is immolation's proper place?" we asked, "since it is the victim which suffers and dies, although his owner may suffer pain and loss." But if the author of the sacrifice choose himself as the victim, this antinomy, or rather perhaps this hesitation, is removed.

The Epistle to the Hebrews, we were saying, saw this mystery in a liturgical setting, using the imagery of Leviticus. The Fourth Gospel did away with symbolism. It went straight to the Saviour's inmost heart, listened to the last prayer of this religious consciousness in full awareness of its worth, its power and its renunciations, and heard the words "I consecrate myself for them [my disciples and all their disciples] that they may be also consecrated. . . . And now, O Father, I come to you. . . ." (John, xvii, 13 and 19).

It is this voluntary love, as S. Thomas will tell us, that has solved everything. Jesus, being by right not liable to death, gave Himself to obey a merciful design in which the effects of sin might in the end become in Him the very death of sin.

But, despite the unparalleled conjunctions of this sacrifice, the only one to realize the conditions for which all others strove in vain, it yet verifies first and foremost the general theory, enfolding and engulfing it though without destroying it.

The two phases of Christ's historic sacrifice, His bloody immolation on Calvary and His glorious reception in heaven by the Father, in spite of their close connection, have not the same significance in the work of our Redemption. For the Son is welcomed and glorified when He enters the eternal tabernacles for His own sake, although this is also for our salvation; but His suffering and death on the Cross is for us only and for our sins. Christian thought and piety have therefore followed a legitimate interpretation of a rich and complex dogma in fixing upon the ninth hour of Good Friday as the hour of sacrifice; they have accurately indicated the point which, from our side, called especially for our attention. It was on Golgotha that the full weight of our sin made itself felt, and on Golgotha that it played its part in the mystery of Christ. Our crimes are responsible for His death, for without them there would have been no Passion.

If then we would underline in Christ's sacrifice the moment which bears the stamp of our sin, the characteristic which shows our signature, if it is fitting to assign our pardon in a general picture of the Redemption to that deed of Christ's which would not have taken place if Adam or his sons had never sinned, then we must say that it was the Cross which saved us and that the immolation of Jesus on Calvary was the cause of our salvation. All our piety is organized around this powerful and central thought, although the Resurrection in virtue of its vivifying and regenerating character is the principle of our new life.

This indicates perhaps in what careful language the two mysteries of the death and Resurrection of Jesus Christ must be contrasted but yet not separated, and in what sense we must sometime emphasize the one, sometimes the other, according as we are primarily considering in the Redemption the sin which made it necessary or the life of grace which it has restored. This is the Church's procedure in the liturgical year, Good Friday and Easter Sunday coming one after the other so that the two complementary aspects of our salvation may be in the same week the subjects of our meditations and thanksgivings.

Of course, life comes to us from the Cross:

qua Vita . . . morte vitam protulit:

and sin was conquered by the Resurrection:

O Mors, ero mors tua;

but the summary of it all is that the immolation on Calvary is the work of our sin, while the Resurrection is the triumph of the Son of God.

If we see in the Redemption first and foremost the payment made for our wrongdoing, as the etymology of the word suggests, the sacrifice of Christ is first and foremost an immolation, and this authorizes us to say, taking a narrower view, that the sacrifice of Christ took place on Calvary, although the Epistle to the Hebrews, taking a wider one and considering the two phases of the mystery in their fuller context, says that this took place successively, not only on Calvary but in heaven also.

Hence by the development of this legitimate conception comes the preponderance of immolation in the sacrifice of Christ, and the impossibility of making it consist first and foremost in oblation, despite the attractive optimism of that other synthesis.

If indeed we understand by oblation not an offering preparatory to sacrifice, but the great positive movement which draws the Son towards His Father, and together with the Son the race which He has saved, whose Head He is, if we mean by it this supreme meeting of the victim with God through the great rush of love in which it gives itself wholly to its Creator—for clearly perfect religion is in the end essentially positive—then oblation has certainly the final

word. And immolation, being the result of sin and acci
dental, falls to the second place; in so far too as it is an act it
can be only transitory.

But we are not denying that when we say that Christ's
Sacrifice consisted in His immolation upon Calvary. We are
simply looking at that side of the question which is the most
momentous for us sinners, that which most touches us and
moves us. Christ, we say, loved us to the point of dying for
us; He delivered Himself up for our salvation *and He was
reckoned among the guilty*—that is, among ourselves. In the
tender compassion of Christians this thought predominates
over the other:

> Fac me tecum pie flere,
> Crucifixo condolere,
> Donec ego vixero.

And this choice of standpoint has another consequence. If
we suppose that there could be a sacramental sign of the
unique sacrifice of Christ, what picture above all should it
convey to us? Must it not be, if we must choose, the image of
the Cross, since the preoccupations of our religion on this
earth, framed by our sin, are turned especially to this?
Besides it would be difficult for human symbolism to
represent the Son in heaven. But if God is pleased to grant
us a *Sign of the Cross*, that perhaps would suffice to call to our
memories, show before our eyes, even apply to our daily
faults the great sacrifice of Christ in which too the Cross is
for us the most moving incident, the most appealing to our
sensibilities, the most relevant also to our lamentable needs.

But it is not yet time to follow up this eucharistic vista;
despite impatience, we must not jump the stages.

*   *   *

So we must give up the idea of seeing the sacrifice which
truly saved us in the incessant oblation made to the Father
by the Son from the first moment of His Incarnation and
throughout His mortal life. Of course in so far as this oblation is wholly ordered to the Cross in which it ends, it forms
part of our Redemption and must be an object of devout

ᴋ

and grateful admiration for us. All the fine passages which the Masters of the French School have written on this subject may remain intact. But after all we must leave words and deeds the meaning which Scripture has placed on them, and think of the plan of our Redemption following the lines laid down by the inspired authors; for them the sacrifice is on Calvary and in Heaven, and it is also the same sacrifice in both its stages, formally bound to one another, the former causing the latter, the latter vindicating and justifying and clarifying the former: *propter quod et Deus. . . .*

In this sense we may still use the French School and its burning devotion to the heavenly sacrifice. But there must be no question of making this mystery a separate sacrifice, or even a continuous facsimile of the first, a sort of anniversary of a great event renewed only by way of jubilee commemoration. No! it is the same event which still takes place and never stops: the sitting at the Father's right hand, as defined in the Creed, is simply the mystery of the Ascension considered as static and in the language of time proper to us human beings. But in good theology, without the use of imagery, it is the reception of the glorified son by the Father, the acceptance of the sacrifice which is nothing else than the apotheosis of the victim. And the Ascension in its turn is the divine sequel to Calvary, the Father's answer to His Son's immolation, the same sacrifice seen from the side of God's intervention. So speaks the Epistle to the Hebrews,* while S. John's Apocalypse has so clear a realization of the unity of this mystery that it has achieved a telescoping of all these phases and stages into a single picture: that of the Lamb slain and omnipotent and glorified at the foot of God's throne, as if these two great ascents which wrought our salvation, that to the gibbet on Golgotha, hideous, unjust, but made in filial and obedient love, and that to the Father's right hand, eternal and magnificent, were blended together in a single vision, that of a bloodstained lamb installed in glory.

* Cf. de la Taille, S.J., De sacrificio vero et proprio quæstiones disputatæ   V, in *Gregorianum*, March, 1928.

CHAPTER THREE: THE PERFECT SACRIFICE

THE mystery of Jesus has been explained to us by S. Paul and S. John in two very different keys. But for the intelligent listener their voices are in harmony. The Fourth Gospel has sustained the theme in the most universal style, freed from any special ritual; only the most fundamental religious experiences and most powerful, because the least materialistic, language are admitted to this exposition. The Epistle to the Hebrews, on the other hand, has translated the teaching of S. Paul into local images, borrowed from the liturgy of the Old Law, whose rubrics are thus invited to become the symbols for Christian thinking.

But these two paths lead to an identical conclusion, which is simply the very essence of Christianity. We might hesitate perhaps to attempt the summary of it once again were it not for S. Thomas's invaluable article in the *Summa* on this very subject: *Utrum passio Christi operata sit per modum sacrificii?* (IIIa, p., q. 48, a. 3). Yes, answers the holy Doctor, because Christ *voluntarie passionem sustinuit . . . ex caritate maxima . . . : opus Deo acceptissimum.*

All the sacrifices of the old religions, including Judaism, rested at bottom on a fictitious pact. The primitive paganisms in the crudeness of their origins allowed themelves to be deceived by this. But the religion which was becoming purified by the teaching of Moses and the prophets had to realize it in the end and to its cost. These victims which were supposed to become the property of God were His already "*for all is Jahve's, the sea and all that is in it.*" And sacrifice might represent this universal dominion liturgically by making it incarnate in some chosen symbol, in the victim offered; but it could do nothing to enhance the world's estate. In some psalms, perhaps the most profound of the collection, a lament for this impotence is heard, and the writer in his despair puts words of terrible irony into Jahve's mouth:

Non sumo ex domo tua vitulum,
ex caulis tuis hircos.

Meæ enim sunt omnes beluæ silvestres,
    jumenta in montibus pecuariis;
Novi omnia volatilia cœli,
    et quidquid in agris movetur, penes me est.
Si esurirem, non dicerem tibi,
    meus est enim orbis terræ et plenitudo ejus.*

If sacrifice really has "making" for its end, that is the
production of a change modifying an existing situation, it
must bring into play values over and above what man already
holds from God's generosity. It is all very well to send
victims to the other world, but sooner or later they would
have gone there anyhow, whether we will or not, since "by
envy of the devil death has entered into the world."†

But in the holy soul of Jesus at the decisive hour of His
redeeming obedience the intimate conviction shines out that
He can *give His life and take it up again*‡ at His own pleasure;
for the death to which He is to submit at the Father's will is
not something owed. As the Son, He had only to ask for
help and more than "twelve legions of angels" would have
hastened to deliver Him.§

Here we are faced with a unique case, at once simple and
extremely complex. Jesus did not have to die, for He is *the
Son*. Nevertheless, if He dies because He is an elder brother,
a first-born whose younger brothers sinned, He is respecting
an order of justice brought about inevitably by our sins. He
has no debt, but He can act as though He had, pouring
straightway into God's treasury values which had never
issued from it. To rise towards the Father, to go to Him, to
enter or return into His keeping, is the Son's right, His birth-
right. But if He return by the way of death to His native
splendour, if He do this because His Father, who does not
claim it and does not even wish it for itself, asks Him to do so
for our sakes, if He give Himself up at the good pleasure of
His Father in a vast onrush of love which carries Him both

* *Ps.*, 50 (Vg. xlix), 9–12, trad. Zorell, S. J., Rome, 1928.
† *Sap.*, ii, 24.
‡ *Jo.*, x, 18.
§ *Mt.*, xvi, 53.

to execution and then at once to the Father's right hand, then
with all these conditions fulfilled we shall have at last in this
undreamt of state of things, this combination of all contrasts
(because uniting "in a single Person the divine and the
human natures") an example—the unique example, rather
—of true and perfect Sacrifice.

It would be wrong therefore to identify the Saviour un-
reservedly with the victims of the ancient holocausts. The
ritual victim of these cults was only the sign, the symbol
liturgically represented, of an inward act. It did not cause a
true redemption. But Jesus on Calvary is not first of all the
symbol of our repentance or our adoration. He is the
principle of both in virtue of His rights of primogeniture, by
reason of His Headship. He it is who gives life to all that
movement of adoration, love, filial and expiatory devotion
which is formed around Him. Thus the old theory of sacrifice
is too narrow for Him. Or rather the Son of God made man
inaugurates a new and quite unheard of form of sacrifice;
beyond the reach of all comparisons, He overthrows all
altars save His own. And this unique altar is the Cross on
which He dies, the heaven to which He enters and the
Eucharist which is the sacramental sign of Calvary and also
the pledge of everlasting life.

For it would be in effect to deny the decisive verses of the
Epistle to the Philippians and further to deny Christianity
itself, if we did not find in the sufferings and death of Christ
that note of freedom in the use of means which we have
found to be one of the characters of sacrifice. The Son,
equal to the Father *in forma Dei*, was not personally obliged
to die so as to realize His end. In accepting the condition of a
servant, *formam servi*, He went beyond His duty as a person,
renounced His proper rights and proved His generosity.
The Son of Man, born of a woman, is not the son of Adam
according to the law of sin, and His divine Sonship gives
Him privileges exempting Him from suffering and death. If
He renounce these powers, leaving His own inner logic, does
He not assimilate His death to that will to strive and struggle
sought by the ancient sacrifices? In so delivering Himself,

He joins us in a work in which all His value is henceforth engaged, the work of our salvation.*

*   *   *

It is sometimes said by way of summary: Christ alone, among Adam's descendants, had the right not to die—for He was spotless and the Son of God. By accepting death He therefore paid a debt which He did not personally owe and straightway He abolished ours. He offered His Father in sacrifice that to which the Father, if one may say so, had no right, and thus created a vast free capital for our disposal. The meaning of the text of Philippians is supposed to be: He who had no obligation to die did in fact die. His life and His blood, which were not owing, served to redeem us. Ours could never have done more than wipe out punishments which we ourselves had well deserved: you cannot buy with what you owe.

But this sort of reasoning, rather like that of S. Anselm in *Cur Deus Homo*, puts unnecessary pressure on the Father's will, which desires our salvation without being forced to it by the death of Christ. The idea would be that His death, not answering to any obligatory law and forming an independent value, should procure spiritual wealth over and above that foreseen by God. This leads to a metaphysical deadlock: the will of God is not tied down by the presenting of a receipt for signature. Sacrifice adds nothing to God's generous providence, with whatever energies it may be ballasted.

This theology becomes fantastic in the attempt to simplify. The truth is more complex: the Son of God, by following the law of His own being, that of returning to His Father as His end, but offering the sacrifice according to laws caused by sin which did not bind Him, which were ours, not His, gives those laws the value of His own mystery. For us this way was normal but unproductive: for Him it was abnormal but fruitful. Thanks to Him, it is now fruitful for us as well as normal.

If then we are saved by the Son, it is because He dies, but

* Cf. P. Galtier, S.J., " Obeissant jusqu'à la mort," in *Revue d'Ascétique et de Mystique*, April, 1920.

He saves us in dying only because He is the Son. Here above all the theory of reciprocal causality shines out. S. Thomas has put this excellently. Whence comes Christ's redemptive worth? From paying to God unowed spiritual capital? That is too narrow and childish a conception. The mystery is far deeper: it comes at once *from the degree of charity in virtue of which Christ suffered; from the dignity of the human life which He offered in satisfaction, which was the very life of the Incarnate Word; from the immensity, lastly, of His passion and His sufferings.* (IIIa, p., q. 48, a. 2.) Here is something far richer: but yet that does not prevent us after all from reducing it to the formula: *He who had no obligation to die did in fact die.* And thus the two mysteries of the Incarnation and the Redemption are only one; at least the first is part of the second. For the Son not only took flesh, but suffered death in the flesh; and if this death saves us, it is because it is the death of Christ the Son.

*   *   *

Sacrifice, a preeminently human action, belongs to the law of nature, as S. Thomas teaches; which means that sacrifice would have been a duty on the part of man, a right on the part of God, even without the supernatural vocation of the human race. And if sacrifice, as we hope to have shown, is a returning, the meeting of the creature with its end, which is the Creator, then creation reaches and realizes its destiny when God accepts the sacrifice.

But if we then suppose that man has beyond his normal end a higher calling, supernatural and gratuitous, surpassing his initial powers, his essential exigencies, his metaphysical requirements, then we can no longer think that sacrifices of a merely human worth can gain the necessary goal, however many altars may be heaped with them. We reach another deadlock. The available resources, even if they were all thrown together on the flames, will never find their aim. Results are never different in kind from the means employed; and these are of the natural order. We have been thinking of a natural religion, a natural end to be worked out and it is just this with which God is not willing to be satisfied.

It is perhaps time to turn back to a problem which controls the whole treatise of the Redemption; its two almost contradictory solutions, the Scotist and the Thomist, engage the manuals on divergent paths. They have to choose between the two; and, having chosen, do not find the means of returning to the cross-roads so as to engross the other system into a final synthesis. What is the problem?

Given man's sin, was the Redemption by the Incarnate Word necessary for an equivalent satisfaction? Yes, answer the Thomists, by reason of sin's infinite malice which attacks God Himself and requires a reparation infinite in value. No, answer the Scotists, because sin, the work of man, is not infinite in malice.

The former attach their answer to their conception of the ends of the Incarnation, the chief of which is sin's redemption; the second to their great theory in which the Incarnation was not in the first place willed to blot out sin but to let God show forth His love. The Scotists maintain that the reparation of the first sin did not necessarily demand the Incarnation of the Son of God, for which they find other principal ends. The Thomists allege on the contrary that if God demanded adequate reparation for man's sin the God-Man was necessary for Redemption.

The preaching of our time, without pronouncing definitely upon the principal end of the Incarnation—whether the creative joy of God or sin's reparation—has for long sided with S. Thomas on the question of Christ's necessity, as by a sort of traditional instinct; and the Christian people hardly conceives of Redemption, perfect at least, without the Incarnation. Whatever the arguments which support this position in the manuals and which may perhaps be unworthy of their thesis, the Thomists certainly seem to have a better grasp of the complexity of this situation, this state of original sin, in which man struggles. The sin which has to be repaired is of no ordinary kind. It is an anti-supernatural sin, which has destroyed a Trinitarian end surpassing all our own resources. It does not appear how man, without some dispensation on God's part of which there is no trace, could offer by his own unaided powers a sacrifice which would both realize this end and take away the consequences of this sin. Humanity could have been restored to the supernatural state by a generous divine pardon, by a gift, by a sacrament, for God's indulgence is not bound. But this would not have been a sacrifice, the normal path of our return to God, in which man finds again in the end the values assigned to him by God in the beginning, after first collaborating with God's will.

This doctrine some have misinterpreted by making an opposition between the God of Mercy who desires to pardon and the God of Justice who refuses pardon. But Scripture does not speak of such a tension; it is content with placing at the head of God's mystery the love which brings wonders to pass and a Justice which explains the course of things along their way. It shows first of all the end, which is charity and supernatural; this end has rights forming a system of Justice; then there are means to reach this end, satisfying Justice.

If religion is the return of the creature to the Creator, and if man can bring to it only what he has received and still possesses, supernatural religion is normally impossible after the first sin. Men reduced to the merely natural state can climb back to God only by natural means, whose scope is too small or too lowly in God's eyes to satisfy the claims of love. To renew our great ascent to God reparation must be ballasted with grace. Whatever then the malice of man's sin, finite or infinite, Redemption by a sinner, a son of Adam, is impossible by way of sacrifice: *nemo ascendit in cælum, nisi qui descendit de cælo.*

That is why Redemption by the Incarnate Word is alone truly satisfactory, *posito quod Deus voluerit exigere satisfactionem æquivalentem*, if God demands equivalent satisfaction and a true sacrifice. We are thus brought back to the Thomist thesis, by studying not the malice of sin but the blessedness of supernatural life; we return also not to the minor Scotist thesis about sin's finite malice, but to the great Scotist thesis in which God's contact with His creature in the Incarnation is an effect not of sin but of His need to see rise up to Him perfect religion and a consummate love.

CHAPTER FOUR: THE SACRIFICE OF CHRIST OUR HEAD

WE begin to see how the sacrifice of Christ caused our salvation. But to give proper expression to the law of this great mystery we have been obliged to lay down two series of complementary propositions, both of them true provided that whenever we use one we do not leave the other out.

On the one hand man's sacrifices could never have regained God's favour. For the return from the state of sin to the supernatural state is impossible for human powers. We never find at the completion of a sacrifice values beyond those originally placed there; and man, who could at best have offered his own nature, could never have realized more than the essence of a rational animal; this was not enough. God wanted to recover for His glory the grace which He had given Adam. But this free gift was lost. Man returning to God could have presented only the religion of the created order; and what God willed to receive was Eden's Trinitarian and supernatural religion, the return of the prodigal just as he was when he set out, if not with his inherited wealth at least with the status and dispositions of supernatural sonship.

On the other hand the Incarnate Son of God, considered by Himself, could never have returned to His Father by the way of death. He had the fullness of the supernatural life. This He could have yielded up to God in its triumphant purity, and by offering it in a sacrifice of joy would have straightway attained His Father whose rights and wishes He would have fully met. It would have been a festival, a jubilee, a vast embrace of love and happiness.

But the point is that we must not make these hypotheses

in separation from one another, dissociating Christ's lot from our own. If we use the language of the one hand and the other, we shall never unfold the Christian mystery which is all unity and solidarity. If the Son of God returning to His Father takes a way spoilt by sin's effects, the supernatural life which He bears with Him will pass by these very paths as Adam left them, bringing them back to their original condition.

And if we ask—the final question and the furthest mystery—how a sacrifice offered by the Son of God, in which so far we have no share, has yet been able to accomplish our salvation, if we seek the secret of this extraordinary generosity in which God extends an individual's immolation to all the race of Adam in effect, then we must answer by plumbing the mystery of the Incarnation still more deeply. For has God been deceived like old blind Isaac? Would he have mistaken His own Son? This sacrifice was the work of Christ, not ours. This rising to the Father's right hand, restoring the full order of His divine and human logic, was His rising, not humanity's. Again, how does the personal mystery of Christ reach us? Jesus died according to the laws of sin, accepting suffering and death. This condescension proves His generosity. But how does it replace our own? Calvary is a historical fact. Let us even allow that it is a sacrifice. But how could it be also a redemption?

We should be asked, in modern language, whence comes this mysterious *solidarity* between Christ and ourselves, which was the cause of our salvation?

This is the answer. Christ is not simply one of a crowd in relation to the human race, merely a man among other men. And His mystery, that of the Word made flesh, is far more complex in God's eyes and for our blessedness If He comes among us and takes a place among the sons of women, the Son of God must fill it as the Head, in the organic sense of that great word. And the eternal and filial dignity of Christ's Person grants to His nature an influence and mastery over the entire race, giving His smallest actions an indefinite repercussion, extending to the most distant members of the great body of humanity. He recapitulates us all, not by absorbing us into some nameless unsubstantial Absolute, but unifying us under His sovereign dignity. He is *the first-born of all creation;* Adam is no longer the name of the guilty first parent of an accursed race but that of the youthful Head of a human race now brought back fully into unity. Jesus is this new Adam, and Christ and we form but one body of which He is the Head. A common life, which does not suppress our personalities, communicates to us henceforth the whole mystery of the Son, the mystery which is the meeting with the Father, the sacrifice which has now obtained its end. That is why Christ's sacrifice is identified with the principle of our salvation. This is in particular S. Thomas's method of explaining how Christ could have merited on our behalf.*

Our forefathers had a keen vision of the recapitulation of the whole body of the Church in Jesus, her Head; perhaps our modern devotion does not sufficiently utilize its implications and resources. When S. Augustine in his famous letter 140 *de gratia Novi Testamenti* comments for a persistent questioner on Psalm 21, putting the words of the prophet upon the lips of Jesus, he unites the Head and the body so closely together that He supposes vital reactions between them throughout. The Head speaks of what happens in the Body as of Himself, because he suffers in it: He is affected, because modified, by it even (in a certain sense) after His Resurrection: *in Ecclesia patiebatur ipse, quando pro illo ecclesia patiebatur* (No. 18); much more then during His mortal life in the sufferings of the Redemption. There are therefore in Jesus psychological states and historical situations which exist only by reason of ourselves and of our sin.† Perhaps we ought to look for the theology of Christ's knowledge in

---

* IIIa. p., q. 19, a. 4, so suggestive, though so brief. Cf. P. Glorieux, Le Mérite du Christ selon saint Thomas, in *Revue des Sciences Religieuses* (of Strasburg), October, 1930. The principle of *solidarity* dominates also the powerful exposition of the dogma of the Redemption which is the theme of the whole second volume of P. Prat's *Théologie de saint Paul.* (Beauchesne.)

† Cf. also S. Augustine, in the Roman Breviary, *feria 6 post octavam Ascensionis,* 2nd nocturn, 4th lesson, taken from sermon 176.

some such direction. The Body in a manner explains the Head while the Head is the Saviour of the Body. It is noticeable that in the *Tertia Pars* the study of Christ as Head precedes the questions on His psychology, and this was probably the traditional arrangement. It is to be feared that our modern manuals depart from it when they discuss Christ's human nature without linking it with the Redemption, and when they postpone the dogma of Christ's Headship to the end, treating it as a corollary, when perhaps the whole secret of the great mystery ought rather to be looked for there.

Humanity has such need of a Head! When at times it seems to us too degraded, we have such need to believe that it rises at its highest point to this perfect human figure, who represents us before God and recapitulates us all.

We are something only in the measure in which we resemble Him; but at the same time any effort to do so that we make, however small, does give us worth. For what counts with God is not that absolute perfection to which we improperly refer in speaking of ourselves (as if the adjective here could fit the substantive) but our relativity—our direction and our tendency towards Him. God has His good pleasure in Christ, where He finds perfection, and He loves us whatever we are through Christ, for the sake of Christ, in whom we are completed; *omnia traham*, said Jesus. And then nothing in regenerated humanity is despicable, because culminating at a point in this perfection. Our distaste at this *monster* which is man arises from our supposition that the individual is a solution, something final, having value in and for itself. But we must see it in the whole, in the mystical body. And as by the Redemption Christ gives this individual the value which his place in the body requires, God, looking down at this vast hierarchical uprising of His creation, declares with yet more joy than on the sixth day of Creation that all that He has made is good.*

* This supernatural solidarity of all Christians in Jesus, which permits exchange of sufferings and merits, has been revealed by the New Testament and by S. Paul

It will be for us only to correspond with the rhythm of the life which beats in this Heart, which comes to us from this sacred Head; vibrating to this movement, to this sacrifice of systole and diastole, we shall attune ourselves to it and so share in it. It is the mystery of the Christian suffering and dying with Christ so as to rise again with Him, and it is the whole doctrine of S. Paul.

*   *   *

But if the Son of God was made man it is because the Father gave Him.

The Father did not act by halves, and since our failures have brought blood and tears into the world He has seen fit that His Son should pass through blood and tears.

How has the Father, if one dare say so, suffered in this extremity!* Or rather how it places the crown upon His love! Christian art and devotion have been sensible of this. In our representations of canvas, stone and wood, where dogma lives in line and colour, we find a Passion of the Father. Emile Mâle has told us of this supreme demand of mediæval feeling which found plastic expression in the fourteenth century, and has commented upon these paintings and sculptures in which the Father, the tremendous ancient of the Old Testament, the eternal Abraham, bears on His knees the mangled body of His Son and gives Him to the world with sorrowing generosity: *sic Deus dilexit!* And finally

---

especially. But it finds solid ground in the fact of the solidarity of all men in their participation of a common nature.

Man's knowledge begins with the individual and reaches to the species from the individual by abstraction and generalization. He does not perceive human nature intuitively, but *conceives* it. His method of knowing the species has foundation in reality, but it does not allow him to consider his abstract idea as existing on its own on pain of the error stigmatized by logic as that of reified abstraction. It follows that reason has great difficulty in conceiving in what sense men are bound together in the unity of the same human kind.

God on the other hand knows the individuals in the species. For Him humanity is no more an abstract entity than it is a concrete one. He is above this classification which belongs to the conceptual order. In His eyes humanity is something very real, exhausting as in one idea the whole temporal development of individuals. Now beings are as God sees them. Men are therefore most really bound together in unity of species. "All men born of Adam," says S. Thomas, "may be considered as a single man, that is as comprehended in the nature taken from their first parents." (Ia IIae, q. 81, a. 1.)

* [This is the language referred to in the Preface as exceptionable. There are a few similar passages.—Trans.]

with the holy freedom of art, it is the Father Himself who offers sacrifice.*

Catholic theology regards this last expression as an extravagance. It can improve upon it, using the teaching of S. Paul: this gift of His Son which the Father makes to us, in that immense love of which this gesture is the proof, is also the effective sign of the pardon granted to all repentant sinners: how could God so love us and not pardon us? That, finally, is why the Passion saves us, why it is a Redemption.†

We can see now how the Redemption has its principle in the Father and how it is first His work before that of the Incarnate Word: the Son gives His blood, but the Father gives His Son to be our Head.

*   *   *

But this young Head who dies upon a cross for the redemption of His countless mystic members dies by Himself alone. Yet He is the victim of the supreme sacrifice. Golgotha is His altar. We might have thought to see a vast assembly around this final and definitive "high place" after the manner of the ancient rituals, in which the immolated victim rises up to God laden with the adoration, penitence and hopes of the spectators, these uniting themselves with it in confidence of heaven's favours. But guilty humanity is represented here only by cries of hatred, some stupid mockery and the aghast disciples. Nor can that dreadful tragedy ever be renewed or be a liturgy in its historical and

---

* " It was not enough to have represented the Passion of the Son and the Passion of the Mother ; the 14th century at its close imagined a sort of Passion of the Father. It is true that the 12th, 13th and 14th centuries had already associated the Father with the Son's Passion. The representation of the Trinity at that time is familiar: the Father, seated on His throne, holds between His hands the cross to which His Son is nailed; the Holy Spirit flies from the one to the other in the form of a dove. But the artist has no intention of an appeal to feeling in drawing this strange scene but only of expressing the theological idea that the Son died with the consent of the Father and of the Holy Spirit. These, he tells us, are the three Persons of the Trinity who gave man the pattern of sacrifice, and the figure of the cross was written from all eternity in the bosom of the Godhead.

The sentiment which artists tried to express at the beginning of the 15th century was quite different. They wished to associate God the Father not with the abstract idea of sacrifice but with the actual sufferings of the Passion, convinced that if God, as S. John says, is love, He could have felt pity . . . . ' I also suffer.' " Emile Mâle, *L'Art Religieux de la fin du Moyen-Age en France*, Colin, 1922, pp. 140–142.

† *Rom.*, viii, 32.

bloody form. Will then the perfect Sacrifice come to nothing
in its very hour of triumph? Will it have taken place only to
fail for ever to fulfil its end—that is to serve as the external
sign always to hand for the religion of man's heart for every
age and race?

At the moment when Redemption is achieved on Calvary,
Christian worship, which must find its source there, seems
still to be seeking for the signs in which it might take shape
throughout the earth.

CHAPTER FIVE: THE SIGN OF THE ONE SACRIFICE

WE have just used a word of awful import in which
perhaps the whole mystery of the Eucharistic sacrifice is found. We have spoken of the chance that there
might be a Sign for this sacrifice, the development of a
liturgy. What does this mean? These statements, these
hypotheses, these hopes, are so momentous that we must
stop at once to scrutinize them.

The Council of Trent gives us the following encourage-
ment at this decisive point:

"After celebrating the old Pasch, which the people of
Israel immolated in memory of the coming out from Egypt,
Our Lord constituted Himself the new Pasch *to be immolated
by the Church under sensible signs* by the ministry of priests,
in memory of His passage from this world to the Father,
when by the shedding of His blood He redeemed us,
wresting us from the power of darkness and leading us to
His kingdom."*

But first did this sacrifice require a sign? Was it not
sufficient of itself? And, since it was a Sacrifice, was it not a
sign already, according to S. Augustine's definition: *sacrificii
invisibilis visibile sacramentum, id est sacrum signum?*

* *Trid.*, sess. XXII, cap. 1.

It is clear that there was on the Cross, in the adorable victim who delivers Himself for our sins, a visible and an invisible value perfectly united with one another, the latter the justification of the former and its principle, the former expressing and embodying the latter. The whole of Catholicism is there, centred in this harmony of spiritual attitude and outward gesture. For there was absolute agreement between the will of Christ, His inner life and hidden sentiments, and His bodily sufferings, His shedding of His blood and dying breath. We must not deny the value or reality of this twofold wealth, of both flesh and spirit. The blood is precious but only because it stands for love. The love is perfect because it went to blood.

When later the Councils condemned Docetism, which denied the flesh of Christ, and Apollinarism, which took away His human soul, the Church remembered that Christ, to save men, had been completely man, that nothing human— sin excepted—was foreign to Him, that He had taken all our nature so as to heal it wholly: *Quod non est assumptum non est sanatum.*

That is the meaning, the other way round, of S. Bernard's famous phrase already quoted about the will of Christ who dies in order to fulfil His Father's pleasure.

Since Christ's immolation falls beneath the senses in correspondence with His inward dispositions, we may say that the sacrifice of Calvary, visible to our eyes under His own species, unites the visible and the invisible in Him, and is already, without the celebration of the Eucharist, a perfect sacrifice.

Protestants, then, have not to fear that the sacrifice of the Mass, if it exists, detracts from the Cross's sacrifice,* since this has already, apart from the Supper, a perfect metaphysical consistency.

The first theologian—inspired by the Holy Spirit—to have conceived a synthesis of Christ's sacrifice built it entire without the slightest reference to the institution of the Eucharist. There is no question whatever of the Eucharist

---

* *Trid.*, sess. XXII, can. 4.

L

in the Epistle to the Hebrews,* even in relation to Melchisedech.

And in brief, if we consider only the principle of our salvation, the Eucharist and its institution were not necessary for the Redemption of the world, neither for it to take place by way of sacrifice nor simply for it to take place at all. It was sufficient that the mystery of Christ in its two stages, one grievous and the other glorious, should fulfil and surpass all the exigencies of immolation and return to God: *omne opus quod agitur ut sancta societate inhæreamus Deo.*

Yet we must consider the following:

For our redemption truly to operate *per modum sacrificii* it was not sufficient that S. Paul should teach a magnificent theology on the subject thirty years afterwards. It was necessary that Christ, the author of our salvation, the victim and priest of our sacrifice, should have instructed us Himself from His own knowledge of His own mystery of Himself as victim. For it is He who first teaches us, and He with whom we are concerned. Nor could He be the victim unless He consented to be such, since He was Himself the offerer.

And then, and above all, in spite of the agreement found between this drama of death and resurrection and the inevitable rhythm of all sacrificial action, we must recognize that there is always this difference between Christ's historic Passion and any liturgy: that the first is a great event which happened once in time and that it is, as a historical fact, individual and unrepeatable; while a sacrifice is normally a rite with a symbolic and efficacious action which by multiplying victims can be indefinitely repeated and always with similar results.

The Passion of Christ is far above such a rite, because it realizes once and for all, completely and exhaustively, all the ends pursued: *hoc enim fecit semel.*

Moreover, it is identical with its results. It is not a means to an end, but the realization of the end itself. When we look at the sacrifices of the Jewish law and even the sacrifices of pagan cults, we can at a pinch think of the liturgical cere-

---

* Except perhaps incidentally in vi, 4.

mony as the cause of the religious effect produced; yet such a way of speaking is not altogether accurate, for the holocausts of the Old Law were not really the cause of the reconciliation between Israel and Jahve: they were its expressive symbol and, if you will, a means of access to it. The truth is that God, on the occasion of them, became propitious and gave effect to the sacrifice Himself.

The sacrifice of the Saviour is not in any case the cause of our Redemption and for reasons diametrically opposite: it is our Redemption itself. When the Son returns to His Father by the ways of death which our sins had made, when He reaches the Father's throne and takes His seat there, when as Head of the race He draws behind Him in the mystery of His Ascension His whole mystical body which is the Church—*ascendens in altum captivam duxit captivitatem*—He realizes God's ends precisely in all this; He does not occasion but performs them. The glory of God is for His Son to come to Him as Son of Man and Head of all men. This is what the Redemption is. The fact which incarnates it at the same time realizes it: *Gloria Dei vivens homo*. Thus the salvation of the world consists in the Son's mystery becoming ours. And now we are dealing with the fruits rather than the effects of the Redemption. For effects are outside their causes, but fruits are part of the tree which is their principle. And as our little diocesan catechisms say, whose traditional formulas are here completely accurate, the Mystery of the Redemption is *the mystery of Jesus Christ who died on the Cross to ransom us* and not *first and foremost* the mystery of the world's salvation by the death of Jesus Christ on the Cross.

So the mystery of the Mass has not to do with a renewing of the merits of the Saviour, beginning the Redemption of the world afresh, but with making them our own, using their fruits ourselves.

There is, then, no question of repeating the Passion as a historic fact: *Christus resurgens jam non moritur*. It has cost the Saviour too much already and, as an event in time, was too atrocious.

Thus we reach the disconcerting fact that Christ's Passion by reason of its very triumph, because it is the only perfect sacrifice, lacks in its historic form some of those liturgical advantages which we are used to find in ritual sacrifices.

But, if it is not a rite, could it not become one? If it *is* not a symbolic sign, could it not *have* one with which it would be so bound up that in renewing this sign we should offer afresh the sacrifice of Our Lord, sacrifice again His death, immolate again (sacramentally) Himself?

Let us realize the tremendous claims of such a question. We have to renew the Passion of Our Lord as sacrifice. But sacrifice, we have seen, is rather a thing than an action; it is a thing in which an action has taken place. The thing in the present case, the reality, is Our Lord, His body and His blood. An action takes place giving as a permanent stamp to the object on which it operates the modifications which it has produced in it. The object itself is now transformed. The redemptive mystery immolated and glorified Jesus Christ: the redemptive sacrifice is Jesus Christ immolated and glorified.

The logic of this is certainly alarming. We shall never have the sacrifice of Christ unless we have His body, immolated and glorious, upon our altars. All that is not perhaps inevitable, but it is what we should expect.

We are here at the very threshold of the dogma of the Real Presence.

* * *

Will Christ be present for His own purposes? Will He renew His sacrifice for Himself? But first will He renew it at all? It is rather we who should have the need to begin it afresh in the sense that we need it as our own, so that we may daily apply its effects to ourselves.

What, then, are the effects of sacrifice in general and of the sacrifice of Christ in particular? We know the answer from our previous analyses. Sacrifice has for its essential end the union of the creature with the Creator and to make religion real by a rite expressing all its hidden riches. What, then, is the content of our religion? On our side it presupposes in our souls all the dispositions without which meeting with God remains impossible: those of repentance, love and adoration. On God's side it demands consent, acceptance, with, as result, the gift of graces. All that is realized henceforth only in Christ. He it is who as the perfect religious brings to God the only acts of religion acceptable to Him. It is through Jesus Christ, the sole object of the Father's good pleasure, that all divine blessings pass, and all saving graces, the sacred fruits of the Redemption.

These fruits of the Redemption, if God willed, could be communicated to us, like all invisible values, under any outward symbol: this would be a unique and splendid application of the theory and practice of the Sign, so precious to humanity. The institution of the Sacraments will be the answer to this hope. But a sacrament is not necessarily a sacrifice. Sacrifice requires a sacred thing, a physical reality, through which communication is established in both directions between God and man: upwards, to incarnate earth's adoration, downwards to incarnate heaven's blessings. For us, Christ is this victim. A sacrifice-sacrament, once again, seems to demand Christ's presence.

And this is not all. Christ, by Himself alone, can place all the effects, all the graces, of His one and only sacrifice in a personal sign in which He would be present. In heaven, eternally present to His Father, as a victim immolated and glorified, He prolongs eternally His adoration, while the Father has His good pleasure eternally in this splendid human nature which is His Son's. In this sense there is perpetual sacrifice in heaven, and all the analyses of the French School of theologians are left intact.

*　　*　　*

But this sacrifice is not only ours in the sense that Christ was immolated for our sins and that we are fortunate enough to be the beneficiaries of this Redemption.

A sacrifice is not just a benefit: it is so in its issue, when it ends in sacrament, but not in its beginning, when it shows man's initiative.

In fine, a sacrificial action of man's, a victim belonging to him and as such something impotent but at the same time able to be a sign, must be changed in the movement of man's adoration into the one true sacrifice, the one true victim. Then man, having the victim of this one and only sacrifice as victim of his own, would gain, thanks to a substantial change of values and yet through species originally contributed by himself, all the effects of religion and of grace flowing from the Cross's sacrifice; Christ's sacrifice would become ours in a daily ritual and so in a quite other sense. And now we are at the threshold of Transubstantiation.

*   *   *

Thus, under the pressure of our study of sacrifice, we are brought back to the Cenacle where this great institution happened. What did happen then? De la Taille would have the eucharistic action to be the first moment of the great work of the Redemption, the ritual oblation made by Jesus. What difference does it make? It is far more probable, more in accordance with the Epistle to the Hebrews, with the Fourth Gospel and with the whole tradition that the sacrifice of the Cross suffices of itself for our salvation without the institution of the Eucharist. But again what difference does it make? For equally, in instituting the Eucharist, the Saviour made the Cross inevitable and, showing His will to be a total offering, solemnly inaugurated His historic sacrifice.

He inaugurated it. We might say with equal truth that He prolonged it. He pledged Himself to remain at our disposal, though without any question of renouncing the glory and blessedness awaiting Him. He gave Himself for our use under signs which do not humiliate Him, but which are very modest; so modest that de Lugo and an entire modern school have thought to find in this some sort of sacrifice superimposed upon the Cross's sacrifice and doubling it, so making it the Mass—the theory of the *status declivior*. This was to take one aspect only of the mystery, although a most moving one, very dear to modern piety, as the whole explanation. It was to stray from the highroad into a byway. But all is not absolutely false about this error. Christ in the Cenacle loved to the end. At the hour when He, the only Son, felt all the glories, all the responsibilities, all the sufferings also of the victims of the Old Law, His predecessors, sweep upon his suffering body and through His innocent veins, at the hour when He saw Himself placed at the centre of the world's mystic scene as the Lamb immolated and life-giving, to whom all the old religions should turn, in whom the definitive religion destined to bear His name should take its source, then once more and for the last time *He, in whom the Father was well pleased, pleased not Himself:* and although He could not add to or diminish the eternal life which as the accepted and triumphant victim He was to begin in the glorious splendour which He had enjoyed for ever not as victim but as Son, nevertheless He took upon Himself to begin another life, a sacramental life, under borrowed species, so that without possessing more of Himself than He had given already, we might yet have, *as human nature needs,** the sensible efficacious sign, the true and certain recognition, of His real presence on our altars as victim of our liturgical and daily sacrifice.

We have been using language scriptural in origin but orchestrated to-day by twenty centuries of faithful piety and relentless speculation. Jesus in the Cenacle had at His disposal no developed theology but only biblical images and the Aramaic dialect to give His disciples understanding of His meaning. But even this sufficed. Using the simplest signs which the Old Testament could lend Him, He chose those blessings and thanksgivings over bread and wine which accompanied religious feasts in Israel. Thus He avoided swamping the reality of His own personal sacrifice in some too grandiose sign which might have proved a hindrance. And in the formulas of institution as in the dogma of His future Church, the Body and the Blood took the first place, their true pre-eminent position. All the visions of the old alliance faded into them; they drew into themselves all the metaphysic of the historic sacrifices which they were re-

* *Trid.,* XXII, cap. 1.

placing. The content of the dogma was secure already, when it became incarnate in the signs of liturgy.

But if it had to vest Him for ever in a sign modest enough to do no injury to the reality, the sacrament had also to be sufficiently intelligible for the Apostles, sufficiently enduring to continue through the centuries. Devout Jews were accustomed to give thanks to Jahve for His best and most necessary gifts, His holy Law, the coming out of Egypt, or simply for the bread on their tables and the wine from their vineyards. Jesus had only to give thanks, to perform a eucharist, over bread and wine, but with the substitution for them of His body and His blood, the victims of the sacrifice of the new alliance. That was all.

The Church thus endowed went from the Cenacle to make her journey down the ages. To possess the victim of Calvary she still performed the eucharist of bread and wine. The most venerable liturgical texts, the Canon, the Anaphoras, Secrets and Postcommunions, express this duality of real sacrifice and a symbolic sign realizing it in words which are full of mystery and full of meaning.

All these liturgical formulas underline the starting point, the bread and wine. These latter seem to bear the weight of the whole thought, being at once the occasion, means and, one might say, the ritual origin of the mystery. They represent that share of religious capital brought by the Church, the addition which she can make, according to S. Paul, to Christ's sacrifice. The bread and the wine are at the source in every sense, at the Church's cradle as in the beginning of the actual liturgy: the first thought always goes to them. Therefore, even if the eucharistic formulas of the *Didache* were orthodox (which is unproven), there would be no reason for disquiet in their insistence on the *vine of David* and *the bread scattered on the mountains*. The Saviour's eucharist, if by that we mean the words of bendiction before the *hoc est corpus meum*, could speak only of mere bread and wine, of the goodness of God in general, of the splendour of creation and its gifts.

But clearly, since Christ went beyond that, it was this

fresh element that was essential. By an inevitable and legitimate evolution the word Eucharist means to-day not a prayer or a symbol but the body and blood of Christ under a sacramental symbol, and the sacrifice of Christ, real beneath the signs which represent it. Merely by following the history of the word, we see that Christ has triumphed. He has imposed on it His will, His institution, and His love.

CONCLUSION

Christ, living His unique mystery both on earth and in heaven, and taking account in it of our sin's demands, has passed through its stages in a series of historical events, grievous and glorious, whose sum henceforth constitutes the one true sacrifice.

In what does this sacrifice consist? First in the return of the Son to His Father with His religion of adoring love, accomplished in the hard conditions which our sins imposed; then in the acceptance granted by the Father with all the depth of His eternal love to this homage of the incarnate Son; so as a result in the meeting of the Son with the Father, conditioned—for our sakes—by previous immolation, and one which went, solely through man's wickedness, *usque ad mortem, mortem autem crucis*.

From His Passion and Death to His Resurrection and Ascension, *per passionem et crucem ad resurrectionis gloriam*, as the prayer of the Angelus puts it, Christ Jesus visibly realized this metaphysic of return and meeting which the ritual and symbolic sacrifices tried unceasingly to delineate and perform upon their altars.

This is the context within which He was established in His own Person the one and only victim. At the same time He was established as the only priest. Henceforth no religion will exist save His. Let us cling closely to this faith which, far from hampering us in our search for sacrifice in the Mass, is on the contrary the only means of setting the dogma of the eucharistic mystery upon a solid basis.

Thus the Christian sacrifice did not lie only in the immolation of the Cross, although it appears there to our eyes in full relief and in all its force. That would be too narrow a conception. We shall never tie down all the mystery here—it would be trouble wasted. We must keep the whole, from the kiss of Judas to the Father's welcome. S. Paul always bound these moments together as interdependent parts of one same work; and our liturgy for Paschal time has found admirable formulas for this powerful unity:

Crucifixus surrexit a mortuis, et redemit nos, alleluia.

The Crucified has risen from the dead and has redeemed us, alleluia.

Qui mortem nostram moriendo destruxit et vitam resurgendo reparavit.

Who dying has destroyed our death and rising has restored our life.

This sacrifice had nothing ritual about it, if by ritual we mean figurative liturgy. But since all the stages of this divine tragedy correspond to the great metaphysical adventure, the toilsome return and the triumphant welcome, which the ancient holocausts tried in vain to picture on their unsubstantial altars, we must say that Christ's death and Resurrection constitute the Christian sacrifice, the only sacrifice.

But this still contains a visible element and an invisible. The visible reality is the Saviour's Passion related to us in the Gospels, and then the empty tomb and the appearances, and then again the Ascension which the Apostles saw. And the invisible substance is the religion of the Son engraven on His soul and dispositions, and also the Father's joy when His Son takes His seat at His right hand.

But these two aspects of the mystery are not quite the sign and the thing signified, but rather the container and the thing contained, the one requiring the other but not substituting for it: the inner life, and its historic evolution. In Christ's Passion we are saved as well by the visible sufferings of His body as by the charity burning in His heart, and God receives all this mystery as efficacious and redemptive.* How then should we liken the history of these events which happened in Jerusalem on the 14th Nisan to ceremonial ritual? So far there is nothing of it in the sacrifice of Calvary, which fulfils nevertheless the ends sought vainly by men's ancient liturgies. And M. Lepin, drawing on S. Augustine, has proposed the noble phrase *personal sacrifice* to distinguish Christ's Passion—and His Resurrection—from the purely figurative sacrifice of the old religions.†

But once the mystery of Jesus has been historically achieved can we not enclose it within an efficacious rite, a sacrificial and eucharistic rite, which will owe all its value to it and give us all its fruits? That is the problem which must now engage our whole attention. Before reaching this dogma of the Mass we had first to stop before the Saviour's personal mystery to realize that He is a true sacrifice. It is now time to view the Altar in the light of Calvary.

---

* Cf. the Hymn for the Ascension :

| Peccat caro, mundat caro, | The flesh has washed the sin of the flesh, |
| Regnat Deus Dei caro. | And the flesh of God reigns as God. |

† S. Augustine, *de Civitate Dei*, bk. X, chh. 5 and 6. Cf. Lepin, *L'Idée du Sacrifice de la Messe d'après les théologiens*, Beauchesne, 1926, pp. 737, sq.

BOOK THREE: THE SACRIFICE OF THE MASS

CHAPTER ONE: CHRIST'S INSTITUTION
OF THE SACRAMENTS

THE Holy Eucharist does not appear as an isolated institution in the religious work of Jesus Christ, but as the crown of a wider sacramental organization which prepares for it, acting as its framework. But the seven sacraments themselves had their precursors—their "figures"—in the Old Testament; and it would be difficult to enter into the spirit of the great liturgical movement narrated in the Gospel if one did not first take into consideration the Messianic preliminaries.

The law of Moses as well as the history of Israel had known the use of sanctifying symbol, in which union with God took visible form in rites or actions. And the future kingdom, announced by the prophets, was also to be recognized by certain signs which should have power to establish it on earth. Being the work of the Almighty, these signs would almost always be miraculous so as to restore on earth the equilibrium of peace and justice, of blessedness and holiness, which the world had enjoyed before sin in the beginning.

The Saviour takes over these needs and these hopes, but He gives them their true sense and real value. He does not refuse, when the good of souls or simply human misery requires it, to answer prayers for temporal or material things; but He tries to reduce men's too exclusively bodily preoccupations to a position of secondary importance. He emphasizes on the other hand the spiritual and invisible value of the *Kingdom* in which we meet with God. And, above all, He shows this kingdom as realized in His own person, and realized in the world by His presence and His action. For He is the Messiah, that is the looked for King; He is so even in an unheard-of sense, since He is the eternal Son and bears in Himself the very life of God to give it to humanity. But because He is at the same time the *Son of Man* and one of us, He realizes by the mere unfolding of His religious and redemptive life, by the mere performance of His sanctifying actions, the close union of the invisible and the visible which makes His very person the Sacrament and His interventions efficacious signs of our salvation. There is no word, no action, no movement of Jesus which does not contain grace, which does not promote the coming of God's kingdom upon earth.

For thanks to Christ and His mystery the Kingdom is henceforth both visible and invisible—invisible in its principle, God and the very life of God, visible in its founder Christ; invisible in the souls which it begets to supernatural life, visible in its extension in space, its organization in historic time.

For this Kingdom, thanks to its Author's founding and decrees, tends more and more to organize itself. The little flock of hesitant disciples quickly becomes an established Church. It is above all of this Church *founded on the rock* that we think in trying to follow the development of the sacramental system. In this perspective we leave aside those of Christ's many actions which were only the response to some passing incident, or a lesson incidentally given, such as the washing of the feet on Maundy Thursday. We pass by also those signs of the Saviour's activity which are too personal to become obligatory upon all the faithful, such as His fast in the desert or His wonderful practice of the counsels which He offered but did not impose, the invitation to celibacy, for example, *propter regnum cælorum*. We leave out too in studying His significant behaviour even those forms of daily apostolate, which the Church will continue to employ, but which only prepare souls for the Kingdom without actually organizing it—such as preaching and the like. And in fine, to fix the list of the sacraments properly so called, the *sacramenta majora* as the Middle Ages called them, it is enough to keep those actions of the King, which, corresponding with a Messianic purpose, have as results both the invisible sanctification of men's souls and the

Church's visible organization. As such they will endure as long as the Church herself, forming for her a powerful and essential armoury. They are committed to her also as a trust, which she must use but may not alter. They belong to her, and she employs them as the instruments of sanctity. They control that Church too and perpetually renew her; without them she would fade away from history.

But, before begetting the future, they were linked with the past, with those Old Testament institutions which they abolished and replaced, with the prophecies which they fulfilled, and more than fulfilled. One of them, marriage, belongs to the very origins of man and to the Father's first designs for the human race. Thus, whatever their diversity, all belong to Christ the King's Messianic functions, organizing His Kingdom to make it at the same time visible in the world and invisible in regenerated souls. They are therefore eminently *signs*, and, since they are actions of the Incarnate Son, of the almighty Word, they are efficacious signs, which contain what they represent, which realize in souls what they show forth to outward eyes.

The Apostles made no mistake about it. When they saw their master rise to the Father's right hand, they kept the double conviction that Jesus would one day return and that they themselves were charged in the meanwhile with respecting the institution of His established Kingdom, guarding its organization against any change. They were content to reproduce the actions of Jesus in His name and by His grace; and these sacraments, through this exact performance and through this identity, would still produce the same effects. The Church lives henceforth only by this fidelity. Beyond all question these infallible actions of the living Christ live also in the Church, who holds over them rights of protection, dispensation and administration. They depend on her intention, which she has the power to make known by other signs personal to herself and added by her. But over the substance of the sacramental institution, as it is found in the Gospel, she has no other right than that of use. Blessed indeed is the Church to be so bound by her founder's will: the Sacraments

fter twenty centuries are still the acts of Messiah, of Christ
he King, establishing His work and organizing it, "the
iving relics," as the old Scholastics said, "of the Incarna-
ion."*

CHAPTER TWO: CHRIST'S INSTITUTION OF THE EUCHARIST

IT is now time, as we try to come to ever closer grips with
our subject, to show how Christ's use and institution of
Sacramental signs, this progressive and definitive substitu-
ion of His personal, Messianic, efficacious acts for all the
ypes and promises of the Old Law, issues on the eve of His
Passion and death in the creation at His holy and venerable
hands of the sacrifice of the new Alliance.

Clearly it is above all the Master's thought that holds our
interest at this decisive moment, but can we be so bold as to
scrutinize Christ's soul? However great the respect, the care,
the sensitiveness, the thrill of faithful love with which we
embark on the attempt, will it not soon crush us beneath its
weight? The task, if we faced it unaided, would be impossible,
but the experiment is in order if it means seeking from
Tradition the riches which it has in store.

And there is a Eucharistic tradition in our Church. It is
present everywhere, beginning with Scripture in which it
takes its rise. It goes on, passing through the Fathers, in the
Summas of the Middle Ages, and it overflows into the vast
literature of piety and popularization which inspires current
preaching. Yet in these devotional books and pamphlets it is
coloured by the mentality of their readers, male and female,
and uses edifying language proper to the time of writing; and

---

* "Ecclesiæ Sacramenta, quæ utraque ab Angelico Doctore quædam divinæ
Incarnationis reliquiæ appellantur." Pius XI, Encyclical *Studiorum Ducem* on
S. Thomas Aquinas (June 29th, 1923).   Cf. Salmanticenses, tract. XXII *de
Sacramentis in Communi*, prœmium. The expression also occurs in the 4th book
of the *Commentary on the Sentences* headed *ad Hannibaldum Cardinalem*, placed
among the works of S. Thomas (ed. Vivès, tome XXX, ca. initium).

this language is sometimes precious, watered down, employing a misguided subtlety. We would find once again the original fresh and vigorous sap and hear the Saviour speak and think as He spoke then to the Apostles and thought in the secret of His Heart. And so it is above all Scripture in the light of this tradition which we must read and meditate with reverent accuracy.

*　　*　　*

The Eucharist has a date. It is a gesture of farewell made on the eve of a departure, at the end of a meal, in an atmosphere of religious fervour and fraternal love, on the vigil of a bloodstained Pasch on which Jesus was to meet His death. This is the context in which we must first place our understanding of this new institution, by which the Apostles will be enabled both to revive the past and to await the future. The Saviour's gesture is a remembrance, a promise, a pledge, an *au revoir*.

Next we must add to this context certain great realities, and first of all the earlier revelations which Jesus had made, all the exigencies of His message, the gradual work of educating the minds of the Apostles in the past three years.

In spite of the simple pride of Jewish nationalism, the religion of Israel still recognized its insufficiency and its provisional character. No doubt the faithful hoped to preserve intact, even after the arrival of God's definitive Kingdom, the majority of their existing institutions, made more splendid and magnificent certainly, but with the old privileges and the old traditions. Belief in Messiah nevertheless had been defined as meaning the expectation of a more perfect state of things.

Jesus had drawn to Himself all these preoccupations and all these hopes. He had presented Himself as the definitive solution of the religious question. At His arrival the era of the prophets had been ended, the Kingdom had begun. He, the only beloved Son, the sole object of God's good pleasure, was the only way by which man might henceforth reach the Father, pray to Him, adore Him and give Him thanks. Jesus did not merely found a religion. He is religion in person, for the doctrine which He preaches, the morality which He inculcates, are not external to Him; they are realized in Himself. In the language of Moses and the prophets, He is the *alliance*.

But every alliance is signed and concluded in a sacrifice. Where then is the sacrifice in this new religion? *Ubi est victima holocausti?*, as little Isaac said to Abraham with youthful piety's relentless logic. Where will Jesus find a victim, He who has already pointed to His own grievous and imminent death as set forth in the Scriptures to be the ransom for the sins of men ?

We are approaching an almost inevitable conclusion. Jesus, who is to die, must pursue the inner logic of His work of religion and redemption to the end: *in finem*. His poor disciples still lack the ritual, visible, sacrifice demanded by their human nature: *sicut hominum natura exigit*. He knows well enough that through His speech and His actions of the past three years the ancient Mosaic liturgy is to perish in the ruins of the temple, which is to be henceforth only a woeful memory. How should it hold firm against this new religion which He embodies and which will engross men's hearts as it already fills the heart of God? *Omnia traham ad meipsum.* . . . If the sanctuary *built with hands* is to fail, it is not only, as Caiaphas thinks, because *the Romans will come and destroy the city and the nation*, but also because Jesus has undermined all transitory and insufficient spiritual powers: *they shall no longer adore neither on this nor on any mountain.* Whatever respect He showed to the ancient rites inherited from the patriarchs, however attentive the care with which He celebrated the Jewish Pasch, He made it perfectly clear that these were only stopgaps, liturgies of the passing hour, and His disciples perfectly grasped that His Father, as in the days of the prophets, *is surfeited, weary and glutted with the blood of goats and heifers.*

It is now another alliance that rejoices the Father's heart and turns Him towards men. And there is no other religion than that *in spirit and in truth*, to-day no more than the little

M

Kingdom of which Jesus is the head and His disciples *the little flock*, but first and foremost concentrated in His soul, the soul *of the Son who knows the Father and whom only the Father understands*.

This interior religion is soon to be translated in a supreme historic act, finding therein both its highest expression and also the beginning of its eternal triumph. For centuries restless mankind has sought by vain symbolic signs for the path which should bring them back to God their Father through renouncement of sin and its effects, to that meeting with Him which should beatify them. Jesus is to mark it out, placing Himself on the way of the Cross which will lead Him to the right hand of His Father: His death found in the Scriptures, His resurrection foretold by the prophets, are the acceptable sacrifice for ever.

But how, unless Jesus explain it to them, are the Apostles to see this coincidence of a horrible death and a glorious resurrection with the persistent secret dreams of the religious animal that is man, this substitution of Calvary for all the vanished ceremonies? To the eyes of the flesh this *baptism of blood* upon a gibbet, this sordid end to an iniquitous trial, are too unlike the ritual splendours which gathered crowds round all the altars of the world behind their priests and victims. How is Jesus to show that *this* is greater than all that, greater even than the events of Genesis and Exodus when Abraham and Moses had sealed the old alliance with the blood of animals?

And then because the march of the world will go on past this night of terror and past the day of butchery that follows it, ending with the abandonment to the Father and self-commission into His hands, and because it will also bring oblivion on this unheeding people, how is the memory to be safeguarded for mankind *of the things which have come to pass in Jerusalem?*

So it is that Jesus resolves both these problems, the one along with the other, with a gesture swift but precise, as clear and luminous as the simplest human actions: He declares the Redemption for the last time, while clothing it in a ritual and lasting sacrament, and He creates the Eucharist, while dedicating His body and His blood to the redemptive work.

In our expositions of Christian dogma we tend to dissociate these two mysteries. Such a division of the subject adds to the clearness of our teaching, but after all Jesus sought and found a double goal, and we cannot really say which is the more precious side for us of the *Hoc est corpus meum; hic est calix sanguinis mei*, whether the definitive knowledge of the mystery which is our salvation, with the pledge given by Jesus to pursue its course to the end, or the institution of the sacramental action which enables us each day, in memory of the Master, to apply liturgically the fruits of this Redemption.

Without the Eucharist the Redemption would have had no liturgical character enabling us to link it with our ritual needs; but without the Redemption the Eucharist would have had no true significance or real value.

The Saviour then delivered Himself up, not only on the morrow but that very night; and of one of the final Jewish rites, one of the most modest but also one of the clearest, pledging therein His body and His blood, He makes the Blessed Sacrament.

It is indeed for our use that He created it. For the principle of our salvation was wholly guaranteed by the sacrifice of the morrow. But this must pass into ritual currency for daily circulation. This is the inauguration of a liturgical cult, but of one which is moreover efficacious: generations to come are to be united to the Father by Jesus, to know Him, to realize Him, and to make Him known. Now for the time being Jesus withdraws to enter into His glory. He does not go for long, for He will return to judge the living and the dead; but all the same He goes. How during the interval is the continuity of religious worship to be assured, the ritual and sacrificial expression of the alliance? For the kingdom once founded does not come to an end. And since it cannot be simply reduced to the institutions of the Old Law, *all must be new*, as S. Thomas Aquinas was to say. The mystery too must have visible continuance until Jesus come. From every point of view the disciples need a sign of the new alliance.

And it is given them. It is as simple as an offering or a libation under the Mosaic Law. It is as intimate as the fraternal communion which it bodies forth in visible form. It is as expressive as the violent death which it represents, figuratively separating the solid and liquid elements of mangled human flesh. It heralds the great eternal banquet in which union will be consummated. It quietly solves all our accumulated psychological problems, as we should expect of a religion which is in spirit and in truth. Thus Jesus performs this act, delivering to us the sacrament of His death with all the efficacy of the grace which this procures for the world's profit. The name "sacrament", so rich in meaning that it has taken the Church centuries to take stock of it, is really the only word for it. Here we possess *the Sacrament of the Redemption* with all that it carries with it, the fulfilment of prophecies and promises, the signing of the new alliance, the perfect and supreme Pasch, the unique and complete sacrifice, the consummation of religion, the remission of our sins, the pledge of Christ's return, the first fruits of the eternal banquet, and the establishment on earth of fraternal charity: *O sacrum convivium!*

Thus Jesus gives Himself to the Father and to us twice over, once overnight in the Paschal liturgy in which He puts Himself wholly at the disposal of our inward and outward religion, filling it wholly with Himself, and again on the morrow, when He delivered Himself up historically to fulfil the mystery of His religious life, taking that grievous course which sin imposed upon our sacrifices.

Or rather, giving Himself wholly, He gives Himself only once, but in two ways, one ritual, the other historic, and both real. The unity of the victim is absolute, so that the two sacrifices, one within the other, despite the external differences which permit us to distinguish them, despite the ritual multiplication of the former, make up only one. The former, that of the Supper, pledges and demands the latter: the latter, that of the Cross, fills with its historical reality the enuous ceremonial framework of the former. The Cross is all-important, because our salvation was dependent on it; but he Supper made the Cross inevitable, and therefore in its own way supports it in its turn.

Here again we find that reciprocal causality which most certainly is the only means of explaining Christianity and, in particular, of understanding how the celebration of the Lord's Supper renews the mystery of Calvary, of which it is the sign.

Can our reading of the documents enable us to go still further? There was still the question of choosing from among so many possible signs and actions. And it was for Jesus to decide. To show for the last time His respect for the old Mosaic law which was to disappear, He borrowed from it the ritual support of the institution destined to endure throughout the centuries of His new era. Thus He welded the two Testaments visibly together, and once more fulfilled the Thorah without destroying it.

At that hour and upon that supper table the Law was summed up in the observance of a few final rubrics of the Pasch: it was represented by a little bread and wine upon the table cloth, the relics of a religious feast faithfully performed.*

The formula, or rather the prayer on which it is modelled, was available. Israel loved to give thanks to Jehovah for all His favours; this was done by the offering of first-fruits: "We give thanks to You, O Jahve, by and for all the gifts received from you, by wheaten bread and the juice of the vine."

This was at the time the only liturgical framework which Jesus had at His disposal. But this light structure was enough for Him. Into this fragment He inserted at a stroke the

---

* This synthesis, if it confines itself to the above generalities, is independent of the solution to the perennial question whether or not the Saviour celebrated a true paschal feast on Maundy Thursday night. It is sufficient, and certain, that the Supper took place in the context of the Pasch, and that Jesus gave a profoundly religious character to this farewell meal : *sciens Jesus quia venit hora eius* . . . there is no need to stress that. There are no materials in the Gospels for a fuller explanation, and it is better not to hazard one. For interesting suggestions v. Fortescue, *The Mass*, Longmans, 1912, p. 317, and especially Moreau, O.S.B., *Les liturgies eucharistiques*, Brussels, 1924, pp. 223, sq.

sacrificial rite of a religion destined to embrace the earth. . . .
At a stroke is not quite true. The Master had for so long
given His disciples the impression that He was the only
intermediary by whom they should approach the Father,
the only priest because the only Son. He had closed all false
approaches: "*I am the way. . . . I am the living bread. . . .*"

It is not surprising then that He should have said to them
in the end: "Henceforth you shall not give thanks except
through me—unless through bread and wine, and that is
because the bread will have become my Body and the wine
my Blood. That will be the efficacious liturgy of the *new
alliance, as you await the great feast of the eternal Kingdom
in the Father's house.*"

This ritual linking of the Eucharist to the Jewish liturgy,
which seems to fit the facts so well, is retained in the Mass
also, thus revealing one of its aspects and recalling its origins.
For the Church still begins her sacrifice with an outburst,
a song, of thanksgiving. And the prayer which is to issue in
transubstantiation starts as if it were to be only a prayer
of praise, a *eucharistia* as the Greeks called it. That the word
should have come to designate the entire mystery shows
that the Apostles conceived of the Lord's Supper from the
beginning as the definitive Thanksgiving, suppressing all
others and replaced by none:

"It is just and worthy, right and salutary, to glorify you
and to praise you, Father, through Jesus Christ, your Son,
who said on the eve of His death: *This is my Body*—because
by Him, with Him, and in Him is all honour and glory to
you in the unity of the Holy Spirit.   Amen."

It is partly because of this birth of the Mass in the Cenacle
that our Catechisms are entitled to say that Jesus Christ
offers Himself to God His Father at the altar by our ministry.
For at the Supper the Saviour really gave Himself to be
next day a voluntary holocaust, and so enclosed all the
mysteries of the days that followed within the ritual and
efficacious sign which we are privileged to renew in memory
of Him. The Mass is possible only because that evening
Christ *had given thanks*. There was a previous prayer

before the *hoc est corpus meum*. The synoptic texts have not
given it because it resembles the Jewish eulogies which it
was suppressing, and with these the primitive community
was perfectly familiar. The Church has built upon their
model the mental and verbal distribution of the anaphoras
and the Canon in their broad outlines. The link is thus
forged between the oldest religious attitudes of humanity
and the youthful liturgy of the new religion. The incarnate
Son had first placed His sacrifice, the sacrifice of His peerless
body and of all His blood, in the place of all the ritual
sacrifices of the Law. In three days His death and resurrection would have put an end to all outworn religions, even
to that of Moses. That evening His answered prayer and
efficacious act were taking the place already of all the
Levitical prescriptions. He destroys only to replace. His
Passion was to replace all our imperfect forms of worship.
His Eucharist was to replace all the vanished cults.

For if Jesus found the materials of bread and wine in a
rubric of the Mosaic feasts, nevertheless in these peculiarities
of Jewish worship He reached all mankind. To offer God
the pure first-fruits of the gifts received from Him, to
renounce them in order to consecrate them to Him, to
obtain from the acceptance which He grants them the
sanctification which transforms them into sacraments of
salvation, all this is the ancestral cycle of all historic sacrifices, the natural and inevitable framework in which in the
end they must all, despite their differences, find a place; it
is the essential movement of man and of religion. Jesus
accepts this attitude. He does not accept it only because on
the morrow, on the day of the Passover, and the succeeding
days, the two phases of His mystery, immolation on earth,
exaltation in heaven, earth and hell, are to reproduce and
magnify the two moments, grievous and glorious, of man's
problem and his sin's problem before the face of God. But
He accepts it also, because from this evening He signs with
this mystery a sacrament whose ascending course heavenward and descending course earthward were already followed by all men's victims and oblations. And the youthful

Church will have only to imitate what the ancient synagogue before her attempted, and, behind the synagogue, humanity, wounded and pitiable, but still hopeful even in its persistent, radical illusions. There is no change in these usages because everything about them is transformed, raised to a higher level, because a new victim is introduced using the old sacrificial gestures, but replacing them.

No need for change then in these usages of ours—but everything to alter in our moral conduct. The religion in spirit and in truth has passed along our paths. This bread and this wine, before becoming the visible species of the body and blood of Christ, must first be the sign* and the symbol of our repentance, our love, our renunciation of sin, our adherence to God. The more helpless and simple and innocent they seem the more clearly do they show the sentiments of our souls; for these they stand for first before they serve as sacrament of the Saviour's body. In that sense above all the sacrifice of men is to become the sacrifice of Christ.

Sacrifice, the Ancients loved to say, is a sign. This is doubly true of the Eucharist. It is both the sign of our internal religion at the offertory and onwards; it is also, after the consecration, the species or the sign of the body of Christ.† Christ became the victim for us when He placed

---

* A true sign, because it really costs something, as de la Taille's admirable theory of Mass stipends shows.

† The Protestant heresy has made us suspicious of these words "sign" and "figure" applied to the Eucharist, for we fear to give the impression of denying the Real Presence by applying them to Christ's body. Yet the Council of Trent had not this fear, for it is content to anathematize those who say that the body of Christ is present *only* in sign or figure: *tantummodo esse in eo ut in signo vel figura*. In fact these words, properly understood and interpreted, belong traditionally to the oldest Eucharistic vocabulary, for they express one of the most certain of the Mystery's aspects, or at any rate the most obvious, namely that the body of Christ is present under a sacramental sign, the sign or "species" of bread and wine. The body of Christ is really present, but under a sign: and it is the bread which serves as a sign, or more precisely the species of which serve as a sign. And in fine the expression "The Eucharist is the figure of the body of Christ" (provided that it is clearly understood not to be *only* that) has a most acceptable sense, if we attribute this function of figure, as we use the word, not to the body, but to the species. And as the Eucharist is both the species of bread (signum) and the body of Christ (res), the phrase is not inevitably heretical; but it is ambiguous. The double sense arises from the obscurity of the genitive: the sign *of* the body can mean equally well "the real body beneath a sign" or "the sign of a body which is not present."

all His personal religion of suffering and of glorification in the purest of our religious rites, in the Eucharistic prayer of our bread and wine; *passio Domini est sacrificium quod offerimus.*

And, thanks to His creative institution, the two signs, His and ours, become only one. His sacrifice of the morrow, which was to save the world as all the vanished holocausts of Levi's sons could not, would yet lack itself that envelope of liturgy required for a ritual sign. M. Lepin, taking up an idea of S. Augustine's, rightly considers Calvary a personal or direct sacrifice, in which the religion of the well-beloved Son was to be realized in a historical immolation, but without the array of symbols in which men had hitherto enclosed their needs of adoration and of expiation. It would be a sacrifice unveiled, one might say, and more perfect than the victims of old, but one in which men, accustomed to confound worship with ceremonial, would have found it hard to recognize the perfect sacrifice of the definitive religion.

Now the early Fathers, especially the Greeks, obeying the law of sacramental realism, which is one of the most assured of their dogmatic positions, always understood the expression in the former sense, and give the impression they did not suppose the latter attributable by anyone. That explains the confident tone of their Eucharistic vocabulary. They gloried in the possession of divine realities under signs or sacraments adapted to our human nature, and spoke fearlessly of the sign or the figure of Christ's body, exactly as we should speak of the Sacrament of the body of Christ in the realist sense. This simple fact utterly destroys the only objection that anyone has ever been able to draw from the language of the Greek Fathers against the Church's belief in the Real Presence.

The word "antitype" is the only serious objection in the matter of the epiclesis against the Latin theology about the moment of Transubstantiation; this has a similar history. It is not opposed to *type* as we should be tempted to suppose from the prefix *anti*. "Type" is not a symbol and "antitype" the reality. "Antitype" only adds a shade of meaning to "type". The latter means symbol, sign or figure: "antitype" means symbol, sign or figure *of*. The bread of the Eucharist is "type", absolutely: ἐν τύπῳ τοῦ ἄρτου, says S. Cyril of Jerusalem, *Catech.* XXII, myst. IV, 314. Relatively, it is type-of (therefore antitype of) the body of Christ. It is true that "antitype" may have also a passive sense, but the sense remains practically the same. And the famous expression in the liturgy attributed to S. John Chrysostom, from which modern Greeks draw an argument for their view of a consecratory epiclesis, τὰ ἀντίτυπα τοῦ σώματος, means merely "the sacrament which figures the body" (in the active sense) or "the body which is figured by the sacrament" (in the passive sense), and both in the realist sense explained above. In English we can translate only by "the Sacrament of the Body of Christ". And after all this expression also has an active sense—"the species of bread serve as sacrament or sign of the body", and a passive sense—"the body is signified (or sacramentalized) by the species of bread", the same doctrine being expressed in either case. Cf. *Hebr.*, ix, 24, and *I Petr.*, iii, 21. And in Cyril of Jerusalem, *Cat.*, XX (myst. II), 6; XXI (myst. III), 1: XXII (myst. IV), 3; XXIII (myst. V), 20; cf. *Cat.*, XXI (myst. III), 6; XIII, 19.

And meantime, or rather at all times, man's vain holocausts were performing their empty task, signs without
reality, actions without content, useless incensations, yet
corresponding in their imagery with those sensible requirements which are our very human nature, this flesh which
moves and speaks, this thing of life and colour.

Thus it is that with a gesture powerful but infinitely
gentle the Saviour took the purest of all human symbols,
the ancient rite of Melchisedech, the eternal sacrament of
our hunger and thirst, placing the whole redemption in that
sign: *sacramentum redemptionis*. Man's sign becomes the
sacrifice of the Son, the one enclosed in the other; the
historical redemption was translated into a daily ritual, and
the Eucharistic bread and wine were changed into the body
and blood of Christ. On the morrow there would be the
historical sacrifice without a liturgy, naked like the body of
the Saviour Himself on the Cross, that the Father's will
might be accomplished and our guilty humanity redeemed;
this evening, in the Cenacle, there is the institution of the
sacrifice to be repeated for all time, upon an altar-cloth,
with candles and chants, *sicut hominum natura exigit*, for the
satisfaction of our humanism.

Jesus, the victim of our sacrifice, is yet its priest also. And
the supreme unity for which we are seeking is finally found
in this single priesthood; not only the unity of the Mass and
the Cross (which is sufficiently established), but also that of
our Masses with Christ's first Mass in the Cenacle. Those
actions of Christ by which He instituted the Sacraments, the
Church and the whole of religion, are valid and efficacious in
our hands to-day only because the Saviour in His capacity as
Head still performs them by our ministry. The Church does
not merely inherit a fortune and the pledges of Christ's love;
she is the very body of a youthful Head who lives within her.
The members of the mystical organism can do no useful
work without the initiative and impulse of its principle. In
the Mass then Jesus still acts, leading us in the offering of
the sacrifice of which He is Himself the victim; as with
all the sacraments those actions of His which we inherit

are sanctifying only because in the Father's eyes and in relation to our souls they are still His. It makes little difference whether we speak in His name: *ego te absolvo in nomine Domini*, or repeat His words by way of narrative using the first person: *hoc est corpus meum*. To be sure this boldness of the priest as he speaks of Christ's body, saying *my body*, *my blood*, seems proud and startling, but it is only the consequence of another more fundamentally daring attitude and of a deeper truth, in virtue of which the Church claims Christ's place—*vices gerens Christi*, because Christ is always the source of her life, active but invisible. So a sacrifice of the Church is inconceivable of which Christ should not be here and now the priest as well as herself, nor therefore a sacrifice which Christ had not instituted with the words *do likewise*.

For without such a creation how should we be assured of possessing Christ's true sacrifice, of possessing Him as victim and above all as priest? His precept to act in memory of Himself was in truth almost unnecessary; His disciples had become so habituated to the idea that the Kingdom depended for its continuance till His return upon their own endeavours. It is not surprising then that the Apostles on the morrow of His departure repeated His last Eucharist using the same terms: *hoc est corpus meum*. By so doing they found Him once again upon the altar as the victim, while as priest He acted through their hands. And the two formulas *the Church offers the sacrifice of Christ at the altar* and *Christ offers Himself on the altar by the ministry of priests* are identical. Tradition realized this and always used them interchangeably. And the question whether the Mass is the sacrifice of Christ or of the Church raises a false problem, because—fortunately for us—it is both.

*   *   *

The two formulas of institution, one over the bread and the other over the wine, should be used in dogmatic theology not only side by side as though they were only parallel, but one after the other, because the second carries on the first and reinforces it. The Saviour's thought widens its exigencies as well as clarifying them as it proceeds. Over the bread, He puts forth a first draft of the new dogma, a prelude announcing the inevitable: *His body will be delivered up and is here present*. But it is hard to express all the mystery of His death over the solid symbol of the bread, for this sign in isolation is not quite sufficient. So our Lord takes up the idea again over the wine and fully develops it, at the same time continuing the institution. The bread suggested only the body of an offered victim; the wine gave the picture of its flowing blood. The revelation could be completed through this species, using too the memory of the blood shed in the first alliance. This treatment of the texts with cumulative significance explains why Matthew and Mark did not think it in the least necessary to proclaim the mystery of the Redemption about the bread which they did declare immediately afterwards about the wine, in terms almost clearer than those of Luke and of the First Epistle to the Corinthians; and conversely why Luke and Corinthians first referred in connection with the chalice to the new alliance, which is in their thought the motive for the presence of Christ's blood. It is also far easier to explain why the Synoptics did not hesitate to introduce variants into the texts of the institution, since they could do no injury to the great dogmas revealed by the Saviour at this final and decisive moment.

CHAPTER THREE: THE EUCHARISTIC TRADITION UP TO THE 16TH CENTURY

THE Church has in her hands a ritual and daily sacrifice of the Redemption, because Christ found the means of giving us a sacramental sign, at once symbolic and efficacious, of His personal mystery, a mystery accomplished both on Calvary and in Heaven. This sign is symbolic because it represents the Saviour's Passion, and efficacious because it applies all the fruits of it to ourselves, thanks to the presence of the same immolated victim. Realizing thus every day the spiritual results of Calvary, the Mass renews among us each morning the single sacrifice of Jesus Christ.

So thought the whole of Tradition. Let us listen for a little to this mighty voice whose evidences have been faithfully collated by M. Lepin.* The texts are to be found in his invaluable work and also under *Messe* in the *Dictionnaire de Théologie Vacant-Amann*. After these definitive achievements it would be of slight advantage to repeat the lists of the Fathers and of the references and quotations from them. Also it is the continuity of the tradition which we need to grasp, and for this a certain scheme of presentation is required, helped by a well-organized typography; M. Lepin supplies them.

But we cannot resist the pleasure of recalling some particularly classical expressions. There is that well-known little passage, inserted in parenthesis by S. Cyprian in his long *Letter to Cæcilius*, in which he takes the trouble to sift for his old friend the pointless arguments of an absurd and long-exploded heresy. He is proving against the contemporary Aquarians that wine and not water must be used at Mass, dwelling upon a point which then had actuality. And suddenly he puts in this remark, a jewel of precision which contains immortal truth: *Passio est enim Domini sacrificium quod offerimus. For the sacrifice of our Eucharist is the very Passion of the Lord.*†

* M. Lepin, *L'idée du Sacrifice de la Messe d'après les théologiens depuis l'origine jusqu'à nos jours*, Paris, Beauchesne, 1926.

† S. Cyprian, *litt.* 63, *ad Caecilium de Sacramento Domini Calicis contra Aquarios*. But there is a difficulty about the exact meaning of the word *Passio* in this letter: does the word signify the supper in the Cenacle or the Passion on Calvary? Mgr. Battifol *Leçons sur la Messe*, Lecoffre, 1919, p. 176, holds strongly for the first translation, which leads to another interpretation of the text, more favourable to de la Taille than to Billot, which we are not using here. But we believe that the word *Passio (dominica)* means here all that took place from the Saviour's entrance into the Cenacle to the piercing with the lance upon the Cross: cf. para. 8: *Christus qui est petra finditur ictu lanceæ in passione;* and para. 6: *leo de tribu Juda et recubet dormiens in passione* (when he dies) *et surgat*. It is therefore exaggerated to restrict the sense of the word *Passio* to the Supper, still more to the account of the Supper. De la Taille returned to this problem in *Recherches de Science Religieuse*, Dec., 1931, pp. 576–581.

Here is our dogma with all its exigencies, all its obscurities if you will, but also in all its light. The triumphant verb *to be* in this proposition leaves room for no possibility of compromise. There is another text in the correspondence of S. Augustine, who summed up all the previous tradition and round whom in turn the tradition of the following centuries gathered. *In Sacramento*, wrote the Bishop of Hippo to his colleague Boniface of Catania, *non solum per omnes Paschæ solemnitates, sed omni die populis Christus immolatur, nec utique mentitur qui interrogatus eum responderit immolari.** The whole Middle Age pondered respectfully the essential idea in this phrase *in Sacramento Christus omni die immolatur*, and the echo of these words sounds throughout Christian literature. The most ancient liturgical texts, especially the Post-Communions, are written with this same perspective of Christ's sacrifice sacramentally realized.†

Again how fortunate were our ancestors for whom these last words were really saturated with significance! They knew what they meant by a sign, a symbol, a sacrament. Those names were not labels on empty boxes or meaningless formulas in their religious life.

A sign was an action, a series of actions and words, a ceremony or a body of rites, allowing the faithful to share in the mystery, recalled to mind and represented by the rite itself. The ancient cults had tried and hoped in vain a thousand times to find this coincidence of hidden reality and visible representation. Judaism had glimpsed it and pictured it in anticipation. Thanks to the Incarnate Word, it had come at last. It was the institution of the Sacraments. God

---

* S. Augustini *Epist.* 98 (alias 33) *Bonifacio episcopo.*

† V. in *Dict. Vacant-Amann* under *Messe*, col. 970, in M. Gaudel's article, the remarkable theological and literary history of S. Augustine's text. Here are some indications taken from M. Lepin's volume:

Paschasius Radbertus (†851): Quotidie pro nobis Christus mystice immolatur, et passio Christi in mysterio traditur (Lepin, p. 48).

Yves of Chartres (†1116): Non mentiri eum qui dicit Christum impassibilem et immortalem quotidie in sacramento immolari (Lepin, p. 28).

Alger of Liège (†1130) : Immolatio Christi in altari non dicitur quod iterum occidetur, sed quod vera ejus immolatio repræsentata idem in altari nunc quod tunc in cruce operetur. . . . Sacrificium Ecclesiæ non constat solo sacramento, vel corpore et sanguine Christi sine sacramento, [sed] utroque (Lepin, p. 19).

Gratian (†1158) : Christus immolatus semel quotidie immolatur (Lepin, p. 30).

n the flesh, eternal life within a human action, grace in a rite—there is the whole of Christianity and the whole of Catholicism to-day, summed up in this achievement.

This incarnation of the invisible in the visible succeeds in both directions,* in the downward movement from heaven to earth, in which it is the sacrament properly so called, the sign containing grace—and in the upward movement from earth to heaven, in which it is a liturgy realizing Christ's religion for us, the Eucharist sacrifice.

The Roman liturgy, in a wonderfully balanced Secret prayer, calls the Holy Sacrifice of the Mass *sacramentum redemptionis*,† the sign of the redemption. So we at least are obliged to translate it, now that the word sacrament has been confined to the seven rites conferring grace. But in S. Augustine and all the ancients the word is still used in both senses, the upward as well as the downward; and the religion of the Church which rises from the Eucharistic altar to the throne of God is the sacrament of Christ's religion and so the sacrament of the Redemption. The priest's sacred gesture, because it is that instituted by Christ, realizes for us what it represents: *it is an efficacious symbol of the hidden mystery which it pictures for our bodily eyes*, or, if you will, *the symbol which, picturing the Redemption, makes it efficacious*.

Efficacious for us, for the Church. For God has no need of it for Himself; the historical Passion and Resurrection of His Son sufficed. This idea that the sacrament is at the disposal of the faithful and for their advantage is another note forming an essential part of the concept of sacrament which came naturally to the ancients. Certainly the canonists of to-day, to resolve their cases of conscience, repeat *Sacramenta propter homines* in all tight corners. But perhaps they do not altogether realize what deep mystical meanings

---

* Cf. Billot, S.J., *de Ecclesiæ Sacramentis*, Rome, 6th ed., 1924, p. 590: sacrificium convenit cum sacramento, quatenus quoddam sacrum signum est. Differt, quatenus sacramentum est signum causarum sanctificationis nostræ, sacrificium vero signum interioris cultus.

† *Roman Missal*, octave of All Saints: Benedictio tua, Domine, larga descendat: quæ et munera nostra, deprecantibus sanctis Martyribus tuis, tibi reddat accepta, et nobis sacramentum redemptionis efficiat. Per Dominum. . . .

are hidden behind this convenient slogan and what religious metaphysic is at the base of it. The end of the sacraments is to put within the reach of men spiritual realities which themselves subsist without either men or sacraments. The latter do not create the mysteries which they reproduce, but put them into our hands in the form of graces. If the Mass is the sacrament of our Redemption, its end is not to begin it again (for it was perfect from the first), but to win its benefits for us by giving it to us, bringing it down upon our altars.

What splendour this reveals in Christian rites! Who can describe the riches found in these formulas, which, striking eye and ear, perform in souls at the same time the invisible things whose symbolic image they externally portray? Shall we ever regain the fervour of faith which our ancestors had, living as they did in the familiar company of these mysteries, their physical sensations in rhythm with the upward stirring of their recollected souls, thus unifying, under the action of grace, all their powers both animal and spiritual? At these blessed moments creation became subject to them as in the days of the world's first innocence, when matter was in complete agreement with the needs of spirit. The phantasmagoria of external things, which to-day constantly drags us away from God and from ourselves, gave place to the perfect harmony of soul and flesh, the latter suffering the action of oil or water and the imposition of hands that the former might be purified, fortified and consecrated. The neophyte made the physical descent to the baptistery, and with the invocation of the three Persons of the Trinity he came up from it animated by a divine new grace. The tomb of the old man, the womb of the new, the sacred bath of spiritual rebirth—the ancients piled up the strongest possible expressions to express this absolute coincidence between the symbol of grace and the grace itself, the hope of which had supported them during the long trials of Lent and the catechumenate and which filled them this Easter night with an unmeasured joy. And Tertullian lent this faith all the resources of a realistic Latin whose profound and daring truths our modern tongues are almost too restrained to render.

"The flesh is the pivot of salvation. It is this that fixes our souls to God and makes it possible for them to be bound to Him. The flesh is bathed to wash the soul; the flesh is anointed to consecrate the soul; the flesh is signed to fortify the soul; and when the flesh is hidden by the imposition of hands, the soul receives spiritual light; the flesh is nourished by the body and the blood of Christ, that the soul may have her fill of God. . . . The oil flows over our bodies, but it is the spirit which profits; and the physical act of baptism which plunges our flesh into the water works invisibly our deliverance from sin. . . . How glorious is this sacramental wave. . . . We are little fishes born in the water like our ἰχθύς Jesus Christ!"*

Thus this poor flesh with our inherited and personal blemishes upon it, but the seat of our imaginations and of our dreams, where the sources of our passions and sensations, so terrifying and rebellious, for ever flow—this sad, sinful flesh, submitting itself to rite, lent itself obediently to gesture and symbol to be moulded and impregnated by the mysteries of the soul and at the last brought into harmony with them. And the neophyte in the water of baptism where the nakedness of his body, gloriously chaste at this divine moment, bent beneath the Trinitarian invocation, felt himself dead to sin and enclosed within a liquid tomb and then reborn of the Holy Spirit and restored to life; he came forth from the waters, a son of the light, and, thanks to the imposition of the holy oil, an athlete of invisible combats, and, finally, one anointed with the royal chrism of the Christian sacring. All his old pagan life in the stadium and the baths, the gymnasia and the *campus*, was transposed into terms of spiritual reality; but his body was always there to support the mystery, canalized as it was through his members, now stirred to fresh life and sanctified. And their faith told our fathers that at the hour when the

---

* Tertullian, *De Resurrectione carnis*, 8; *De Baptismo*, 1 and 7. The Latin has a conciseness and force which is the despair of a translator.

N

Bishop's hand came down upon their trembling and submissive flesh with words of consecration or of purification,
an immense interior reality, parallel with these symbols,
transformed their souls to the pattern thus expressed. This
mystery was the very life of Jesus revealed of old on the
banks of the Jordan.

The making of the sign was also the realization of the
grace. The one carried the other as the body supports and
contains the soul. The whole of religion was enclosed within
an action.

We can mock, if we will, in our irreverent way. But
humanity is against the mockers, and so is Pascal, as he offers
the holy water that he may give men to God.

Anyhow, it was the faith of our fathers.

*   *   *

Joys like these, but with a different course, taking the
direction of sacrifice, seize upon the priest who goes up to
the Eucharistic altar to celebrate the holy mysteries. From
head to foot, from the amice which helms him with its white-
ness to the noble folds of the alb which fall to his feet,
he has found once more in these ancient vestments the
attitudes of the early Church as she prayed in the catacombs.
The stole and chasuble, to-day hieratic and stylized, make
him go back in an instant through the centuries, linking
himself with their traditions. He is now subject to rubrics
as to an exacting heritage; but his obedience to the
rites, disciplining his whole being, straightway enriches
him with all the religious fervour of past ages. His whole
body lends itself to inclinations, genuflections, kisses and
heavenward movements. Above all his hands, consecrated
in his youth by the Bishop's chrism, are bound to the
mysteries which their gestures faithfully portray. On the
altar cloth a golden chalice and paten, an ancient book of
time-hallowed formulas, two candles, vessels of wine and
water; and to the rhythm of the words prescribed a man's
all-powerful hands open and close, bless, break, distribute,
as the Missal directs. The priest feels himself at the service

of the Spirit, and the Spirit works through his hands: it is at once all symbol and all reality. Here is that traveller in the sacred wood of whom the spendthrift heir of Parnassus spoke to us.* Over the altar stone the same sacred actions, shaped to a setting for the text, in rhythm with the words and figuring them, express the symbols of invisible realities; *and the mystery of the Word made flesh will be again incarnate in the visible sacrament.*

We are familiar with this mystery. We know how it moves from Passion and Death to Resurrection and Ascension, realizing the one and only sacrifice. This mystery then it is, by the institution of the Saviour Himself, the only possible author of so magnificent a thing, enclosed whole and entire in the efficacious symbols of word and action over this bread and wine, changing them into the body and blood of Christ. What is a sacrament of the New Law? It is a series of visible signs and actions which, by reason of the Saviour's will, contain within them the grace whose image they portray before our eyes. What is the Eucharist, the ritual sacrifice of the New Law? A series of visible signs and actions, a unity of chosen materials and sacred formulas, which, by reason of Christ's will, contain the sacrifice whose image they portray before our eyes.

He who, being God, could enclose the divine life in His human words and deeds, communicating it to us in visible symbols, is still powerful enough to enclose also the whole reality of His human religion and therefore His whole

---

* Baudelaire had written

> Nature is a temple where a medley of words
> Seems to rise sometimes from living pillars ;
> Man walks there through a forest of symbols
> Which look familiarly upon him.

But M. de Mun gave one day a Christian and sacramentalist interpretation of these famous lines: ". . . None better than a Catholic can recognize himself as this traveller through the forest. Whatever my dear friend Emile Faguet may say, man's whole religion invites him to think, trains him to meditate upon the deep sense of things. From the rising of the sun to its setting and into the very hours of the night, marked by hours of the liturgy, he goes onwards to his end with symbols on every side of him. Everything recalls them to his mind, the splendour of Biblical images, the living lesson of the Gospel parables, the architecture of his churches, the vestments of his priests, and his ceremonial worship." (A. de Mun, *Réponse au discours de réception d'H. de Régnier, Académie Française*, Thursday, 18th January, 1912).

sacrifice under a double sensible sign, that of the tran-
substantiated elements. The marvel this time is even less in a
sense, for it is less astonishing to see the Son of God gather
together the whole reality of His human religion in appropriate symbols than to see Him charge the actions of a human
being with the very life of God. But what makes the mystery
less difficult in itself is just what makes it hardest for our
minds. For the divine life communicated to us under the
name of grace is so much beyond us that we easily resign
ourselves to failure when we seek to know how it comes to us
under an efficacious symbol. But we do sometimes suppose
ourselves capable of understanding Christ's religion as it unfolds itself in time in all its griefs and glories in the Gospel
story. We are impatient that we cannot grasp how it is whole
and entire here and now upon the altar, not only in figure or
picture, but in its complete reality. Yet it is really so. But we
must not, in order to admit this, ask like children where
upon the altar are the nails, the hands, the Cross, the
Resurrection and Ascension; we must simply accept, with
the faith of our fathers, that the author of the sacraments,
the efficacious signs and action of the divine life, could also
make chosen symbols the source of His religious, sacrificial
life.

Sacramentum Redemptionis! Shall we now grasp the force of
these two words when we read them again in the Missal,
believing at last that all the Redemption is contained beneath the signs which represent it? It is the sacrament of the
Saviour's sacrifice, the sacrament which is at once representative and efficacious. The ancients called it so, admitting
the truth of it and adoring it. To have the sacrament of a
reality, when this sacrament comes to us from the Saviour, is
to have the reality—in a way which, as the name indicates, is
sacramental, that is not only symbolically but by the realization of it.

Our controversies with Protestants have as it were broken
the force of this vocabulary into pitiable fragments. When we
speak of symbols we think nowadays of deceptive appearances, empty signs and mystical illusions. That is why we

no longer dare to say that the Eucharist is the symbol of Christ's body.

But our forebears put into the word all the meaning figured externally before their eyes. And they considered that man can possess the same reality in two ways, as such in its historic actualization—as with the Passion according to the four Evangelists—and in its bare metaphysical nature veiled by a symbol which makes it at once real and present, and pictured at the same time by our ritual figures— and so is the Saviour's Passion on the Altar.

So to the question which haunts our modern manuals "How is the Mass a sacrifice, and the Saviour's sacrifice?" they answered *symbolically*, putting into the word all the realism with which they had already filled it. We have kept this language in the still universally received expression "unbloody sacrifice", which we apply to the Mass in contrast with the bloody sacrifice of Calvary. The unbloody sacrifice is the sacramental sacrifice or sacrifice in sacramental form.

It is both the same as the first and different: *the same*, because as regards the history of Christ, His oblation, immolation on Calvary, return to heaven and welcome by the Father, this mystery took place only once and is as such present before God eternally—*semel oblatus est, semper vivens*—and there will never be more than one Redemption; *different*, because in so far as a sacrifice presupposes a liturgy, a rite, and even a minister and assistants, this Mass is not that, and neither is a bloody sacrifice.

The latter in its historic sense does not begin afresh. What would be the good of repeating it as such? Nothing can alter the fact that the Son of God died on a cross, and, having died, rose from the dead. These events are for ever before the Father's eyes, and the victim for ever lives for our salvation. This is the sacrifice which the altar receives in its entirety, that we may share in it. It receives it under a symbol. In that sense it begins it afresh, and as often as may be, distributing its fruits and gaining its benefits for the Church to-day.

Thus sacrifice is multiplied by sacrament, but in its own sacramental way, resuming it without replacing it, renewing it without reiteration. The sacrament communicates to its contemporaries a mystery already accomplished which their salvation constantly requires.

Thus we must not make a contrast between Calvary and the Eucharist by adding them together like two distinct quantities similar in kind, for we are not faced here with mere copies of a single reality, but with efficacious symbols of a previously existing mystery.

This Christian language is certainly alarming. It says everything outright, is daring to the uttermost, because it believes and declares all that the Son of God has taught us. But we must find our way to the secret of its genius if we are properly to understand this revelation. The way to reach it is, according to tradition, the theory of the visible rite which effects sacrifice and represents it.

*   *   *

When we say *efficacious*, we must understand "efficacious for us, for our use, at our disposal." For the Mass does not repeat the Redemption, which was once and for all perfectly accomplished. But it allows us to enter into this great work of our salvation and to obtain its benefits. It has not to produce another immolation of Jesus fresh from the start as if the first were insufficient. For let us think what was this sacrifice of Christ—an onrush of love which carried the Incarnate Son into His Father's arms across the gulf of sorrow and death formed by our sin, and placed Him finally at the Father's right hand in that glorious meeting which the Epistle to the Hebrews has described for us. And who are we to re-enact such things, which are as much beyond us as heaven is beyond earth? *They* do not begin anew by their very definition, and the Resurrection on the third day has long ago made any new physical immolation of the Son impossible.

We have better things to think of than these futile impossibilities.

We must make this unique sacrifice our own, that is enter

into it so as to join ourselves to it, and to go back to the
Father in our turn in a movement of religion which, without
adding to it, will prolong God's glory. And, as *without Christ
we can do nothing*, His sacrifice must be given to us. A sacrament instituted by Him will be enough for this. The original
sacrifice moreover still exists and always will. The historic
cross was long ago removed from Golgotha, the executioners
are dead, Annas, Caiaphas and Pilate are no longer there, and
the body and blood of the Saviour, reunited to His soul, have
been lifted up. But the victim remains eternally, in all the
great reality of incarnate grief and religious love, keeping
still in being the drama which governs and explains the
whole world's history. And the fruits also remain of this
great mystery of the Redemption. If we could only gain
some share in these realities and, since we cannot here touch
them with our hands, receive them in a sacramental symbol
which should deliver them to us whole and entire, without
profanation but without diminution! *Poor soul* (God answers
us) *it is so!*

The truth lies here, as always, in an exact mean between
our contradictory exaggerations, one of them being a sort of
ultra-realism which would make Jesus die time and again and
would end by dissolving the realities of the altar into a mere
Passion play. And perhaps some writers of mediæval folk-
lore did look at the sacrifice of the Mass in some such way.
They heard Jesus's dying cry at the *Nobis quoque pecca-
toribus*, and they had seen Him stripped of His garments
when the priest uncovered the chalice at the offertory, and
then nailed to the cross when he spread out his hands at the
Preface. Explanations of the Mass along these lines exist, and
we must avoid such puerilities. Put into theological form
they would ruin the dogma which they are trying to explain;
for by multiplying the Saviour's death they would prevent
us from possessing it in its single truth. We should have
copies only of a lost masterpiece.

But there is also, at the other extreme, a sort of empty
ascramentalism, by which the Mass is reduced to a mere
offertory of a victim sacrificed already without any true

resumption of the great mystery. Jesus died once, at Jerusalem, on the 14th Nisan. Thanks to the presence of His body on the altar we renew the offering of this death; and that is why we call it, using a magnificent but rather strained expression, the Eucharistic sacrifice.

This time the theory errs by defect. For we possess in the Mass the very reality of the Saviour's one and only death. We possess it not only because the present, past and future are telescoped in God's eyes into a single glance and we may therefore say that in God's eyes Jesus dies always. That explanation is insufficient and even unsound. For we are concerned with our view of things, not God's; with Jesus in our relations with Him, not with the wholly unified knowledge of the infinite God.

Shall we then say that Jesus having once been immolated on Calvary nothing can henceforth do away with the fact of it; and thus that we offer at the altar one who once was immolated and is therefore for ever in an immolated state?

This conception is fuller and close to the truth, but it does not exhaust it. The claims of tradition are still stronger, and Christian thought is both simpler and more mysterious. S. Thomas, at any rate, and after him the Council of Trent, use a different style, the sacramental and realist style: the sign of the Saviour's Passion, instituted by Jesus Himself, applies to us every day, thanks to the victim's presence, that Passion's fruits, and thus prolongs His sacrifice and even His immolation to our own time. That is the meaning of the magnificent period which forms the collect for Corpus Christi, the work of S. Thomas Aquinas:

Deus qui nobis sub Sacramento mirabili passionis tuæ memoriam reliquisti, tribue, quæsumus, ita nos corporis et sanguinis tui sacra mysteria venerari, ut redemptionis tuæ fructum in nobis jugiter sentiamus.

O God, (1) who has left us under a wonderful sacramental sign the memorial of your passion, (2) grant us, we beseech you, so to venerate the mystery of your body and your blood, (3) that we may always taste the fruit of your redemption in us.

This prayer, to-day that of the whole Church, springing from the holy Doctor's religious soul, simply takes over in liturgical style the simple and vigorous doctrine of the *Summa Theologica*, III^a p., q. 83, a. 1, where S. Thomas, taking the dogma of the Real Presence as proved, asks whether Christ is immolated in this sacrament. And he answers in the affirmative for two reasons, later to be repeated by the Council of Trent at the beginning of its great Twenty-Second Session. "The celebration of the Eucharist", says S. Thomas, "is called the immolation of Christ on two grounds: first, because it is a representative image of Christ's Passion, His true immolation . . . second, as regards the efficacy of Christ's Passion, because this sacrament makes us participate in the fruits of the Lord's Passion. Thus the Secret prayer for a Sunday [9th after Pentecost] says: *whenever we celebrate the memory of this victim, we set in action our Redemption:* quoties hujus hostiæ commemoratio celebratur, opus nostræ Redemptionis exercetur. In the first sense we might say that Christ was immolated even in the figures of the Old Testament, and in this sense *the Lamb was slain from the beginning of the world* (*Apoc.*, xiii, 8). But in the second sense it is special to the Eucharist that Christ is immolated in its celebration."

The passage contains a great deal, and we must try to fill ourselves with all its wealth of meaning without losing anything. Its formulas are so far-reaching. The Redemption was both the Father's supreme gift to man and the super-abundant satisfaction offered to the Father by the Son, the principle both of our sacraments and of our sacrifice, the principle of the sacrifice and of the sacrament of the altar in which it is completely realized. So the Eucharist will be the efficacious symbol of the Redemption. But what, once again, does this phrase mean? Is it that the Eucharist effectively contains the Redemption, as any sacrament does grace? Or rather that the Eucharist makes the Redemption effective by communicating to us its beneficent results? This last expression is that which S. Thomas prefers and the Council of Trent also: it is the clearer of the two. But in reality the two propositions are equivalent. The Redemption is not a treaty of peace concluded some nineteen centuries ago between God and men, the clauses of which are applied by the Church to new-born children and repentant sinners without any relation between this ancient contract and our present salvation save a connection of cause and effect and a respect for pledges. This infantile idea would be very close to the Protestant theologies condemned at the sixth Session of the Council. The Redemption is the very mystery of Jesus internally communicated to us: when this mystery is applied to us, it is as it were extended and prolonged. When we derive its fruit, it is because we in our turn enter into it, carried on by its own movement.

We cannot then gain the salutary effects of the Redemption without possessing it within us, without receiving the communication of it, without participating in what is its essence, the very mystery of the Saviour's sacrifice.

If then there exists, instituted by the Saviour, a symbolic rite which applies to us the effects of the unique redemptive sacrifice, the Redemption itself will be effectively contained by it; and the sacrifice which we can offer in these conditions will be the very sacrifice of the redemptive Passion.

In the light of these principles we can now admire the accuracy and profundity of the expression current in Christian language *in the Mass the Church offers the sacrifice of Christ*. This little phrase does not mean that, the Saviour's sacrifice having taken place on Calvary and only on Calvary, the Church contents herself thereafter with multiplying the offering or offertory on the Eucharistic altars, as a child might offer its father a hundred times over some picture or needlework of its own making. That interpretation is far too feeble. What it means is that the Church makes her own the unique sacrifice of Christ which took place on Calvary and was concluded in heaven, and that in this sense she offers it; for to offer sacrifice is to *make* it. And, as in this case it is already made, the Church, who takes hold of it, must at least draw into herself this mystery of Christ's sacrifice, making it her own, and must gain possession of its effects.

First it is a remembrance or image of Christ's Passion: *sub Sacramento memoriam reliquisti;* then, thanks to the real presence *corporis et sanguinis*, participation in the fruits of the Redemption: *Redemptionis fructum iugiter sentiamus;* such are always for S. Thomas our holy mysteries in the sacrament: *sub Sacramento . . . sacra mysteria*. Such were the familiar categories of his thought vivified at the Augustinian, the traditional sources. We meet them in the *Summa Theologica* as in the collect for Corpus Christi. The holy Doctor followed in his prayer without strain or effort the same mental lines as in his teaching.

Three centuries later, in years of heresy and storm, the Church gathered together at the Council of Trent was content, after the curious deliberations chronicled by M. Lepin, to take this doctrine over as it stood. And she has wrought it out in one of the finest documents of our theological literature. The first chapter of the Twenty-Second Session, in which some forgotten humanist translated S. Thomas's rather restrained expressions in magnificently flowing periods, is one of those divine pages with which the whole of Christian doctrine, were it ever to disappear, could be reconstructed. But this biblical and scholastic tapestry, however finely worked, does not surpass S. Thomas's statements in solidity: the writer has only subdivided the first of the Summa's reasons, distinguishing between the image and the remembrance of the Cross, and declaring both realized under the figure of the visible species. For the rest there is no difference between the teaching of the III[a] p., q. 83, a.1, and the following passage from the Council of Trent:

"Since under the first Testament, according to the testimony of S. Paul, the impotence of the Levitical priesthood made all complete achievement impossible; it was necessary, in conformity with the merciful designs of God the Father, that another priest should arise according to the order of Melchisedech, Our Lord Jesus Christ, who should be capable of leading all those who were to be sanctified to the state of complete perfection. He then, our God and our Lord, *although* (*etsi*) He was to offer Himself once only to God the Father upon the altar of the Cross going by way of death to work eternal redemption: since *however* (*tamen*) His death was not to end his priesthood, at the last supper, the night that He was betrayed—in order to leave to His beloved Spouse the Church, as human nature requires, a visible sacrifice, to represent the bloody sacrifice which He was to accomplish once for all on the Cross, to preserve the memory of it to the end of time and to apply every day the virtue of this salutary sacrifice for the remission of our sins; declaring Himself appointed priest for ever according to the order of Melchisedech—offered to God the Father His body and His blood under the species of bread and wine, and under the symbols of these same elements delivered them to the Apostles whom He appointed priests of the New Testament; and He bade them, as also their successors, to offer them, saying: *hoc facite in meam commemorationem.* Thus the Catholic Church has always understood and taught. For after celebrating the ancient Pasch, which He immolated in memory of the coming forth of the children of Israel from Egypt, He instituted the new Pasch, that is Himself, which the Church is to *immolate* by the ministry of priests under visible signs in memory of His passage from this world to the Father, when by the shedding of His blood He redeems us and saves us from the power of darkness to transport us into His Kingdom. . . .'*

How much time might have been saved if the explanation of Canons 1 and 3 of this Twenty-Second Session had been

---

* The theologians of the Order of S. Dominic, when they escape the influence of the Counter-Reformation theologians, take over the great Thomist tradition in this matter quite naturally.

". . . [Christ] did not make the Mass an external sacrifice somehow superimposed upon the sacrifice of the Cross and redundant in regard to it. For why should there be two sacrifices when one would be sufficient, which would itself alone surpass all imaginable sacrifices in its value for intercession and propitiation? What Christ did was simply to give the sacrifice of the Cross, henceforth itself invisible, a symbolic dress, to translate it externally before our eyes without any injuring of the sacrifice's reality by the symbols, but on the contrary so that they might be bound up with it, showing its precise outlines. . . .

But it does not follow that the Mass is only a symbol of Sacrifice. It is a real Sacrifice, the Sacrifice of the Cross continued. . . ."

R. P. Gillet, O.P., in an article on *The Harmonies of Transubstantiation*, in *Revue des Sc. Phil. et Théolog.* [of Kain], 20th April, 1914, p. 263.

sought simply in this first chapter, written and promulgated by the very authors of the dogmatic definition and intended to be its commentary and proper context? And was not that account worth all the arguments, proofs and discussions used to convert the Protestants of that time and of this?

There were unfortunately too many such arguments, and they still load our manuals; they appear too under the disguise of vaguely edifying phrases in works of piety for the faithful, unless they end in complete disillusion by the admission of ignorance and failure.

CHAPTER FOUR: THE BREAK WITH TRADITION

WHY was it then that the current which the Council of Trent had canalized vanished at once into thin and feeble rivulets? The controversy with the Protestants was the reason for this dispersal of energies. As a contemporary theologian has said "the necessity for remaining within the limits conceded by an adversary at the beginning of a discussion involves the risk not of falsifying but of impoverishing the notion (of the subject). . . . . And the apologetic perspective is seldom the best for getting to the bottom of a problem."

Briefly, there had been handed down an ancient formula which had to be understood in the sense in which the Ancients and the Council of Trent had always understood it: the formula of sacramental immolation, in which the noun and the adjective explained one another by their interaction. The symbolic character of the immolation did not prevent it from being real; but this reality, given to us in a sacrament, was no novelty. Through the new sign we shared in an ancient immolation. From the day when immolation and sacramentalism began to be treated as two connected but separable factors under the pressure of the methods imposed on theology by Protestant objections, the straight road, the main highway, was abandoned. Some, theologians of Spanish Flanders, in direct contact with their opponents, put the emphasis on the sacramental idea, and sometimes tried to satisfy themselves, in order to appease the Protestants, with a figurative or *representative* immolation. Others, theologians of the Italian school, underlined the dogma of sacrifice so as to crush the distant heretics more effectively and looked for an immolation at the altar so much the more real, they thought, in that they showed it to be a fresh immolation, distinct from that of the Cross.*

To-day all this is dead and buried. The details are in M. Lepin's book and all the manuals. Here an attempt will be made to synthetize these movements. After all these theologies of the mystic Lamb are not hostile and contradictory conceptions between which one must choose, but like the scattered panels of the polyptych by the brothers Van Eyck. Some bashful canons and a sacristan Emperor let the scattered fragments of this masterpiece go to Brussels, Berlin and Paris. This partitioning had at least the advantage that during the years of their unhappy separation each panel received the honours and attention due to a complete retable in the foreign museums where they spent their exile; they were treated lovingly and proudly studied. To-day it is time to restore S. Bavon's treasure intact, to bring the corresponding panels together, to explain them by one another, revealing the true colours of their complex beauty in the wise balance of their composition.†

---

* De la Taille, *Esquisse*, pp. 17–18.

† The table below is a venture. This sort of synoptic summary, the delight of students on the eve of examination, is usually the most grievous injustice to the authors thus racked on a Procustes bed; for it is quite certain that these convenient schemas are obtained only at the cost of suppressing all the personal elements in the systems so neatly balanced one against another. The reader is therefore asked not to weigh the respect and attention which these great theologians deserve by the position and size of the pigeon-holes allotted to them. M. Lepin, for example, while conceiving of sacrifice as *a gift acceptable to God*, does not overlook the place of the shedding of blood in expiatory sacrifices, etc. . . . M. Lepin, in the work already cited, has also done much to give the older writers their due: Vasquez, among others, is shown to have a richer teaching than the manuals had seen fit to grant him.

One group of theologians had rightly sought a symbolic resemblance to Calvary in the sacramental signs, but they had made the new sacrifice consist exclusively in this, as though a resemblance could of itself produce reality. This similitude was pictured in the liveliest colours as if to create the actuality by ever increasing the illusion of it. Thus first of all Vasquez tentatively, Lessius quite definitely, and behind them Flanders and the Spanish Netherlands, underlining the adjective *mystic*, taken as synonymous with *symbolic*, and raising symbolism to the dignity of sacrifice in virtue of its resemblance to it.

Then under the pressure of the theory itself, which could develop only by exaggeration, the ground suddenly shifted. Now it is not only because it contains an image of Calvary that the Eucharist is a sacrifice, but because it is itself physically another immolation. Lessius had spoken of an image which would transform itself, if it could, into reality. De Lugo thought that this virtuality actually existed: there is a new immolation at the altar. There is a death upon the corporal: *semper* moriens *ad interpellandum pro nobis*. So the Italian school would speak; it becomes excited, enflamed and intoxicated by its own forced eloquence, and Christ now lies upon the altar as in the most adorable of deaths. But (a bad

	THE SACRIFICE OF THE MASS IS, IN RELATION TO THE SACRIFICE OF THE CROSS, A REPRESENTATIVE SIGN, AND, *BY MEANS* OF TRANSUBSTANTIATION :—							
	A fresh (different) immolation					AN EFFICACIOUS SIGN (because instituted by Christ) of the SAME SACRIFICE (The *same* immolation, but sacramental)	AN OBLATION	
SACRIFICE IN GENERAL IS :	of bread	of Christ					of the immolation of the Cross	without fresh immolation
		real	equivalent	virtual (conditional)	sacramental			
A destruction (more exactly a consumption).	Suarez	Bellamine						
An immolation.			de Lugo	Lessius	Billot			
Opus quod agitur ut sancta societate in-hæreamus Deo. (Augustino-Thomist definition)						The Augustino-Thomist tradition	de la Taille	
An oblation.								Lepin

sign!) a single species would be strictly sufficient to realize this fresh destruction of our Saviour. And the aspect of immolation, thought of in isolation, makes that of sacrament almost disappear.

Thus the precious formula of sacramental immolation, so rich in content but so poor and pitiable when treated in this way, suffers a succession of interpretations all falsified by their desire to isolate themselves from one another. Sacramental immolation becomes symbolic and then mystic, that is elusive and purely figurative. Or it is real in desire as well as in image, but unrealizable in itself, and so virtual. Or it is the immolation which the sacrament imposes on Christ's glorified body by a fresh modification, physical and humiliating, of the victim.

At this final stage of the vicious circle other theologians, more sensitive, protest. "It is too much", they cry, struck to the heart at the vision of their Saviour's corpse laid upon the altar at their Mass each morning. But they are carried with the storm and do not think to look behind them. They can only think that it might be possible to seize upon an element of Christ's sacrifice more spiritual but in sufficiently close relation with the immolation of the Cross to give (by its repetition) possession of that immolation, though without beginning it afresh. This saving gesture is oblation. Here at last seems to be the sacramental immolation which they seek. Some find it at the end of the mystery of the Redemption, in Heaven, where Christ still offers Himself, and so bring this upon the altar; others see it at the beginning, at the Supper, where Christ delivered all His body and His blood as a holocaust ready for offering to His Father's glory.

The circle is complete. Brought back to the Supper where Christ instituted the divine Eucharist, theology can start the round again. Some apparent varieties will give us the impression of fresh lines. In reality we are still on the wheel which wore down eventually even the inexhaustible patience of M. Lepin.

We must escape from this labyrinth of systems which have no future because they have no past. And there is a way out

to the open air and to the high road. There is another interpretation possible of sacramental immolation—the doctrine
of the efficacious symbol. A sign instituted by Christ is rich
enough to contain within it the reality which it resembles.
Its extraordinary power comes to it not precisely from this
resemblance, however moving this may be for us, however
exquisite our Lord's selection, but from the fact of institution by Him. It is a sign possessing, in virtue of its author,
the value which it signifies.*

To-day we may say that this tradition has been rediscovered and reaffirmed.†

* The sacramental sign is not efficacious because it symbolically resembles the
mystery to be produced by it. It is efficacious because it has been instituted by
Our Lord. But since it has been chosen and instituted by Him by reason of this
resemblance, its causality derives in the last analysis both from its author and from
its resemblance to the effects.

Thus the Eucharistic sign is not the sacrifice of Christ because it symbolically
resembles the sacrifice of Calvary. It is a sacrifice because it has been instituted as
such by Christ, who chose it for the resemblance of the species to the external
appearance of His immolation and to the prophetic images of the Old Law. In that
sense (which is not the poor one given by Vasquez) the Mass gives us the sacrifice
of the Cross because it represents it.

Setting aside the system of Lessius, which has too little theological solidity to
count, we may say that none of the systems studied in the manuals, except that of
Billot, succeeds in making the reality of the sacrifice of the Mass depend upon its
resemblance to the Cross's sacrifice. In de Lugo, the French School and perhaps
(I am less sure) in de la Taille, the Mass (1) represents the Cross thanks to the two
species and (2) it is a sacrifice. But the connection does not appear between these
propositions: if both the species are required for the resemblance, they are not
both required for the reality: one would suffice to verify the sacrifice. In Billot,
the connection is much more essential, because the author reintroduces into
sacrifice—in the reverse direction, distinguishing the causal mode—the familiar
and fully articulated theology of sacrament as sign both symbolic and at the same
time efficacious, efficacious because of the choice of Christ who chose it for its
symbolism. This synthetic power in his system already suggests that we rejoin
with Billot the line of the great tradition and that we must go this way to find the
high road.

† Vol. IX of *Histoire Littéraire du Sentiment Religieux en France* by Henri
Bremond, which appeared while this book was in proof, proves magnificently in
chap. II, section 2, *Le Saint Sacrifice*, that this tradition was never really lost.

O

CHAPTER FIVE: THE RETURN TO TRADITION

THE leader in this victory was Billot in his teaching at the Roman College. With a determined gesture he swept away the accumulated rubbish of fruitless controversies and at once regained vast territories of traditional doctrine; the value of the sign as such, the Eucharistic species intervening to give us a real sacrifice, but with no physical change in Christ Himself, the essential importance of transubstantiation; the relation of the Mass to Calvary, establishing the propitiatory value of the Eucharist; and the possibility of possessing Christ's sacrifice in two different ways, both under His own species and under those of the sacrament. Through this last door the whole of tradition returned triumphantly into the palace of theology.

De la Taille was to discover later that this system erred by defect. This was no doubt, in his eyes, because Billot underlined too heavily the importance of the sacramental sign. But it had been so much forgotten! If we suddenly discovered Origen's *Hexapla*, should we not forget occasionally S. Jerome's Vulgate?

In any case Billot, instead of finding in the sign nothing but the image or virtuality of an immolation, finds a real one. And he does not allow that this immolation is independent of that of Calvary, nor above all that it makes Christ undergo a change of any kind. In the last edition of his *de Sacramentis*, under pressure from the respectful but very definite criticisms of de la Taille, he even gave a new form and a new precision to his thought which prepared the way for a still deeper sounding of the doctrine:

Oblatio cænæ (quæ est prima ac prototypa sacrificii missæ celebratio) opponitur sacrificio crucis sicut repræsentativum repræsentato, sicut memoriale objecto in perpetuum memorando, sicut

The offering of the Supper . . . is opposed [in the Scholastic sense] to the sacrifice of the Cross . . . *as the representative to what is represented;* as the memorial to something for ever me-

id quod in finem usque re-
petendum ac continuo fre-
quentandum præcipiebatur,
ei quod semel tantum erat
peragendum, nusquam iter-
andum.

morable: as what will be
renewed and repeated con-
tinually for ever by Christ's
order, to what had to be
once and for all performed,
without possibility of reiteration (p. 602).

Habet consecratio veram in
se sacrificii rationem, for-
maliter et præcise secundum
quod est incruenta Christi
immolatio, cruentæ immo-
lationis crucis repreæsenta-
tiva per sacramentalem seu
mysticam corporis a sanguine
sub distinctis speciebus panis
et vini separationem.*

The consecration has in it
the true essence of sacrifice,
formally and precisely in
that it is an unbloody *immolation* of Christ, representative of the bloody immolation of the Cross, by
the *sacramental or mystical*
separation of the body and
the blood under the distinct
species of bread and wine
(p. 621 and 632).

This sixth edition of the first volume of the *de Sacramentis* is perhaps more remarkable for its suppressions than
for its additions. The author in the third of his preliminaries
on sacrifice in general has cancelled a whole page often mis-
used by his disciples to make his doctrine more palatable for
the general public. There had been in it perhaps some relics
of Vasquez to which the author gave a fresh and acceptable
sense but his readers an out-of-date and narrow one, easier
to follow: the sacrifice of the Cross was expiatory, the sacrifice of the Mass was not, in virtue of the respective species or
figures in which they were offered. All that has disappeared
and in its place there is a valuable note on the relations between immolation and oblation. Thus it remains that the
Mass, deriving all its essential value from Calvary of which
it is the sign, does no injury to the Cross by claiming to
utilize, that is to realize for us the effects, including the
expiatory effects, of the sacrifice of Golgotha.

* Billot, S. J., *De Ecclesiæ Sacramentis*, tomus prior, Roma, 1929 (edito sexta
aucta et emendata) esp. pp. 601–605.

Why then is Billot so afraid of employing the expression *"unity of sacrifice on the Cross and in the Mass"* accepted by S. Thomas,* canonized by the Catechism of the Council of Trent† and by so many of our diocesan catechisms? We may reckon the length of our human existences by successive days, by the risings and settings of the sun; but there is after all one great orb blazing in the sky. The difficulty is always to give a precise sense to the two words *sacramental immolation*, whose meaning varies before our eyes like the plumage on a pigeon's neck according as we put the emphasis on the noun or adjective, according as we think of them as separate or as united. We must take up the question later once again. For the moment pleasure and profit await us in de la Taille.

*   *   *

The theology of de la Taille is far richer and more elaborate than the wretched little schema to which some casual readers would confine him. For, according to him, the Church does not offer in the Mass only the Saviour's immolation, but the immolated one accepted by the Father, the eternal "theothyte". Then the system supposes a sort of metaphysical bond, that is, a necessary one, between the offering of the Mass and the immolation upon Calvary. At the Supper the Saviour, pledging Himself, made inevitable His immolation of the morrow—*oblatio victimæ immolandæ;* in the Mass the Church enters into this complex of relationships: her offering presupposes the immolation of Calvary—*oblatio victimæ immolatæ;* and in so far as a consequence can involve its principle, the Mass, sprung from the Supper, requires Calvary and is essentially related to it.

To strengthen this bond, which might not seem too obvious, de la Taille teaches that the Supper, of which the Mass is a replica celebrated by the Church, was not only the sacramental heralding of the Cross but an integral and even an essential part of the Sacrifice of Calvary. Thanks to this bold and ingenious theory, the Mass participates in the

* III^a p., q. 83, a. 1, ad 1 um : unum sacrificium.
† *Catechismus ad parochos*, par. 2ª, cap. IV, *de Eucharistiæ Sacramento*, No. 76.

ontological unity which existed between the offering of Christ in the Cenacle and His immolation on the Cross, making of the two a single sacrifice.

Thus all the lines of de la Taille's theology are closely held together. The theory of the Supper as an integrating part of Calvary, which some have tried to separate from the general system, is logically demanded by his whole teaching. And this is the alarming part of it. This synthetic unity is a powerful thing. But perhaps it may become a weakness, for if one point is lost the whole position crumbles.

Now in showing us the Eucharist of Maundy Thursday as the first act of the next day's sacrifice, de la Taille is obliged to give a further emphasis to the unity, which the tradition always saw in the Passion narrative, extending from the Cenacle to Calvary. The institution of the Eucharist certainly forms part of the sacrifice of the Redemption. But perhaps the author comes into collision here not only with Billot but behind him with the first chapter of Trent's Twenty-Second Session, with the *etsi* and *tamen* already indicated as the two shoals between which we must pass.*

It is difficult to believe that the institution of the Holy

---

* On the crucial passage in the *Esquisse*, pp. 18–19: "The Church immolates the Saviour in the Mass mystically, that is sacramentally but not effectively," one might say:

The Church immolates the Saviour effectively, *distinguo*: effectively and historically, as the Jews did, *nego*, effectively and sacramentally, in an efficacious symbol, in a sacramental efficaciousness, which preserves the mystery of Christ's immolation and makes it ours, *concedo*.

Then what follows in de la Taille, *loc. cit.*, is most satisfactory. "It is sufficient that Christ, being the victim of His (historical) sacrifice, should become through our action the victim of our (sacramental) sacrifice. He is a victim apart from us; it is for us to make Him *our* victim. That is what we do in taking over to our use His action at the Supper".

But, as against the note on this page 19, our symbolic immolation, being effective, is not limited to the sensible externals of the sacrament and is not external to our Lord : nevertheless it does not modify Him intrinsically, for it causes no change in His glorious state, which is simply that of a glorified victim (and therefore of one immolated). Possessing Him in His glory we possess Him as immolated also, for it is all one. Possessing the glorification, we possess the immolation, for they are obverse and reverse, one the consequence of the other. They are not opposed, they suppose one another. If we could only understand that *propter quod* thrown out by S. Paul to the Philippians (ii, 9) as unifying the whole mystery of Christ! The glorification of the Son by His Father on Easter day is the Son's voluntary immolation taken to its term. It is the mystery developed to its end. And if it did not seem a slightly flippant way of treating such adorable realities, on which the redemption of the world and the joys of eternity depend, we might say that you may lift up the mystery of Christ by the top or the bottom, but you lift all of it in either case. What God has joined, man will not part asunder.

Eucharist, though a means for the revelation of the doctrine of the Redemption and necessary for the application of its fruits, was necessary to it in itself. But de la Taille's work is too rich, his traditional conception of sacrifice in general too magnificent—applied to Christ's Passion and glorification it explains Scripture too well, applied to the Eucharist it frames the theological texts and rubrics too perfectly—for these pages of splendid writing not to be used and exploited like a vein of fine marble for many years to come. It contains a theory of Mass stipends which is admirable enough to justify by itself alone, in spite of the secondary importance of the question, the theology of sacrifice on which it rests. And there is a unity of thought in these two volumes, the Latin and the French, which may sometimes make unacceptable demands upon the reader, but which he must admire even when at certain points he is regretfully obliged to differ from it.

* * *

Had the French school achieved this synthetic unity? Did the great masters of the seventeenth century, those splendid ancients before the throne of the Lamb, succeed in keeping in their vision of the eternal mystery all the wealth with which Christ had filled the sacrament of the altar on Maundy Thursday? Their theology with all its flashing enthusiasm ill fitted them for a well-balanced view. As the heirs to a century of extreme Augustinianism they were badly prepared, through their very conflicts with Port Royal, for preserving a calm equilibrium in their definition of the Christian sacrifice. Yet M. Lepin, thanks to a filial respect which wins our own, has managed to extract from the work of de Condren, freed from the extravagances foisted upon him—doubtless gratuitously—by a Jansenist editor, a theology of the Mass wholly dependent upon the Heavenly sacrifice.

We may frankly regret that this splendid structure rests upon a thorough-going opposition between oblation and immolation. The sacrifice of Christ in Heaven does not consist solely in the renewed offering of His earthly death, in a sort of *post factum* offertory of His previous immolation made by the Son to the Father; but it is that state of meeting with the Father which is the logical result and the true end of the immolations which Christ underwent, their very conclusion, or more exactly the glorious and beatific aspect of His single mystery, which is His journey to the Father by way of the humiliations of the Cross and His consequent reception by the Father. With us the mystery has had a history and has evolved in time. In God's eyes it is a single all-embracing mystery with two sides, one deriving from our sins, the other the result of love and justice. And it is the conclusion of it, conditioned by the previous immolations, which is eternally presented to the Father's eyes, filling Him with infinite joy and satisfaction. The Son's religion exists in heaven in its perfection. It did so essentially on earth as well but in a situation inconsistent with itself—consistent however with our sin. Now it is complete, *consummatum est*. But it is achieved only after passing through its stages, those of sorrow and humiliation even unto death.

And this, it seems, is what the Epistle to the Hebrews really means. When the sacred author suggests that Christ is truly priest only in heaven, he does not deny that He was so from the first and always on this earth. But, if one is above all a priest at the moment when sacrifice is offered, as the sacrifice of Christ was not *finished*, did not succeed except in heaven, it is in heaven that we must adore the Son in the full exercise of his sacerdotal functions. And the Apocalypse of S. John, in another literary framework (differing even in theological approach), reaches the same conclusions in the famous vision of the Mystic Lamb. Only the Epistle to the Hebrews looks for preference at the final stage of the mystery, at Christ as priest because His immolation of Calvary has been completed and followed by His heavenly exaltation. The Apocalypse on the other hand shows the past immolation transparently appearing even in the apotheosis, because it is the Lamb who was slain, the bloodstained source of the mystic bath, who triumphs at the foot of the eternal throne.

And it is true that in our human language, in which we must refer separately to the two aspects of the mystery, we are forced either to speak first of the glory, like S. Paul, before referring to the Cross, or to speak first of the Cross, like S. John, before referring to its glorious issue. God alone sees the whole drama in its perfect unity.

But it is the whole mystery that the Mass gives us in this perfect unity—oblation and immolation, the mystery both of death and glory. *Unde et memores, Domine, nos servi tui, sed et plebs tua sancta, ejusdem Christi filii tui Domini nostri tam beatæ passionis, nec non et ab inferis resurrectionis, sed et in cælos gloriosæ ascensionis: offerimus.* . . . These solemn words are uttered by the celebrant in his own name and that of all the faithful immediately after the narrative of the Supper and Transubstantiation: "Therefore remembering the blessed Passion of our Saviour Christ your Son, and at the same time His Resurrection from the dead, and also His glorious Ascension into heaven, we offer to your supreme Majesty . . .": all the mysteries of Christ are reunited into one and all are realized in the same way in our sacrifice.

It seems then that we have no need to accept the limitations and restrictions which de la Taille and M. Lepin, each from his own point of view, feel obliged to introduce into their vision of the Mass-oblation.

The Supper was not only the first act of Calvary: it was also its Sacrament or sign; and the Mass too is this. And this sign is rich enough to give us the whole sacrifice of Christ. Immolation is not opposed to oblation, not even to the great final oblation in heaven, which is the positive and beatific aspect of a single mystery, that is, the Son's movement of adoration towards His Father by the ways of immolation in which our sin delayed Him, and the acceptance of the Son's religion by the Father on Easter Day in their joyful meeting at the hour of consummation.

But this respectful reading of three great contemporary authors must not result in merely negative criticism. We might extract from these imposing theologies, by allowing them to react upon one another, a synthesis in which we

should rediscover that ecclesiastical tradition which has preoccupied us from the start. It is now agreed that we
must not look for a real or virtual physical immolation on the
altar, distinct from that of the Cross, which would produce
(de Lugo) or try to produce (Lessius) any fresh modification
in Christ's body. This common consent on the part of
modern Masters represents considerable gain. It may serve
as a solid foundation for a satisfactory constructive effort.
The difficulties and misunderstandings concern only the
relations of the *immolation* of Calvary with the *sign* which, in
the Mass, bestows on us its blessed fruits.

M. Lepin offers the simplest system. There is no question
of immolating Christ anew; we are to be content to offer
Him, or rather for Him to offer Himself at our hands; and
this oblation, which is all that is required for sacrifice, will
give us all the salutary effects of His immolation.

De la Taille demands far more. He sees an intrinsic connection between oblation and immolation, in which the first
involves or presupposes the second, and he claims such a
unity throughout the entire mystery that our Eucharistic
sign of the oblation instituted at the Supper need only gain
possession of the Immolated One, now received in glory,
for our sacrifice to be complete as Christ's was.

Billot breaks up this system. The Supper was not part of
Calvary. It is, if one may say so, an anticipated replica, and it
institutes the new sign of Christ's immolation, *in specie
aliena*. This is what we repeat at the Saviour's bidding.
Christ is immolated at our hands thanks to the species whose
separation is the sign of immolation, necessary to all sacrifice. The function of the sign is simply to represent; here it
fulfils it admirably. Further since Christ was immolated
historically on Calvary and is here present on the altar, the
Eucharist is no empty and sterile sign, but a fruitful and
profitable one. Vasquez sees in the Mass only the representation, under the species, of Christ's immolation, and was
satisfied. Billot sees on the altar the immolation of Christ
Himself thanks to the sign set forth in the species.

De la Taille reproached his illustrious *confrère* with contenting himself with a sign instead of a reality. Perhaps it would be enough to say that Billot's theory leaves a residue of "extrinsicism" between the sign and the reality. The Church performs a gesture of immolation with the species while Christ really offers Himself to His Father. This cleavage between the symbol and its content is lessened in Billot, because when he studies the Eucharist as sacrifice he has already established the Real Presence by Transubstantiation. He has already the body of Christ. He has only to study the sacramental conditions of His presence, which prove to be a sign of immolation.

But de la Taille's objection is of value because it indicates the real issue. These two authors have a fundamental difference in their theories of immolation and the sign. In Billot immolation shows that the sacrifice is made to God; it is, if one may so put it, the label on the parcel.* In de la Taille it bears witness to our fallen state, the signature of Adam's children. Again, in the former, immolation is extrinsic to the real content of sacrifice,† and, being only an indication, it can be found in a mere figure in the species. In the latter it is, since sin, a real part of our religion's soul and body. As a result the two theologies have not the same conception of the sacrificial sign nor of its connexion with sacrifice's inner essence: they take in different ways S. Augustine's *signum visibile invisibilis sacrificii.*

Billot does not incarnate the reality in the sign so formally. Immolation, which he sometimes calls destruction, could not be required for its own sake but only as a symbol of our adoration. This is perhaps exaggerated or rather insufficient.

---

* Specialis ratio submissionis et reverentiæ prout Deum solum et nullum alium respicere potest, optime exprimitur dum fit oblatio per consumptionem exsistentiæ rei oblatæ in honorem ejus cui offertur. Hujusmodi enim ritus per se idoneus est ad significandum affectum hominis sese devoventis Creatori suo tanquam ei cujus obsequio dignum est ut omnis vita creata consumatur. . . . (Billot, *op. cit.*, 6th ed., 1924, pp. 587–588). This is de Lugo's general idea of sacrifice so vigorously attacked by de la Taille at the beginning of his work (ch. 1).

† Destructio in sacrificiis non propter se quæritur, siquidem destructio secundum se nihil profecto habet quod facere possit ad cultum et honorem ejus qui mortem non fecit, rec delectatur in perditione vivorum. (Billot, *ibid.*, p. 634.) Here de la Taille would agree. But he would not leave as it stands: sed quæritur propter sæpe dictam symbolicam significationem; illius, inquam, devotionis qua nosmet ipsos debemus offerre Deo. . . . (Billot, *ibid.*)

The author had done well to recall the Augustino-Thomist definition of sacrifice *in genere signi*. But in ancient rites the sign of immolation has not as its end merely to show interior religion: by the renunciation which it demands, the immolation which it involves and the sacrifices (in the petty modern sense of the word) which it presupposes, it makes some start towards realizing what it represents, that is satisfactory adoration. Thus it incarnates an element of sacrifice, necessary since sin, and is not content with symbolizing it. In the same way at Mass the symbolic gesture of the separation of the sacramental species is not content with showing us the image of Christ's sacrifice (only Vasquez thought that sufficient): but it realizes what it represents, that is the victim of the sacrifice of the Cross and, with the victim, all the fruits of grace and religion deriving from that immolation And, as S. Thomas loved to repeat, "what the Passion of Christ did on earth once for all, this sacrament works to-day in each man in particular" (III[a] p., q. 79, a. 1).

What the sacrificial sign tried in vain to do in men's sacrifices, to incarnate as well as to symbolize their immolation, by making some beginning of it through the privations which it cost them, the Eucharistic sign performs for the profit of the world and its salvation: it symbolizes the immolation of Christ, and then realizes the whole mystery for us through the unique and irreplaceable power deriving from its institution to this end by Christ Himself.

CHAPTER SIX: SYNTHESIS

THUS the problem of the essence of the Holy Sacrifice continues to show real progress. Year by year satisfactory results can be observed and increasing agreement among competent theologians. They have rediscovered in the earliest sources and the old authorities, and also in humanity's primitive religious needs, the fullness of truth to which the text of Trent held fast.

Representatives of the old Schools also are joining in this revival. For three centuries the Benedictines and the Dominicans had almost all stayed under cover, preserving the sacred fire of tradition, while the theologians of the Counter-Reformation, in the forefront of the fight against the heretics, hastily improvised de Lugo's little system or Lessius's, which so regrettably swamped the whole of pious literature. But now that illustrious Jesuits themselves have given the signal for return to the true wisdom, why refuse them the acceptance which such loyalty deserves? A Benedictine, Dom A. Vonier, the (late) Abbot of Buckfast, has published a whole book on the theology of the sign;* and in introducing this work to the French public the reviewer in the *Bulletin Thomiste* noted with applause the agreement between the author's views and those of contemporary theologians on the Continent.†

The most powerful synthesis which has appeared in French is that of P. H ris, O.P., in his work *Le Mystère du Christ‡* in the chapter headed *Our participation in Christ's Sacrifice*, pp. 332-368. And perhaps it would be better simply to follow S. Thomas here as he speaks to us in the words of his modern disciple. But if it is legitimate in a matter of such burning interest to vary the exposition of his teaching, making it more intelligible perhaps for certain minds, then this is the sort of way in which we would suggest a final presentation.

Mathematicians, faced with a difficulty, assume that the problem has been solved, and in the light of the supposed solution, indicated provisionally by some conventional sign, they find eventually the means for lighting on it in reality.

---

* *A Key to the Doctrine of the Eucharist*, London, Burns Oates and Washbourne, first printed 1925, second edition 1931.

† *Bulletin Thomiste*, January, 1928, pp. [233]–[238], under the signature of P. Héris, O.P.; and January, 1929, pp. [451]–[454], under the signature of P. Ch. [enu], O.P. The *Revue des Sciences Philosophiques et Théologiques* of July, 1928, (p. 459, note) refers to P. Barnabé Augier's (forthcoming) *Etude Théologique sur le Sacrifice*, which seems to contain ideas moving in the same direction.

[The author refers also to the Revue Thomiste for 1929 as containing the only information then available for P. Augier's views.—Trans.]

‡ R. P. Héris, O.P., *Le Mystère du Christ*, Publications of *la Revue des Jeunes*, Paris, Desclée, 1927.

To clarify our own complex data let us reverse this process. Let us suppose that the Eucharist does not exist, and guided all the same by our knowledge of Christ's institution let us try to rediscover it, first fixing the religious needs which it is meeting. Thus we can gain a better understanding of our mystery and make a sort of reconstruction of it.

What then was the problem to be solved? Christ was to offer Himself as a victim, once and for all, upon the Cross, as an event of history; the world would then be saved. The very perfection of this sacrifice seemed to make any repetition of it useless and impossible. Men still to be, who would not have witnessed this great happening, could at most participate from afar in this single sacrifice, and could not replace it by any other.

How were they to participate in this sacrifice? The classical, traditional, method would have been communion, physical or moral, with the victim. Now that the victim has been gloriously taken up to heaven, one might suppose a moral communion, as of the Jews with their burnt up holocausts.

But communion with the victim need not mean offering sacrifice, for communion is possible with another's sacrifice, with a victim already offered and immolated by some third party, relative or friend or ally. So the Church might have communicated in Christ's sacrifice, but she would not have offered a victim that was really hers. This would have been, at least psychologically, a serious gap, a great omission, in this vast Church scattered through time and space. Human nature seems to demand more, and the rights of God seem to claim from us more efforts, greater adoration.

Again, if the Church is one day to offer a sacrifice herself, this cannot be other than that of Christ and the Cross, since we already know that only this is acceptable to the Father for all time.

In short the Church must offer in all ages and in every place a sacrifice which is at the same time hers and Christ's, enabling the faithful to participate by communicating with the victim in all the fruits, otherwise unobtainable, which were won on Calvary.

There is a means of satisfying these combined requirements, perhaps a unique solution given the conditions of our
human nature, so vitally engaged in this great business. This
means is the *sign* which makes it possible to place a higher
value within a lower one, making them absolutely coincide.
Cannot the Church use for her needs a sign, in the word's
great religious sense, which should contain the sacrifice of
Calvary? Can she not have a sacrificial action which is in the
first place hers, yet is or becomes at the same time Christ's
sacrifice?

Let us remember too that sacrifice is both a thing and an
action, an object acted upon and at the same time an action
bearing on the object, that is, a transfer of property and also a
property transferred. The Church then must make expression of her inward religion—*invisibilis sacrificii visibile sacramentum*—by means of an object belonging to her, and this
must become the sacrifice of Christ, with the original sign as
a permanent connecting link, for us to have the sacrifice of
Christ beneath the sign of the Church's sacrifice. But the
sacrifice of Christ is itself a thing and an action. It is Christ's
body immolated, offered and glorified. Only here the actions
took place once for all on Good Friday and at Easter and the
Ascension, though they still stamp the object—which is the
immolated and glorified body of Our Lord.

If the Church's victim, acted upon by her, becomes
the very victim of Calvary, in whom we can participate
under the species of the Church's victim, we shall have
beneath a sacramental sign the very reality of Christ's
sacrifice.

We have this sign, this sacrament: "If anyone dare to
deny", says the sacred Council of Trent, "the wonderful and
unique changing of the whole substance of bread into the
body, and of the whole substance of wine into the blood of
Our Lord Jesus Christ, the species of bread and wine remaining and these only—a change which the Catholic
Church calls most properly transubstantiation, let him be
anathema."

So the fine text of Canisius, which de la Taille put so

felicitously to head his work: *Missæ sacrificium est dominicæ passionis repræsentatio et simul oblatio* does not seem strong enough. The Mass is not only the offering of Calvary's immolation: it is the sign, in the Augustinian sense.

On the evening of Maundy Thursday Christ put all His sacrifice of the morrow, which for brevity we call His immolation but which is more than that, beneath a sign. His religion and our redemption, incarnate in His body, had already all the reality of sacrifice, that is oblation, immolation and acceptance by the Father; but they had no liturgical sign. Jesus gives them one. Thus there is reciprocal causality: without the Eucharist the Redemption of the following day would have had no sign; and, conversely, without that day's events the Eucharist would have been empty of sacrificial reality.

The only way of putting a liturgical reality and a liturgical action one inside the other, making a single sacrifice of the two combined, is to place the victim with all the effects of the sacrifice beneath a sign. This is what Christ willed and instituted that Thursday evening.

Thus the one sacrifice which took place on the Cross and in heaven could become the Church's daily sacrifice, because with her victim changed in the course of the liturgy to the Body and Blood of the victim of Golgotha her sacrifice could draw upon the whole reality of the Cross's sacrifice and all its fruits of grace and of religion. We could have the sacrifice of the Cross, that is the victim, beneath a ritual sign, and so the effects also of His sacrifice. The sign will be ours, in the sense that it is we who provide its materials, perform the actions and pronounce the words: but the reality will be the body of Christ Himself, and the results obtained those of the sacrifice of the Cross itself.

The mediæval mind had grasped this when it analysed the fullness of the Eucharist into the three elements called in the language of the schools *sacramentum et non res*, that is the species of bread and wine, the sacrament properly so called, together with Christ's words and action; *sacramentum et res*, that is, the reality of Christ's body and blood; *res et non* *sacramentum*, that is, the effects of grace from the great mystery in our souls and in the Church.*

S. Thomas Aquinas must have had in mind this powerful teaching when he composed in liturgical style the Collect for the Mass of Corpus Christi where it is gathered up completely:

Deus qui nobis sub sacramento mirabili, passionis tuæ memoriam reliquisti, tribue, quæsumus, ita nos Corporis et Sanguinis tui sacra mysteria venerari, ut redemptionis tuæ fructum in nobis jugiter sentiamus.

Sacramentum et non res.

Sacramentum et res.

Res et non sacramentum.

We are simply summing this up rather shortly but in a way which, properly explained, represents the whole of the Church's tradition when we say: the Mass is a sacrifice because it is the efficacious sign of the Cross's sacrifice. Since the latter is to-day invisible, we may even use the old formula of S. Augustine: *Missa est sacrificii jam invisibilis visibile sacramentum, id est sacrum signum.*

In ancient sacrifices, pagan and even Jewish, the rite itself almost always pushes into the background the religious feeling which the action was intended to translate; that is why these liturgies are first and foremost ancestral theatre pieces, conventions and traditions which were inclined to lose their wider meaning in mere formalism. They are a ritual expression of a metaphysic too often unconscious of itself. And the great work of the prophets in Israel consisted above all in restoring the balance in favour of spiritual riches: *Do I need, says Jahve, the blood of goats and heifers?*

On the other hand the sacrifice of Christ on Calvary is not a liturgy. There was no priest on Golgotha on the 14th Nisan other than the victim. The executioner wore no ceremonial

---

* Cf. e.g., Innocent III, in Denzinger—B., p. 415 : letter to John, Archbp. of Lyons, 29 Nov., 1202:

Forma visibilis—panis et vini—sacramentum et non res. Veritas corporis—carnis et sanguinis—sacramentum et res. Virtus spiritualis—unitatis et caritatis—res et non sacramentum.

costume, went through no preordained performances of ritual; there was no choirboy carrying a torch. No Isaac was there to offer the wood of the holocaust or the sacred sword of immolation. Instead a great historical event took place, at the confluence of two great realities, man's sin and the Son's divinity.

It is only in dependence on this historic fact that the sacrifice of Christ, thanks to the Eucharist, took a ritual form in which we every day renew it. But this priority of historical fact over our liturgy will always prevent Catholicism from falling into religious formalism. These species of bread and wine will never be dead images or empty gestures covering religious sloth. Thanks to the truth of Jesus of Nazareth's death and resurrection, a vast displacement of forces occurred enhancing inward values. And yet outward or sacramental religion still exists, though only as secondary and wholly relative to these inward values. And if the Mass has replaced the sacred butchery of the past, it is because the death and resurrection of Christ had first replaced all the ancient sacrifices.

*   *   *

We must find this synthesis in the blessed soul of the Saviour at the time of His institution, when He took bread and wine and pronounced upon them the decisive syllables. As He spoke, Christ was constituting Himself already the victim of the morrow's sacrifice; and, in this sense, in so far as they are an irrevocable statement and a final offering, these words of the first consecration are part of the Redemption, and de la Taille is right. The first Eucharist was in truth an irrevocable offering of Calvary, a pledge, an engagement, and here all the "oblationists" are right.

But in giving the Apostles the power and the precept to renew this action, Our Lord gave to His Church at the same time the right and the duty of making Him the victim every morning on her altars; the Church was to go as far as the Saviour Himself along this road. He, as He spoke, inaugurated Calvary and made it necessary; the Church, repeating

P

His words, perpetuates and renews Calvary—even as He does. The Church does not put Christ to death any more than He was His own executioner. But as Jesus was immolated in His offering of Himself at the Supper, so the Church immolates Christ by offering Him upon the altar: the real presence of His body, and Calvary prolonged in heaven under the form of an apotheosis, prove to us that these liturgical actions are not empty and that these words are true.

These actions are not materially the same as those which constituted Calvary's historical drama, ending in heaven and in glory. They represent it in ritual image; they are its signs. And, because they are signs instituted by the Saviour, they share the religious value of the one Redemption.

This liturgy of bread and wine was already a symbol of sacrifice before it became the sign of Calvary, because it was a gesture of offering, renunciation and consecration. Calvary, now represented by the separation of the species, thus wears the form of another sacrifice, that of the Church.

But that sacrifice would be vain unless it changed to that of Christ. Transubstantiation is the achievement of that mystery. The Eucharist must be not only Christ's sacrifice, but the Church's. It does not start in heaven like other sacraments, channels of grace; it rises from earth, because it is first of all an act of worship and adoration. It begins in our sphere, in our barns and our cellars. But, if it remained as such, it would not attain its end. If it is changed to the sacrifice of Christ, then it will succeed.

But any sacrifice, including Christ's, is a thing as much as, more than, an action. The sacrifice of Christ is Christ Himself. The real presence of the body and the blood resolves the problem.

That, finally, is why to offer Christ is to have Him present upon our altars, under the signs of His past immolation, after the transubstantiation of our oblations into the Saviour's body and blood, which we present to God as the victim of our own sacrifice—in virtue of those words which of old constituted Jesus as the victim because they contained in principle the whole of Calvary. And Calvary is to-day the principle of our Masses, for they owe to it all their value, they draw upon its wealth and they apply its fruits to us.

All these formulas are traditional. If we have succeeded in this work in showing that they are truer and richer in meaning than the faithful generally believe, we shall not think our labour lost.

CHAPTER SEVEN: THE SACRIFICE OF THE CHURCH IN THE MASS

WITH our synthesis behind us and keeping a firm grasp of the whole truth in it, we may now take up the treatment of its parts considered separately without loss or danger and study the Church's sacrifice and Christ's immolation as provisionally distinct from one another. The latter comes first historically; but in the liturgy the Church initiates. We follow the order of the liturgy.

* * *

The Eucharist is not only the sacrifice of Christ. It is also that of the Church. It even appears at the beginning of her ritual prayers, at the offertory, at the opening of the Canon and even again at the *Placeat* at the end of Mass as if it were only the sacrifice of men, for ever imperfect and of uncertain issue. The general theme of the liturgy is an immense effort, an ardent petition that God, accepting our good will, should make our sacrifice His own, that He should purify it, making it worthy of Himself, that He should then accept it and receive ourselves, despite our sins, in the offering that we make. Here as in the past the great aim of sacrifice is to obtain the meeting and alliance of earth and heaven. The acceptance by the Creator of the creature's return to His embrace is the last end of this divine tragedy, of this sacred play. This is to be the eternal seal placed on our attempts at worship, our will to adoration. This is also the supreme achievement which makes subsequent communion possible. For the victim, once received in heaven, sanctified by God's touch and in that sense divinized, may now come down again from heaven to earth to bring to men the blessings and the graces which henceforth saturate it. In our hands it was the victim of our sacrifice; God returns it to us the sacrament of His benediction.

The Church can at least begin this movement, the climax of which is hidden with God, to which He alone can give value by His ratifying. She can invite the Father to come to her by her own gesture of return to Him. If the beloved daughter hold out her hands, her God will open His arms to her:

Accipe, parve puer, risu cognoscere Patrem.

And what then will she offer as the visible sign of her inward religion: *sacrificii invisibilis visibile sacramentum?* Christ when He left her showed her bread and wine, the symbol of our love, our repentance and our adoration, as in the religions of old the finest, richest and purest fruits of the earth represented and conveyed the trembling and prostrate adoration of men before their God. Laden with these gifts the Church, the immortal wayfarer, sets out upon her road. But she knows that she will not reach the goal unaided. To hope for success with such weak elements as these, however pure—*infirma et egena elementa*, would be to move back forty centuries to the valley where Melchisedech, a splendid figure of the things to come, offered bread and wine.

To-day the King of Salem himself appears only as a prophet heralding the future. And, if we consider our poor offerings, what does God care henceforth for the heaped-up loaves of proposition and for the wineskins full of the finest *soreq?*

The only sacrifice which God requires and which He accepts is that of His Son, that of the Body and Blood which were offered on Calvary.

"So, Father", says the Church, hesitant yet bold, "Change

my bread and wine into the Body and Blood of Jesus Christ, and at the same time substitute His love and adoration for my own—or rather raise mine to His, so that You may accept the one in and for the other, and the one holocaust which You can receive may rise to heaven. My belated sacrifice—*vespertinum*—cannot fail to please You, joined with His: is it indeed still mine in these conditions? Is it not rather that of Your Son?

And how should I know that this offering gives You joy? Only if You, my Father, work this conversion, if You yourself, taking possession of my bread and my chalice, change them into the sole oblation which can win Your favour."

There, then, is the supreme acceptance, the final point of my sacrifice. It triumphs by sinking itself utterly, it succeeds by transubstantiation. Or, more exactly, it gains its goal and so takes place at the moment when it is changed to the eternal *theothyte*. In the instant at which the feeble materials in which our inefficacious worship tries to be incarnate are transformed into the accepted victim, the Church's Christianity becomes ritually but in reality what it always is—the religion of Jesus.

So it is that transubstantiation, properly understood, seen in the light of Christ's intentions at His institution of it, *is* the very sacrifice of the Altar. As this alone can give meaning and value to the movement of our religion, so it is too the most dazzling and decisive ratification on the part of God—perhaps the only decisive one—of our desires to adore Him.

For, if He gives us His Son in place of the bread which we offer, is not this proof positive that He accepts our victim? How should He not accept it, since it is now His own beloved Son? And how, if He had rejected our oblation, could He have preserved the species and accepted the substance, even transforming it into the holy Body which died on Golgotha for the world's redemption?

All then is concentrated upon this vital point of transubstantiation: the hopes and strivings of earth, the Church's effort upwards to God, His favourable answer to it, and between the two the eternal Pontiff, the one and only mediator, destroying all distances, healing every breach.

The Church climbs heavenwards with her bread and wine to sketch in two short phrases the realities of Calvary; the Father bends downwards to put in place of these oblations the Body and Blood of Jesus, showing that He holds the Church's sacrifice as His, and as such accepting it. Whence comes this marvel that the two holocausts can form one only in the sight of God for our salvation, and that our sacrament of bread and wine gains through its transformation our reconciliation with the Divine?

The secret of this unity lies in Him who created it upon the tablecloth at the Cenacle the evening before His death. The two great converging movements, that of the Church and that of the Father, meet at the consecration, uniting on the altar in a single mystery.

In the light of this doctrine the liturgy of the Mass seems clear and simple.

Our Mother the Church is at first so anxious that her offering should be soon received. She would not feel these fears if her gaze bore already on Christ's Body and Blood. But for the moment she thinks only of her bread and wine, her own poor wealth, the first-fruits of her harvests, but the symbol above all of her poor love; and behind this bread and wine, the sacraments of our religion, she presents this religion itself, our griefs, our expiations, in fine all that we do and feel. Will they be accepted? Are they acceptable? In view of what we are, are they really pure?

Then these anxieties give place to a prayer whose answer will banish fear. And how bold a prayer, how fantastic! It is that this bread and wine should be changed into Christ's body and blood. This will be the undreamt of, certain, proof that our offering is favourably received. What more firmly guaranteed acceptance is imaginable than this conversion? It is easy now to understand how the picture of the fire coming down from heaven to consume the victim of the holocaust rose in the memories of the Masters of the French School, filled as they were with scriptural images. This Old

Testament prodigy would so well picture that substantial taking over of the victim which we present to God. If God gives us His Son in the place of our oblations, if He burns them in the transubstantiating flames, the eternal signature will have been set on our religion. God cannot refuse His Son; He will not refuse our sacrifice.

But, Lord, who would dare to utter this prayer, if the example, or rather the institution of Your Son and His express command, did not support our filial boldness? Thus we shall commemorate Him and the events of that last evening of His life; and, repeating the words at His own bidding, we shall realize the mystery, the mystery of Your well-beloved Son, or rather You, Lord, will realize it beneath our sign, as You hear His voice.

So then we commemorate both the Supper and the Cross: *pridie quam pateretur* on the one side, *unde et memores* on the other, but in different ways. We commemorate the Supper because we use Christ's authorization, the precept, example and power of our Head, to formulate our request, to believe in its realization, to complete by the triumph of transubstantiation, by a solution beyond all our hopes, our sacrifice of bread and wine, which without that conclusion would have ended, like the Jewish sacrifices, in the realm of figures, empty in themselves, of a reality still hidden in the future. We commemorate the Passion and Death of our Saviour Jesus Christ, His Resurrection from the dead and His Ascension, in the sense that by repeating the symbolic gesture of the Thursday evening we purpose to enclose within it, under sensible and sacramental species, all the reality of Christ's single sacrifice, all the great cycle of return from earth to heaven unfolded between Good Friday and Easter Sunday, the Christian mystery itself, Christ's mystery.

And while the sacrifice of Jesus takes the place of ours by transubstantiation of the offered elements, our sacrifice, thanks to the preservation of the species, is the efficacious sign, the realizing symbol, for this single sacrifice.

The Mass is the blending of two sacrifices into one by a

reciprocal causality. We shall never grasp its meaning unless we see in a single glance these two great movements meeting one another, or rather, since our human reason does not let us move at once in both directions, unless when speaking of either we do not think also of the other. Such is unity of this religion.

There are therefore in the Mass, if one may dare to put it so, two sacrifices, one of which acts as a sacramental palimpsest beneath the other, while the second, ultimately the one true sacrifice, gives its real value to the liturgy expressing it. To offer sacrifice is to consecrate and vow to God gifts which He accepts from us in order to return them if He will, sanctified and blessed. The Church, instructed by Christ, performs this traditional sacrificial gesture so far as lies within her power; but, further, by His means she wins' magnificent success. For her bread and wine, vowed and offered, are so far accepted, so far sanctified, that God changes them into the Body and Blood of the one and only sacrifice, the victim of Calvary. At this divine moment when the Church sees her work successfully accomplished, the Saviour's sacrifice is substituted for her own, and is made one with it.

This is the end of the movement which gives its value to the beginning of it. Without transubstantiation it is all too clear that under the New Law our offering of bread and wine would have no longer any worth or meaning.

It is a delight to realize that the prayers of the Mass, from the Offertory to the *Pater*, can be taken in both senses, that we may take them for our religious life as bearing either upon the sacrifice which the Church is offering or upon Christ's sacrifice on Calvary; and in each case our thought is based on a firm textual foundation. In these ancient and venerable prayers, previous to scholastic codification and to the controversies with the Protestants, there is a literary felicity recalling in its double strand of meaning S. John's finest pages, in which the humanity and the divinity of Christ are found within a single verse. Here in one prayer our offering and Christ's join in a single whole; and yet these passages would not be what they are, some of their formulas would be even meaningless and unacceptable, if we did not remember at the same time both the Church offering her bread and wine as the offering of herself and also the Passion of Christ, which has put an end to all other sacrifice. Yet to speak of the two as in any way separate is to be unfaithful to the dogma which we are trying to uphold; the truth is that the sacrifice of Christ has become our own. As Christ's, it is *pure, holy, immaculate, without blemish;* He fills all those who receive Him *with heavenly benediction and every grace;* it is too a work accomplished long ago, which *in the unity of the Holy Spirit gives glory to the Father by the Son eternally.* As ours, it needs *to be received, ratified, made reasonable and acceptable;* it is comparable and perhaps inferior to the holocausts of *Abel the Just,* of the *patriarch Abraham* and of the *priest Melchisedech.* It is a work to be brought to a successful issue, for which we must always beg and pray; otherwise, if not on the altar, where transubstantiation will necessarily take place, at least in our souls which are perhaps rebellious and impure, this sacrifice would always be a hazardous affair and insufficient.

To the careful reader of our offertories and anaphoras the problem of the Epiclesis of the Holy Spirit, instead of throwing an unexpected obscurity over the end of the Canon, will become almost a further light in this progressive movement of analysis. The famous invocation concerns ourselves and our needs rather than the Body and Blood of Christ; it is we who need transubstantiation and must profit by it with the all-powerful help of the sanctifying Spirit. That is why to the end, even in our Post-Communions, we pray to God that the sacrifice of Christ may be truly ours, that the bread and wine may be *for us* the Body and Blood of the Saviour.

It is this transition from one sacrifice to another, or more precisely this magnificent transposition as the rite proceeds of a poor, simple gesture, that gives the Christian Mass an appeal to the eye shared by nothing else.

We are not speaking only of the detailed splendour of it;

it is certain that the Mass, considered as a work of ritual art, is a pure masterpiece of tranquil beauty. Colour, sound, movement, all the æsthetic resources of the human body in its symbolic actions, are united and bound together in a context of splendid, stylized archaism around this altar barely lit with a few candles to produce one of the wonders of religious history.

But behind all this beauty, there is a hidden drama, whose spring and movement we must penetrate—but not the eternal and invisible drama, the Passion of Christ which is here renewed or His heavenly sacrifice which is here communicated. Although this tragedy of the world's Redemption is given to us in the Mass in sacramental symbols, it is itself beyond all visual analysis.

What we are speaking of is the movement of the liturgy itself, of the divine plot which is developed and resolved throughout this spectacle, the ceremony's hidden soul, the secret of all this anxiety, the inner explanation of it. This mystery of the bread which is changed to the Body of Christ is the occasion in the secret of the soul, externally translated by the outward gestures, of a series of acts, prayers, strivings, joys and triumphs which the rubrics, texts and symbols will relate and picture for us with religious accuracy.

The priest, at the foot of the altar steps, first prepares himself in confession and humility for the great work which he initiates; then he goes up to the altar to prepare the faithful in their turn by prayers and chants and reading from the Scriptures. He lingers in these introductions as if he still shrank before his own audacity; then he begins to busy himself with the oblations and to make the signs of offertory, pregnant with holy ambitions and strengthened with the courage born of confidence. He meets his God face to face for the first time and tentatively. Then he sanctifies the altar with pure incense and renews his summons for the faithful's prayers.

At last he brings himself to action. He takes responsibility, alone this time, for this ceremony which has seemed to move a little slowly, its conduct shared so far with the deacon and sub-deacon. It gives us the impression of a great avenue on a gentle slope, opening clearly and directly upon some near-by mystery.

The long-drawn ceremony has enhanced the splendour of our approach to God, and by building this great stairway before the temple has added to the dignity of the work in hand and to the view behind. The priest may now raise his voice and intone the preface, calling upon God the Father in a chant of supreme assurance and magnificent respect, giving thanks in order to obtain from Him, praising and glorifying Him in order to receive from Him, calling the Well-Beloved to witness and claiming His authority. Such is the Church's attitude, most truly religious and most truly human. This is that central strand of the Eucharist from which it won its name. But if it is a prayer, it is also a task. It is a work to be successfully accomplished. The offertory had left us in full activity—a sacrifice of bread and wine began, but this, as such, could not succeed. The second act, the Preface, takes up the project where we left it and turns it in a direction previously foreshadowed but so far only barely indicated. It drives it towards a splendid transformation of the problem, resolving and suppressing it, yet keeping to its inner logic. The bread and wine will not be what they were before, but our sacrifice will still exist under the same symbols of our desires to worship. This then is the centre. The liturgy gives the impression of it. The chanting ceases, the ministers fall to their knees or bow, the people stay reverently silent. The priest himself speaks low but clearly. And in this silence, barely emphasized by the tinkling bell, the mystery which we waited for takes place, bathing us in the atmospheres of Sinai and of the Cenacle: *hoc est corpus meum.* We are in heaven, at the foot of the throne, and on earth also, at the foot of the Cross.

When we have passed this climax, the movement of the liturgy is like coming down from a mountain in the calm and joy which follow favours won and undertakings brought to a successful issue, for the conversion of our offerings is both the symbol and the principle of our own sanctifying, the result of the divine touch and of the encounter with the transubstantiating flame. The most ancient forms of the rite prolonged the sense of expectation further still and left the prayers suspended, as it were, until the end of the Canon, when the little Elevation, which precedes the *Pater*, like a mere raising of the ground at the end of a long avenue or the apsidal chapel of a Cathedral, marked the triumphant conclusion of the epiclesis. The Middle Ages preferred to build in the very centre of the mystery, marking it more clearly, the twin spires of the double Elevation, and the Latin liturgy has brought back to a position before the consecration several prayers which in earlier days kept the attention on the central act of sacrifice after this had happened. The perspective has been slightly modified, as when Michael Angelo's cupola, Maderna's front and Bernini's colonnade replaced the old Constantinian basilica of the Vatican, whose destruction archæologists constantly deplore. But we cannot prevent the Church or art or the liturgy from living and moving; and if the Confession of S. Peter still remains in place, traditions are safeguarded and ancient forms respected.

Besides, the modifications in the Mass have been far less important; the general line has been preserved, keeping for us the original theme of the Eucharist and giving us successively the anaphora, the *Sanctus*, the Canon, the anamnesis, the epiclesis, the whole Action whose very name points to a heavenly work which we must carry out.

For the work has not been finished yet. For the third time the drama starts afresh; the divine plot is not yet resolved. This holy victim, which is henceforth ours, and which God has accepted anew by giving it to us, is for us to profit by, through grace, for the spiritual nourishment of our souls. Sacrifice usually ends with a sacred banquet, and we must now achieve communion. The liturgy, which had slackened its pace a little, quickens into preparation with prayer and action for some new thing. The deacon and sub-deacon begin once more to assist the priest at the altar for the ministration of the family meal. And there is a reverent stir among the people in its turn. They have replied to the *Pater* as to the chant of a brotherhood, of a country's citizens. They make an act of humility, they exchange the kiss of peace, and they are absolved. The priest breaks the oblations which are now the victims. And the people in its turn follows Moses to Sinai, where Wisdom setting her table invites her friends to eat and drink, for all is ready for her Kingdom's feast.

When all the faithful, after beating their breasts like the Centurion of old, have been filled with the new manna, the liturgy grows calm, coming to rest in the great concluding prayers. And this tremendous movement, which has stirred heaven and earth, set forth the Church's bold but humble claims and brought down heaven's answer, ends with a grand gesture of farewell and benediction: *Ite, Missa est.*

It is indeed finished and with magnificent completion, like the finest of ancient tragedies when art, music, liturgy, religion and the theatre itself, joined together to hold captive all man's nature, were also joined to divinize him. The most primitive and most persistent powers of our soul's depths are energized by Christianity.

*   *   *

The ideas maintained or rather rediscovered in this chapter force us to an inevitable conclusion: that the Mass is a liturgical sacrifice offered by the Church, which is yet at the same time the sacrifice offered on the Cross and consummated in heaven by our Lord—and this because the Church's oblations, the bread and the wine, whose species act as sacrament or sign for the immolation of Calvary, are changed into the Body and Blood of the victim of Christ's sacrifice, that is Christ Himself, so that the Church has as victim on her altars every day the very victim of the one eternal sacrifice.

The full understanding of this far-reaching proposition presupposes, it is true, the acceptance of certain truths rather lost sight of by modern minds but familiar to our forefathers: first, a definite idea of sacrifice in general as having for its end the transference to the Divinity of earthly wealth, renounced by man to make it holy and to use it for religious purposes; next, a faithful application of this definition to Christ's death and resurrection, thought of as the perfect sacrifice in the sense explained by S. Paul and S. John; lastly, after a legitimate transposition of the properties of the victim to the sacrifice itself, the acceptance of the following simple idea: that the definitive sacrifice, that of Christ, having reached successful issue, and, as such, having never ceased, the Church's whole act, when she too would please God and be united with Him, consists in taking possession of this unique exemplar, making it her own, to realize all its effects and to taste all its fruits. That is what she accomplishes, following the example and the precept of her Master and under the all-powerful action of the Head who animates her, when she immolates bread and wine so as to change them to the very victim of Christ's sacrifice. If once that position be accepted, all the other problems invented by three centuries of misplaced theological ingenuity are, as de la Taille puts it, *non-existent*.

But do not we return, in so saying, to the view which lingers in the manuals under the name of Suarez, mentioned by writers only to be immediately rejected, that the consecration of the Mass is a sacrifice because it immolates and annihilates the bread and the wine, putting in their place the Body and Blood of Jesus Christ?

If Suarez really held this petty view, it must have been because this great man fell into an error which always lies in wait for the best theologians, that of repeating ancient themes and, in a moment of distraction, changing the direction of traditional thinking by a misplaced emphasis. If in my mind I put the weight on the final part of the expression in the formula before us, I turn all Christ's institution upside down. The Church's sacrifice becomes a sacrifice of bread and wine miraculously transformed in the course of the ceremony into the sacrifice of the Body and Blood. And however accurate may be this last proposition, it is not this that dominates the mystery: it shows only its secondary or initial aspect.*

We must say on the contrary: the sacrifice of the Church is the sacrifice of Christ, thanks to the symbolic species of bread and wine already offered. By thus reversing the formula we set in order the entire doctrine. And we make contact again with the idea rediscovered for us by Billot thirty years ago, which has probably made possible all our present theological advances: the Mass is the very sacrifice of the Cross under sensible signs, which are convenient because representative. Then we return to the great stream of our tradition: *a reality beneath a sign*. This, I think, is what Dom Vonier calls the *key* which admits us to the mystery of the Eucharist.†

The Church has always attached the greatest importance to signs and the theology of signs; she has built her whole sacramental doctrine and so her whole treatment of Eucharistic dogma on this notion. The sensible signs instituted by the Saviour are not merely splendid but empty symbols to the eye of faith; on the contrary they contain what they

---

* "It is we who take the inititative, at least on the surface. . . . Perhaps it is this action of our own, this initiative, which we are underlining in the various offertory ceremonies of the Roman rite where our attention is fixed on an oblation which is strictly ours. There we show our awareness, it seems, that it is we who make the start and make the offering. We set in motion a whole action which is crowned by the words of consecration, in so far as they belong to us. . . . Let us follow this marvellous movement in harmony with our point of view, in so far, that is, as it is *our doing*. It is the ascent of ourselves, of the Church, in the body and blood of Christ along with the oblations, since we have been identified with these in the offertory; an ascent which is a communion *in voto*, since we have willed it and even begun it. . . . So by one and the same movement we produce the body of Christ [a Suarezian formula] and we throw ourselves upon Him. We produce Him by the act of throwing ourselves upon Him."—In fine, the Suarezian formulas express the mystery of the Mass well enough in so far as it is the mystery of the Church. And we must never forget this side of it. The Eucharist, looked at from the side of Christ whom it contains, is a thing, *res*, the Body and Blood of Christ, immolated and glorified. But the Eucharist-sacrifice, seen from the Church's side, is an action and finally a transubstantiation. This must be true unless Mass lasts throughout the time that the sacred species remain in the tabernacle—which is certainly not so.

† In Suarez's rather pale and monotonous firmament, with its wide smooth stretches, an occasional comet flashes by, riveting attention. One seems to fit our subject here: "Fatemur non solum Christum esse rem oblatam, sed aliqua etiam modo panem et vinum. Neque inde fit esse duo sacrificia, quia illæ duæ res concurrunt, ut termini a quo et ad quem ejusdem sacrificationis, quia panis convertitur in corpus Christi, per cujus præsentiam species sanctificantur" *Tract. de Missæ Sacrificio*, disp. 75, sect. I, n. 12.

represent. But they first represent their content and do it well.

So the Mass, which gives us the victim of Calvary and the Cross's sacrifice, begins by a superlative picturing of them both. The sign was chosen by the Saviour with the greatest care; the distinction of the two species, solid and liquid, gives us a delicate and expressive image of the dreadful separation of the Blood from the Body, when Jesus commended His soul on Golgotha to His Father's hands.* Lessius and all his school had seen this clearly; their only mistake was to try to find in this sign, and thanks to this sign, a new immolation distinct from that of Calvary and almost independent of it; whereas the property of a sacramental sign is to give us the reality which it represents and not another. What is given us anew on the altar is the one and only immolation of Calvary itself.

Moreover the Eucharistic sign is not lifeless. It is a gesture full of movement, representing not only its end, Christ's sacrifice, but its beginning, the Church's sacrifice. That is the fragment of truth perceived by Suarez and treated by him improperly as a full definition. As a partial explanation the idea must be retained. For the Church does make a sacrifice of bread and wine to offer the sacrifice of Christ. This is only a gesture. But it is a sign and, coming as it does from the Church, it too contains what it signifies, a will to adore and worship, a desire of immolation and oblation, a hope and possibility of communion. And, because it is a ritual sign and a rite is by definition always repeatable, it contains the principle of indefinite renewal, and of liturgical, but not essential, multiplying. It will now be possible to put Christ's sacrifice into currency; not that this great act, this great object, could be distributed in fragments or reproduced like a book in a numbered edition, but its fruits can be applied and so obtained times without number. It is multiplied in our

---

* In the Gospel Our Lord says more exactly: "Behold my body delivered and my blood shed". His thought bears on the two together rather than on their separation. But, because His institution separated them, theological thought has legitimately adopted the second attitude, and separation is only another word for bloodshed.

souls, because it is given to fructify within us, and because its fruits are infinite, or, better, indefinite, inexhaustible.

Since this is a sacrament, there will be always the condition that we make the *sign*, and so that we bring bread and wine to offer them and even immolate them, renouncing the use of them for non-religious purposes. S. Irenæus had realized this aspect of the mystery very clearly; he saw the bread coming from our barns, the wine from our cellars and, as he put it, from the visible creation of this world.* Perhaps our concentration on the end makes us too neglectful of the beginning, so that we forget that the bread and wine are the symbol of our renunciation of ourselves, of our riches, and, behind them, of our covetousness. We should blend our sacrifice with Christ's. This adaptation of our hesitant effort to the great victory already won by Christ, which we shall profit by if God will, is very clearly indicated in the central prayers of the Mass, where the two sacrifices, our ritual sacrifice, the sign of our invisible one, and the sacrifice of Christ, represented by the species of our own, make one only in God's sight. And we shall have to show in conclusion not only how our gesture is identified with the great Act of Christ's religion, but also, conversely, how Christ's religion consents to clothe the species of our own to make it His.

This must be so. It is the very purpose of Christ's institution. What did He wish to do on Maundy Thursday save to put His single sacrifice of the morrow constantly at our disposal that we might use it daily and daily find its whole effect? That is how S. Thomas Aquinas puts it. That is how the Council of Trent puts it. Again, it seems so simple that one wonders why people should add difficulties to this mystery, which is admirable enough in itself without being weighted with useless and imaginary excretions.

It is true that this sacrifice, to be really ours and not only Christ's, must begin with us, with our material resources, with the abandonment of our visible wealth, the symbol of our

---

* *Adv. Haer.*, IV, 17, 5 ; 18, 4–5 ; V, 2, 2–3.
  V. Mgr Ruch in Vacant-Amann. vol. IV, *Messe*, col. 910 sq. For a rapid glance at the full context, v. Dufourcq, *Saint Irenée*, coll. Pensée Chrétienne, Bloud, 1905, pp. 204–210.

Q

spiritual self-renunciation. For offering, or rather performing, sacrifice, means the loss of one of our possessions, our bread or our wine for example, so as to find in its place the very goods of God. It is the transformation of our property into divine property. But if this divine wealth exists already, if it is unique, irreplaceable, already offered, accepted and consecrated, made already and forever the living and eternal victim and sacrifice, then our sole aim will be to put this sacrifice, this victim (for it is all one), in the place of ours. And by this magnificent exchange we shall have succeeded absolutely.

Our success is all the greater because we can always repeat this splendid operation. On our side it is a rite, and a rite can be renewed at will. Bread and wine will be always at our disposal. With God's grace we shall arouse in our hearts our inward religion, incarnate in the fruits of the earth. *And we shall go up every morning to the altar of God in all the joy of our youth.* The rest depends only on God. If He accepts our victim, if He gives in its place Christ, the ever consecrated victim, if Christ remains with us as the thing made sacred, the sacrifice of God, and becomes our sacrifice, then—*O res mirabilis!*—we shall have for our sacrifice the Christ who has been offered, immolated and accepted and, as such, for ever consecrated.

In fine, our sacrifice of bread and wine, when we ask that it should become Christ's sacrifice, that is Christ's offered and immolated Body, succeeds beyond all its hopes. It triumphs by its very acceptance of failure, by its acknowledgment that already *all is consummated* and that it comes upon the scene too late. It is not that it is humble in victory; on the contrary it glories in its defeat. Incapable as it is of achieving its end by itself alone, it renounces such a programme and changes itself into another sacrifice, the only one which can henceforth exist. All these are statements which are precisely true, above all if our minds consent to see in the syllables of the word sacrifice not so much a rite or an action as a thing and an object. Thus the value of the Mass is properly assessed, if we see it as a sacrifice only by reason of another sacrifice, that of the Cross. Thus the theses of the Real Presence and of Transubstantiation, as Billot said, and that of the Mass also, as de la Taille would add, are shown to be nothing but a single dogma thrice defined. O cursed heresies which have forced us to break up revelation into numbered propositions, different in appearance, but in reality the same!

So, then, we have for our use, at our disposal, as the object of our sacrifice, Christ as victim and therefore Christ as immolated. All theologians who have followed recent controversies will be able to accept this formula as a common basis.

Perhaps too the great leaders, Billot, de la Taille, Lepin, would accept it, each with a different though complementary emphasis. Does not it then appear after this analysis as the traditional formula? The next chapter must take that for its subject.

CHAPTER EIGHT: CHRIST'S IMMOLATION IN THE MASS

WE are now face to face with the supreme and most difficult and most controverted question, and one which our long analysis has now made the most inevitable: is Christ immolated in the Mass?

All the ancient texts, faithfully interpreted, answer in the affirmative up to the sixteenth century. The mediæval tradition, based on S. Augustine, loves to speak of a daily immolation. S. Thomas included this formula in the *Summa Theologica*, III^a p., q. 83, a. 1: *quotidie immolatur Christus in sacramento*. The Council of Trent naturally accepted this: "After celebrating the ancient Pasch, which the multitude of the sons of Israel *immolated* in memory of their coming out from Egypt, Jesus Christ made Himself our new Pasch *to be immolated* under sensible signs by the Church through the ministry of priests, in memory of His departure from this world to His Father, when He redeemed us by the shedding of His Blood and snatched us from the power of darkness to lead us to His Kingdom". (Trid., sess. XXII, cap. 1.)

No Catholic author dreams of ridding himself of such decided testimony; no one wishes to change Christian language, in which Christ's immolation on the altar is a current phrase. We say unhesitatingly that Christ is immolated in the Mass. The traditional formula seems to be in the following even stronger terms: *Christ is immolated by the Church;* or, *the Church immolates Christ.**

But from the sixteenth century at least, from the time of the Protestant objections, a certain number of theologians, listed in Lepin's great collection, put firmly aside any thought of a real immolation in the sense of a physical change in the victim. Such an alteration or modification of Christ's glorified body seems to them inconceivable. There can be question only of a mystical immolation, and of this various explanations have been offered.

It is well known that, as against this interpretation, another school energetically maintains the physical and corporeal reality of the Eucharistic immolation, and even insists upon it as distinct from that of the Cross, special therefore to the sacrifice of the altar.

These differences of opinion in the heart of an authentic and traditional doctrine are tolerated by the Church, but they cause disquiet, not as regards the faith itself, but as regards the piety of the faithful, who are lost among so many different, if not contradictory, accounts.

But here again perhaps a determined effort to return to the highway, to the tradition of Christian thought, would bring back light and peace.

---

* The word *immolamus*, clearly applied to our Saviour on the altar, appears in the Secret prayer of the new Mass of Christ the King (end of October): "Ut quem sacrificiis praesentibus immolamus, *Ipse . . . Jesus Christus . . .*". And with this may be compared the older Secret for October 25th: "hostia, quae in natalitiis sanctorum Martyrum tuorum solemniter immolatur. *Per Dominum . . .*". The literary connexion between Christ and the idea of immolation is not the same in each case; the modern formula is far clearer—a good example of increasing precision.

It is time to recall the body of teaching amassed throughout this work, following up our advantage to the full, using the positions which we have regained. Our previous loyalty to the tradition will enable us to accept its findings without attenuation.

The Mass is an unbloody sacrifice, not because it is a mere oblation of a victim previously offered, not because it is sufficient for Christ in heaven to offer Himself without further bloodshedding, but because it is the Sacrament or the Sign, and so the unbloody rite which represents the bloody sacrifice and enables us to share in it.

*   *   *

In the first place, we know what immolation of a victim means in general. It is the renunciation of it so as to give it to God and, thanks to God, eventually to regain it. It is to perform an act which, by depriving us of its use for non-religious purposes, changes it in our regard into God's property. And because a living creature, above all since sin and under the sway of sin, can go to God only by dying, immolating an animal (in particular, a rational animal) means putting him to death. Yet the putting to death is not the formal element, that which really defines the action. And so the ancients would have spoken quite naturally of immolating wine when they poured it forth in their libations. They deprived themselves of it; they would not drink it; the precious liquid is absorbed by the earth and so returns to God's possession—it is immolated.

In this purely religious perspective the patriarch is the first to immolate himself when he kills the victim detached from his flock as an offering to the Eternal One. As he is also precisely represented by the lamb, which is the sign of his religion, there is no distinction made either in thought or in current speech between the immolation of the man and that of the animal: the one is in the other, as the reality signified in the symbol which at once pictures and contains it. The hidden reality, the adoration or repentance in this case of a faithful Israelite, is a spiritual value incarnate in the action and, according to the general theory of the sign, making only one with it.

For we must come back always to the theory of the sign. This putting to death of the victim, not being wanted for its own sake, but for the attitudes of mind which it translates and causes, is simply the efficacious expression of a religion of penitence and adoration. In virtue of the reciprocal causality between the visible symbol and its inner meaning, the immolation of the animal is both the cause and the effect of the patriarch's spiritual immolation. For we must not forget that sacrifice is a drama on two levels, the one visible and the other invisible, ordered absolutely one to the other: *sacrificii invisibilis visibile sacramentum*. Thus there is also a double immolation, one in the heart, the other on the altar, but bound closely together, the first producing the second and reciprocally.

The immolation of the lamb is not only a brutal fact of liturgical butchery, the driving of a blade into a bleating animal. We must realize that there is not only blood-value but ritual and significative and so religious value in this great business. We must plumb these depths of moral conduct and psychology to gain any understanding of the sacrifice of Calvary. For if immolation meant only putting to death, the sacrifice of the Cross would have been performed on Calvary by the executioners—which is repugnant. Christ is the priest of Calvary. He it is, undoubtedly, who immolates Himself. He it is who consents to die to return to His Father. He it is who renounces the human life which He took from His holy Mother. And having chosen as the victim none other than Himself, He has realized better than anyone the absolute identity between the immolation of the victim and that of the religious soul offering the victim.

But why is Christ's death an immolation? No doubt because Jesus consents to die; but also because He dies in an attitude of adoration and obedience which makes this fact of history the supreme religious act, the act of the Redemption. To return to His Father He consents to pass along the ways which sin has laid on Adam's sons; and He who could have been glorified without dying accepts death first and foremost by reason of our sins. Consenting to suffer before ascending to the Father's right hand, He offers a sacrifice after the manner of men, He immolates Himself. Henceforth there exists in the new religion which He has instituted a victim, and so a sacrifice. Sacrifice is nothing but the victim constituted as such, that is offered, immolated and accepted. And because all sacrifice is a sign, that is a spiritual value incarnate in the victim who represents it, Jesus, as the victim of His sacrifice, possesses a redemptive value. This invisible wealth is incarnate in His body and blood which were immolated and which contain the sacrificial value; the price of our salvation, this reality which is the body of Christ, is since the sacrifice of Calvary the sign which contains all His religion, all His love, all that the Father has loved, all that has given Him satisfaction, and so all that has saved us.

In fine, we are wrong to treat the ideas of sacrifice, victim, immolation and above all Redemption in modern language as if they represented values which though related could be held apart. No doubt sacrifice is rather an action and the victim rather a thing, but because the victim is a thing made sacred and sacrifice consists in making sacred, sacrifice is in the victim and the victim is the realization of the sacrifice. Conceived as a sign, immolation begins by integrating all the sentiments in the patriarch's heart, which must be expressed, translated and realized, and must issue in the victim's death—and this is called also immolation. For a sign will always contain both the visible and the invisible, a hidden soul taking sensible form in a symbol, the one justifying the other and expressed by it.

The death of Christ on Calvary is a sacrifice not in so far as it is a judicial murder carried out by executioners, or a sin on the part of the Pharisees, but in so far as it is the self-immolation of God's Son; and because sacrifice is an efficacious sign of the inward religion incarnate in the victim, it succeeds in giving to the body and blood of Christ all the religious and redemptive value which it possesses in the

Father's eyes. That is why Christ is a victim. Nothing henceforth can take from His body this quality, this immolated
state, since it was the sign—so grievous in the making—of
the perfection of religion.

And on the Cross also there is a double immolation, that
of the body torn, mangled and done to death, and that of
the religious soul in adoration. Or rather there is the external and historical sign—the death of a man who commits
His spirit to God, whose side is opened by the lance of the
centurion; and there is the hidden meaning—the Son's love,
the Father's compassion, the consummation of Redemption.
For this sacrifice is redemptive. The death of Christ is the
efficacious sign of the Redemption, because it is the real
sign of redemptive immolation.

But let us now suppose that the body of Christ, without
undergoing any fresh modification but remaining the immolated and now glorified victim of the one and only sacrifice,
becomes through a marvellous transubstantiation the
matter of another sacrificial act to which it will bring the
virtue of its own immolation and all the redemptive fruits
of which it was and is the efficacious sign. If these conditions
are indeed fulfilled must we not say, in virtue of this
reciprocal causality between the sign and the thing signified,
that we have the right to speak of His immolation in the
Mass, possessing in it as we do all the hidden realities of
that immolation?

That, precisely, is what S. Thomas always taught: *how and
why can we say that Christ is immolated in the Eucharist?
Utrum in hoc sacramento Christus immolatur?* (III^a p., q. 83,
a. 1.) He answers (first), because the celebration of the
Eucharist is the representative image of Christ's Passion,
and (secondly), because it produces in us all the Passion's
fruits. And just as the immolation of a lamb meant first and
foremost to immolate oneself, conforming with the sign in
mental attitude, so, or rather conversely, to possess the body
of Christ as victim of our sacrifice, and to participate
straightway in all His immolation's fruits, is in fact to
immolate Him.

The Council of Trent simply took up this teaching: the Mass, it tells us, repeating and developing S. Thomas, *represents*, *recalls* and *applies* the Cross's sacrifice. That is why it is a sacrifice, an immolation, and the very immolation of the Cross.

If this most powerful doctrine has seemed weak to modern men, it is perhaps that they have lost sight of the Augustinian theology of the sign, which alone explains the metaphysic of sacrifice. They hear the word immolation and, reducing it to the mere material fact of putting to death, they would either relieve themselves of it by removing it altogether from the sacrifice of the Mass (which is the origin of certain oblationist theologies, in which immolation is thought of simply as a condition of sacrifice, a dispensable accident) or else, misconceiving the thought of Trent but determined to be more Catholic than the Council itself, they require in the Mass a new immolation of Christ, distinct from that of the Cross, and this is the theological principle behind those theologies which are attributed to Lessius and especially to de Lugo in pious books.

The truth does not lie in the excess or in the defect. It lies in the theology of the sign.

The bread and the wine which were at the beginning of the offertory only the insufficient signs of our imperfect religion become by the transubstantiating consecration the sign or the species of the victim immolated on Calvary; and from this moment the sacrament contains within it all the fruits of Christ's historic immolation. In virtue of the theology of the efficacious sign which allows us to use the same word for what is visible and what is invisible in our mysteries, to say, for example, that the water of baptism makes us adoptive sons of God, we may and must say that we immolate Christ on the altar since we become participants in His own immolation. He who is always the victim and the sacrifice of His Father, and for ever accepted by Him, becomes at this moment our victim and our sacrifice. He, the eternal immolation, is immolated now for us.

* * *

Thus the objection which persistently demands, on the
pretext of a true immolation, some grievous or humiliating
modification of Christ's Body does not gain, by so degrading
traditional expressions, any increased realization of the
truths hidden behind these venerable words. For example, is
the purpose and function of immolation in sacrifice always
fully understood? As S. Augustine and S. Thomas teach, it is
a sign. That means that the putting to death of a living creature, libations of pure wine, mutilations of the victim and
the rest are not in the least willed for themselves as physical
facts, but because they are the efficacious expression of our
inner sentiments, in particular of repentance for our sins.
They express our spiritual life *outwardly*, they make it incarnate in suitable external acts, and by making it incarnate
and by reason of the mutual influence of soul and body they
engender and produce the inward religion which they represent; thus they are truly signs, and signs which effect what
they signify. The corporeal is willed for the spiritual, which
is found therein.

This essential function of immolation is clearer perhaps
at the beginning, when primitive man, cast naked into the
midst of nature spreading huge and hostile around him, and
having as it were nothing of his own but his bodily members,
could immolate only some part or other of his splendid,
suffering frame. Personal mutilations, of which circumcision
is the most expressive, are thus at the root of the great rite of
immolation; we find them everywhere. We modern civilized
Christians must not be too hard on these ancient things; we
must excuse them for their magnificent spiritual significance.
Later on man, having in a sense extended his body beyond
himself into the material goods of private property, will look
rather in this direction for the materials for his immolation;
but the invisible will which is the foundation of the visible act
remains the same, and here lies the purpose of the action.
Immolation then is not first and foremost the killing of an
animal but the repentance for our sins by means of it.

Our Saviour on Calvary, when he offered the perfect
sacrifice, returned at once, magnificently and in undreamt

of and superlative conditions, to the very origin of the institution. He identified anew and for all time the priest and the
victim, him who offers and him who is offered, him who immolates and him who is immolated. And, without inflicting
death upon Himself, He so accepted it as to put into the
sufferings and tortures of His flesh first all His personal
religion and secondly the satisfaction which He offered for
our sins. This was eminently the corporeal willed for the
spiritual, an immolation of which Christ was both the
author and the subject. But how can we immolate Christ?
Not, certainly, like the executioners, who did not in fact immolate Him at all, since He immolated Himself in the true
sense of the word. Not then, certainly, by subjecting Christ's
body, as did the soldiers, to physical mortifications, injuries
and wounds. Such a supposition is meaningless and impossible. His glorified condition contradicts it. God would
forbid and stop it. Besides the Father has no need of it. Is
not His Son for ever immolated, in the true sense of the
expression, since the Sacred Humanity of the Word, His
Body and His Blood, have suffered for our sins and been the
instrumental cause of the Redemption?

To immolate Christ in sacrifice to-day can mean only this:
to gain the Body of Christ as the victim of our sacrifice and
thus as the cause in our souls of that perfect religion of
adoration, love and penitence which we must win from Him.
To immolate is to repent visibly and invisibly, to produce
the invisible through the visible; more precisely, it is to have
a visible object as both the sign and cause of our interior
penitence, and, if there is such a thing, of perfect penitence.
Transubstantiation, by putting the victim of Calvary in the
place of our bread and wine, the species—separated and so
representative of Christ's death—remaining, and by making
the victim of Calvary our victim, gives us this Body which
Christ made the efficacious sign of His redemption, the
visible instrument of our salvation. And since this Body has
become our victim, it engenders in us at this moment the
inward immolation of adoration, love and penitence of which
it is the efficacious sign.

In that sense—the true sense—Christ is immolated for us to-day; this is exactly what S. Augustine repeats in agreement with the whole tradition before and after him. And so too S. Thomas and the Council of Trent explain it: Christ is immolated on the altar because, under figures which represent the immolation of the Cross, He produces in us its invisible fruits. Thus He continues His great function of victim; He engenders new spiritual fruits, but in our souls, making us participate in all the effects of His Redemption.

Christ's immolation in a sense enlarges its scope and gains fresh ground. It extends its *efficacious significance*. By taking possession of so many different altars at so many different points in time and space, by multiplying the species of the one and only immolated Body, it spreads its fruits far and wide. So we find *in omni loco* the efficacious sign of our salvation, the sacrament of the Redemption; and in that sense Christ is immolated wherever there is a priest capable of placing beneath the visible sign of Calvary the victim who is the cause of all its invisible results.

*   *   *

Immolation is renunciation of sin through a sign, that is by means of a sensible object representing us, its mortified state picturing and causing our repentance. It is therefore the obtaining of spiritual results by means of a victim; more precisely, it is the finding in a visible object, thanks to its value and also to the grievous effects wrought in it, the efficacious sign of our own inward state, provided always that this object represents us, that it is really ours and in a sense identified with us, that our attitudes of soul are incarnate in it, while it also engenders them in us.

Transubstantiation, by exchanging our oblations for Christ's Body, makes of this *our* victim; it brings us all its worth of immolation and of sacrifice; it communicates to us under the sign of our oblations all the spiritual fruits of which Christ was, and so is still, the cause, and in particular the propitiation which has Him for its principle.

Thus we sacrifice Christ on the altar because the victim of

Calvary there becomes our victim thanks to the transubstantiation of our oblations. The short formula: transubstantiation immolates Christ (or: transubstantiation is a sacrifice and the very sacrifice of Calvary) contains, when fully understood, nothing which need surprise a Christian.

We must however notice this: in ordinary sacrifices, the spiritual value of the sign, found in men's souls, is superior to that of the material object figuring it; and the *spiritus contribulatus* of which the Psalmist speaks is of far greater worth than all the holocausts which it occasions and produces: *scientia Dei plus quam holocausta*, as the prophet says. But in the Mass this relationship is reversed; and the Body and Blood of Christ, which act as victim for the Church's sacrifice, are incomparably more worthy than all the feeble movements of adoration which try to rise in our contrite hearts. And further it is Christ, our Head, who is the principle of the Church's spiritual sacrifice and not conversely. Our victim causes of itself the religion which it represents.

But because the immolation of the Body of Christ on Calvary was in its turn only the bodily and bloody outward showing of the wonders in His filial soul, our sacrifice and our Mass are bound up, like our salvation and our Redemption, with a spiritual value. And these succeed in the measure in which our souls, through the Body of Christ which is given to us, are conformed with the Saviour's, share in His religion, in His adorable inner life and dispositions. So at last S. Paul's desire is realized: *Hoc enim sentite in vobis quod est in Christo Jesu;* then our souls are immolated with the Immolated One: *in Ipso, per Ipsum, cum Ipso.*

CHAPTER NINE: THE SIGN

AND now by way of ending these long discussions let us try to contemplate for the last time in a final effort of thought the riches bound up together in our Eucharistic Sign, hidden at first but to be better revealed to us as we follow the thread of the sacrificial movement. At the beginning of the mystery, when the bread and wine leave our stores to be carried to the offertory table, they are just God's gifts which we prepare to give Him back; then they represent, as expressive symbols, the feelings of religion, adoration, thanksgiving and love of our repentant souls.* But because they have been chosen from our healthiest food and most human drink, they already foreshadow a banquet which they are to make possible, an agape of union with the Divinity, a feast in which we are to find the nourishment and strength, in the symbolism of bodily hunger and thirst, of which our souls have need.

But before the time comes for this communion, the elements will act as a sign for another fundamental mystery, that of the Redemption. The sensible species of the bread and wine are to become the sacrament of Christ's Body and Blood, which will be really present, and to represent His death by their separation; in virtue of the law of the efficacious sign they are to make us share in all the fruits of the Redemption. These figures of bread and wine have become the signs of Christ's immolation and of His sacrifice which they contain, since they enclose the victim's Body and Blood.

Thanks to this sacrament we may communicate with this victim, sharing in all the effects of His mystery, above all in the charity which the Redemption has established between God and men on earth, and, through God, between man and man. The visible unity of what was bread and wine shows

---

* Cf. S. Augustine, *De Civitate Dei*, lib X, cap. 6 : *Quod (sacrificium) etiam sacramento altaris fidelibus noto frequentat Ecclesia, ubi ei demonstratur, quod in ea re quam offert, ipsa offeratur.*—"This is the sacrifice which the Church repeats in the sacrament of the altar which the faithful know so well, where it is shown to her that she is herself offered in the thing that she is offering." But when he speaks in this way S. Augustine is thinking already of transubstantiation through which the Church will be more than ever offered because her Head will be present and will offer His members in offering Himself. This is the mystery of absolute unity, in virtue of the Head. Cf. also S. Augustine, *Serm. de Sacramentis in die Paschæ* (Serm. 111 ad infantes), Migne, *P.L.*, Vol. XLVI, 827–8 ; or in Dom Morin's edition, Rome, Typ. Vatic., 1930, pp. 18–20 : Accipite itaque et edite Corpus Christi, etiam ipsi in Corpus Christi facta iam membra Christi ; accipite et potate sanguinem Christi. Ne dissolvamini, manducate vinculum vestrum ; ne vobis viles videamini, libate pretium vestrum.—And at the end the admirable play on the words καθ' ὅλου, "*unde catholica nominatur [Ecclesia].*"

forth clearly the charity which ought to reign among the faithful who approach the altar; the species are now signs of grace, after being signs of the presence and the immolation of grace's Author and before that of the religion of us men. Thus they are indeed a sacrament in the word's strictest sense throughout the ceremony.

But how are we now to bring to unity these diverse aspects of a mystery of unity? Why have these figures of bread and wine successively and efficaciously these different meanings while yet preserving the inner life of their ritual movement?

It is that they contain the very Author of spiritual unity, Him whom we call the Head because He recapitulates in His person all His members. If our religion is not vain from the start, if it is not to be buried in eternal frustration like the Danaids along with the vanished sacrifices of past centuries, it is because it is always the religion of Christ's members and because, by reason of the Head, the Father has pity on the body. So to hasten the success of our endeavour God soon changes the substance of our offering into the only sacrificial substance which has real value, that of the flesh and blood of the youthful Head, who takes command over our sacrifice and gives it the worth and value of His own.

If the union shown by the grains of wheat in a single piece of bread and the grapes pressed into a single chalice is more than an empty symbol, an ineffective wish, it is because Christ is present beneath the species giving our sacrament, now become His own, all its effective power.*

And if our final communion succeeds in a return to God, it is because it is communion with the Body and Blood of the

* De la Taille (*Mysterium Fidei*, 1921, Elucidatio, XLIII), and following him M. Anger (*La Doctrine du Corps Mystique de Jésus-Christ*, Paris, Beauchesne, 1929, p. 171), observe rightly that this symbolism of the unity of the grains and grapes has not the original symbolic value of the separation of the species figuring Christ's death. That is true. But if the sacrament (*signum tantum*) figures the Body and Blood of Christ rather than the grace of Christ, this grace has been none the less underlined in the texts from the earliest times. It is pre-eminently the grace of unity in charity, because, one might say, inverting the symbolism of the grains, there is always only the one Body of Christ beneath all the bread and wine. By reason of the unity of the Body, we have the right to say, passing from the thing to its sign, by a bold but legitimate reversal of sacramental symbolism, that the bread of the Eucharist is only one. And so we then rejoin S. Paul, *I Cor.*, x, 17, that is the very origins.

Head who delivers Himself to us to share with us His filial grace.

In fine, all this movement of the mystical body is possible, fruitful and efficacious only because it has a mystic Head, and because the members, communicating with the glorified flesh of the Head, become still more His body. The Eucharist is a mystery of unity—the unity of the Church's sacrifice and Christ's, the union of God and men, the union of Christians among themselves—because it gives us the one and only Head in the very mystery in which He has recapitulated all things, earth and heaven, in the mystery of His Passion, Death and Resurrection.

So, thanks to Christ, the Eucharist is also unified. Nevertheless as liturgy it evolves in time and may be contemplated at this or that instant of its movement. Then it shows diverse aspects for Christian piety to admire one by one: it has different values exploited in turn by the devotion of the ages.

S. Paul and S. John have already given witness to this splendidly various magnificence. P. Lebreton once dwelt with supreme delicacy of touch upon the contrasts shown by our two great Eucharistic sources, chapter xi of First Corinthians and chapter vi of the Fourth Gospel, reducing them to their proper limits: in the one we have the celebration of the Lord's death, in the other communion with the bread of life.* But are not these two aspects of the same dogma rather the successive moments of a single mystery?

S. Paul, writing to the Corinthians, was looking at the liturgical and dogmatic centre of the Eucharist, the instant at which it is the sign of Christ's death through the consecration of the bread and wine: *Mortem Domini annuntiabitis donec veniat*. That is what was later to be called the dogma of the sacrifice of the Mass. S. John developed above all the final result of the mystery, its natural outcome: to communicate with the victim is to find the eternal life which the Son receives from the Father; that would come to be known as the sacrament of the Eucharist.

In virtue of that law of influence which we have seen

* *Recherches de Science Religieuse*, vol. XVII, 3-4, June–August, 1927, p. 332.

verified already of the doctrine of our Lord's Divinity, the
Johannine manner made a greater mark upon Patristic
catechesis and through it upon Scholastics and Theologians.
In the whole tradition of instruction on the Eucharist, it is
studied first as the sacrament of grace and only secondly as
the sacrifice of religion, and the Council of Trent arranged
its canons in this time-honoured order.

But this convenient arrangement is not the only possible
one. Also it causes certain awkwardnesses, for it made it
harder in the end to give an elementary account of the dogma
of the Holy Sacrifice suitable for children, who do not con-
nect it closely enough with our Saviour's institution. If there
is no question of replacing S. John by S. Paul, who is too
concise in this passage for catechetic purposes, we can at least
bring these two great witnesses together in a synthesis such
that each, despite his special point of view, provides the
whole dogmatic content.

And if we must gather up the result of our researches in a
single phrase for the last time in the form which our enquiry
demands (rather like trying to bind too many ears into a
sheaf), we should be disposed to say: the bread and the wine,
which try in their feeble way to be the sign of our religion,
are changed into the Body and Blood which were the sign of
Jesus Christ's religion; but as the species of bread and wine
remain after this substantial change, the religion of Jesus
finally subsists under the sign of our religion: we have all the
reality of the one under the species of the other, all the
sacrificial reality of the Head's religion beneath the symbolic
figures of the religion of the members.

Innocent III one day, in the letter to John of Lyons
already quoted, put all this doctrine into two or three propositions of a conciseness that discourages translation: "The
species of bread and wine are sign or sacrament twice over—
the sacrament of Christ's Body and the sacrament of the
grace of charity: the Body of Christ itself is both its own
reality and a sign of grace. And so grace comes to us both
from the sacrament and from Christ's Body."*

* Text in Denziger–B, 415, or in Migne, *P.L.*, 214, 1119, A sq.

R

The divine liturgy of our Roman Missal, above all in the Secrets and Post-Communions of its oldest offices, has lavished this wealth like a hostess honouring her guests with varied fare, drawing on inexhaustible reserves. On some days the Church reminds God that this bread and wine come from her own store and represent her offerings, this especially in the Secrets before the consecration, at the beginning of the action. This is the first sense of the word sign:

Secreta:

Domine Deus noster, qui in his potius creaturis, quas ad fragilitatis nostræ subsidium condidisti, tuo quoque nomini munera jussisti dicanda constitui: tribue, quæsumus, ut et vitæ nobis præsentis auxilium et æternitatis efficiant sacramentum. Per Dominum. . . (*Feria V post Dom. Pass.*)

Lord our God, You who have chosen the creatures made by You for the support of our weakness and bidden us consecrate them to Your name as offerings: grant, we pray, that they may be both the support of our present life and the sacrament of life everlasting.

For the Church does not mean to stop there. She must go on. The sign must change its value and its meaning.

Secreta:

Benedictio tua, Domine, larga descendat: quæ et munera nostra, deprecantibus sanctis Martyribus tuis, tibi reddat accepta et nobis sacramentum redemptionis efficiat. Per Dominum. . . (8 *Nov., Oct. Omn. Sanct.*)

May Your benediction Lord bountifully descend, that by the intercession of Your holy martyrs it may make our offerings acceptable to You, and make them for us the sacramental sign of our Redemption.

Or more briefly :

Secreta:

Munus, quod tibi, Domine, nostræ servitutis offer-

This offering which our religion makes to You, O

imus, in salutare nobis perfice sacramentum. Per Dominum. (*Feria II post Dom. III Quadrag.*)

Lord, make for us the sacrament of our salvation.

Why? Because of Christ's institution:

Secreta:

Ipse tibi, quæsumus, Domine sancte, Pater omnipotens, æterne Deus, sacrificium nostrum reddat acceptum, qui discipulis suis in sui commemorationen hoc fieri hodierna traditione monstravit, Jesus Christus Filius tuus, Dominus noster, qui tecum vivit. . . (*Feria V Maj. Hebd.*)

Holy Lord, omnipotent Father, eternal God, may He make our sacrifice acceptable to You who to-day by His institution showed His disciples how to perform it in memory of Him, Jesus Christ Your Son our Lord.

How? By a divine acceptance, like the fire coming down from heaven:

Secreta:

Sacrificia, Domine, tuis oblata conspectibus, ignis ille divinus absumat qui discipulorum Christi Filii tui per Spiritum Sanctum corda succendit. (*Feria VI, IV Temp. Pent.*)

May the sacrifice offered before You, Lord, be consumed by that divine fire which kindled the hearts of Your Son's disciples under the action of the Holy Spirit.

At this hour of transubstantiation, the sacrament acquires a fresh significance, that of Christ's death:

Postcommunio:

Largire sensibus nostris, omnipotens Deus: ut, per temporalem Filii tui mortem, quam mysteria veneranda testantur, vitam te nobis dedisse perpetuam confidamus. (*Feria IV Maj. Hebd.*)

Grant us, all-powerful God, the assurance to our minds that through the temporal death of Your Son, witnessed by these venerable mysteries, we have received from You eternal life.

And then this sacrament is efficacious; it is for us the sign of the Redemption (the expression has occurred above already) and the sign of grace; and because grace in its turn inaugurates and prepares in us the life which has no ending, this sign shown in time upon our altars is charged already with eternal promises and eternal realities.

Hence come two oppositions to be noted, each at its own time; the first is between the sign and grace, its content. Then we ask that the sign should not be fruitless, that our unworthiness should not empty it of its riches. But this rather narrow outlook is usually subordinated to a wider one. The thought of a quite sterile, sacrilegious sign is not attractive. But we do feel often enough disposed to ask that the present effect of the sacrament should be extended and intensified in the eternity which it is pledging us; that, we think, is the meaning of such phrases as the following:

Postcommunio:

Immortalitatis alimoniam consecuti, quæsumus, Domine: ut quod ore percepimus, pura mente sectemur. (*Dom. XXI post Pent.*)	Having received from You the food of immortality, we pray that we may aspire with a pure heart to what our lips have touched.

After reaching this supreme significance as the pledge of everlasting life, the Eucharistic sign—simply as sign, *sacramentum et non res*—triumphs by its own annihilation. Some prayers speak of that definitive state when there will be no more signs, because we shall have the realities uncovered, face to face, without intermediaries. This is the final prayer:

Postcommunio:

Perficiant in nobis, Domine, quæsumus, tua sacramenta quod continent: ut quæ nunc specie gerimus, rerum veritate capiamus. Per Dominum. (*Sabb. IV Temp. Sept.*)	May Your sacraments, Lord, we pray, accomplish in us that which they contain, that we may possess (one day) in truth what we now show forth in figure.

Already in the eleventh century the monk Lanfranc hesitated between two possible interpretations of this ancient phrase to which the clue was lost: "The priest asks", he said, "that the Body of Christ, represented here under the form of bread and wine, should be possessed one day as it is in the splendour of an unveiled vision. Other commentators, with much probability, understand by the truth of the Body and Blood their efficacious virtue, that is the remission of men's sins." (*De Corpore et Sanguine Domini*, cap. 20, Migne, *P.L.*, vol. 150, col. 436).

But other similar examples leave no room for doubt:

Postcommunio:

Quod ore sumpsimus, Domine, pura mente capiamus: et de munere temporali fiat nobis remedium sempiternum. (*Ordinary of the Mass.*)	May we possess, Lord, with a clean heart what our lips have received and change a temporal benefit into an eternal remedy.

Or again:

Postcommunio:

Sumentes, Domine, cælestia sacramenta, quæsumus clementiam tuam: ut, quod temporaliter gerimus, æternis gaudiis consequamur. (*Feria IV, IV Temp. Pent.*)	Receiving, Lord, Your heavenly sacraments, we beg of Your mercy to grant us in eternal joy what we here show forth in time.*

Thus in the Post-Communion for Saturday *Quattuor Temporum* (September), *quod continent*, the content of the sacrament, is not the Body of Christ, which cannot be completed or perfected. It refers to the other reality included in the sacrament, the spiritual reality of grace. The conclusion of the prayer shows this clearly, *veritas rerum* in the future being opposed to *species* in the present. If the text referred to

* Nor can there be any more hesitation about the meaning of the rather elliptical Post-Communion of the Dedication of S. Michael the Archangel (29th Sept.).

Beati Archangeli tui Michælis intercessione suffulti: supplices te, Domine, deprecamur; ut, quod ore prosequimur, contingamus et mente.	Upheld, Lord, by the intercession of Your blessed Archangel Michael, we humbly beg that our souls may attain what our lips have taken.

Christ's Body it would seem to say that this is on the altar in appearance only, that it will not be really present until later. That is inadmissible. In fact two ways of possessing the life of grace are here contrasted, the first being the method of the sign which consists in the performance of a rite so as to gain under sacramental form (*specie*), under a borrowed figure therefore, what we shall have later face to face, without intermediary, in the eternal vision. Then the *régime* of signs, the subject of our impatience as well as of our joy on earth, will be replaced by that of the beatific and direct possession which it is preparing in our souls.*

And it is effectively preparing us. The Eucharist is in no sense an empty sign: it enables to do again what Christ has done. It is an action—and what does it perform? Sacramentally, the very Redemption itself. Thanks to the sign we bring eternal life into activity: *res gerimus*, or in the words of the other Secret which delighted S. Thomas: *opus nostræ redemptionis exercetur*, "we perform the very work of our redemption." But to perform the redemptive work through Christ is to offer His own sacrifice. The Mass is therefore truly a sacrifice, and "what Christ's Passion did in the world, this sacrament operates in individual men." (III* p., q. 79, a. 1).

Lanfranc however was not entirely wrong in seeing a possible reference to Christ's Body in *quod continent*. For it is subject to the *régime* of signs in our Eucharist, present only beneath the species and hidden for us there as well as given to us. There is thus a still more glorious state than that of the priest at the altar, of the Christian before the monstrance, for the elect in Heaven see Christ and God as they really are, without the aid or the concealment of any sacrament, unveiled by any sign. And the communicant must realize this, asking for to-morrow a means of having this same treasure other than to-day's.

Again S. Thomas reminds us of it, putting on our lips this

---

* There is a similar interpretation, though on rather different lines, in a contemporary of Lanfranc's, Guitmond, bishop of Aversa (Italy): *De corp. et sang. Domini ver.*, l.2. *P.L.* 149, 1468, quoted by de la Taille, *Mysterium Fidei*, first edition, p. 486.

final hope of one day seeing the disappearance of the splendid but incomplete *régime* which is our joy on earth:

> Jesu, quem velatum nunc aspicio,
> Oro, fiat illud quod tam sitio,
> Ut te revelata cernens facie,
> Visu sim beatus tuæ gloriæ.

*   *   *

A sign is a reality which has two values, the one visible, the other invisible, because the first represents and (it may be) actually contains the second.

Sacrifice in general is a sign, as S. Augustine teaches, because the victim offered and immolated represents and carries within it men's adoration and repentance, putting them before God, so that it may bring heaven's blessing upon men and the divine alliance which it now symbolizes.

The death of Christ on Calvary is a sacrifice, and so a sign, in many ways, in particular because in the Body and Blood of Jesus, immolated and offered, are found incarnate His love, His adoration, all His religion, and also the pardon of God which He has won for us, and of which his Sacred Humanity is henceforth the instrument.

In our dispensation we visibly incarnate in the bread and wine men's efforts of repentance, oblation and immolation; they are the signs of the Church's religion.

But if beneath these signs, which are only species, God places the very victim of the Cross with His religion, which is perfect, we shall have beneath the sign of the Church's religion the religion and the sacrifice of Christ, perfectly represented moreover by these separate species, and with their full effects, pardon and redemption, all God's graces.

Thus the sacrifice of the Mass, which seems in its species to be but the Church's sacrifice, is also and at the same time the Cross's sacrifice and so Christ's sacrifice.

*   *   *

The mystery of the Redemption develops for our salvation on two levels, the second depending on the first without which it would not exist: there is the historical level, the Passion, Death and Resurrection of Jesus Christ the Son of God, and the sacramental level, which seizes upon all this mystery in ritual or the signs of liturgy.

This proposition has always been admitted; it is even of faith when we are speaking of grace, that is the gift of the divine life to men, or of the Redemption working downwards. In this direction the immensity of the sacramental mystery does not come up against our imaginations, which readily allow that God could place His grace, that is His life, in ritual or in a sign containing it. But the proposition must be true also the other way, upwards, in the reverse direction, when we speak of Jesus Christ's religion towards His Father, and therefore of His sacrifice. Must there not be also a rite containing Christ's religion and Christ's sacrifice? The special difficulty must be noted: sacrifice is a victim filled with all its fruits, fruits of religion and of union. So there must be a rite or sign containing the victim of Calvary with all these fruits. And we have seen (wonder of wonders!) that such a sign exists.

CONCLUSION: CHRIST OUR HEAD

In making a last study of the eleventh chapter of First Corinthians, and the sixth chapter of the Fourth Gospel in the foregoing pages, we had the joy of rediscovering the way in which these two statements of Christianity complement one another; their agreement had delighted us before when we were examining the scriptural sources for the dogma of the Incarnation. S. Paul and S. John prove to reunite once more when they treat, each in his own way, of the mystery of the Redemption and, further, of the mystery of the Eucharist.

The course of the Fourth Gospel's Prologue, the flight of the eagle, is the most sublime, but on the whole the simplest. The eternal Son of God took a human nature, we might almost say human nature absolutely. From this moment all that He touches amongst us is healed and sanctified. He saves men by living in their midst. He is their light coming into this world, the water which quenches thirst eternally, the author of the second birth, the resurrection and the life. Eventually He divinizes even suffering and death, the daughters of sin: they become the cause of our salvation from the hour when He made them His. In this line of thought, His sacred Body, the Body of God's Son, is the instrument of our salvation, and the Eucharist, which is His really present flesh, is a sacrament, an efficacious sign of grace. And, since it is referred to after reference has been made already to the Person, we must say that it descends from heaven: *Ego sum panis vivus, qui de cælo descendi*.

The other direction, that of S. Paul, rather less familiar to modern Eucharistic piety, is equally dogmatic and well grounded. It begins with the human nature of the Son of God: *hoc est corpus meum*. The sacred humanity of the Word lived on this earth in the conditions of suffering which sin had imposed on Adam's children, conditions corresponding with our faults, but not with the rights of the Son of God—which thus are not respected. Nevertheless, for love of us, Jesus chooses this slow road and pursues it to the end, to the death which He willingly suffers for our sins. But His Father, whom these delays have cost so dear, hastens to revive this human nature placing it at His right hand. Then was the Son of God adored in His sacred humanity, *in heaven, on earth, and in hell*, which recognize this Filiation—S. John's Prologue had made it the beginning of the whole account. In this second direction the human life of Jesus, ended by His grievous Passion, is a sacrifice; and the Eucharist, which gives us the victim of Calvary under the symbol of the species, is a sacrifice also and the efficacious sign of the perfection of religion.

When we consider the Eucharist in the liturgical context of the Mass which gives it to us, this second direction of thought, scripturally the first because that of the Synoptics, must be the one to follow. On the altar the Eucharist is first

an act of religion before becoming a sacrament of grace.
However great the importance so rightly given by our piety
to the Real Presence, this exists only through the previous
sacrifice. And communion is before all else our union with
the victim who gives God perfect honour and satisfaction.
But to have a complete picture of the Eucharist (as of the
Incarnation) we must combine the two ideas of sacrifice and
sacrament.

Now there exists among the titles of the Incarnate Word
a splendid name which sums up both the complementary
aspects of His mystery. It is the title of Head. If Jesus is a
Head or an elder Brother, it is because He is the Son of God
but also because He has a mystical body of brothers or
members, for He has no brothers except men.

To speak of the sacrifice of our Head would be to bring
within a single phrase all the teaching of this book, in which
Jesus our victim has been shown to us at the centre of the
Eucharistic action, as we had first gazed upon Him on the
Cross at Calvary, animating the vast body of the Church and
even that of all humanity with His all-powerful religious
energy.

He is not laid upon our altars, like the victims of sacrifices
now outworn, passive and resigned, playing the part of a
sign at the brutal bidding of a foreign master. On the contrary, He it is who is still the animating force of the great
movement of which He was the principle, prolonging it to
the end of the earth and in men's hearts. The creator of
religion, the author of grace, the source of salvation, Redemption itself in His own Person, He acts potently upon all
those who choose Him as their victim, or rather those to
whom He has offered Himself as victim and oblation. In His
immolated state, He is more than ever our Head; for He sus-
tains us by His presence and His action. He is a victim, yes,
but a lifegiving victim, who gives worth to those who immolate Him instead of receiving from them His value and
significance.

So S. John saw Him in the Apocalypse as the mystic
Lamb, immolated but omnipotent, giving life to the world,

the centre of human history and of divine religion, the extraordinary victim who does not undertake for others their wishes and intentions but communicates to them on the contrary all His own spiritual wealth.

And it is the Eucharist which sets in motion every morning the outflow of this influence, this unique exchange; we must conclude with a last summary of its marvellous deployment. When in the first part of this work we tried to restore our concept of sacrifice in general to the most inevitable categories of human thought, we were led to say just this: offering sacrifice is doing for the sake of having, it is the doing of a ritual action so as to have a sacred object. S. Augustine and S. Thomas had constructed with almost the same logical elements what is perhaps the finest of their definitions of a sacrifice: "*omne opus quod agitur ut sancta societate inhæreamus Deo:* anything done that we may have communion with God." Thus the mind's eye hovers between the two verbs *do* and *have*, and it is probably for this reason that the Hebrew and certainly the New Testament Greek has the same word for the *act* and for the *victim* of the sacrifice. It is quite obvious for θυσία, so often applied to Christ Himself (e.g., in Eph., v, 2), and even for ἱλαστήριον (e.g., in Rom., iii, 25). So with us the word 'offering' signifies the action or the thing indifferently, often even both at the same time, probably because it is a relatively rare expression which has escaped control by either word.

This reduction to verbal and even intellectual unity appears legitimate when we remember that, for the ancients, sacrifice is a sign, the sign of a hidden reality, of the ascent of our religion to God, so that, after having appeased Him, we may be united with Him. Now what makes this inward religion or invisible sacrifice incarnate, as S. Augustine says, is both our ritual gesture and also the victim who lies immolated on the altar; this victim, acted on by us, will rise to God, and, if accepted by Him, will unite us to Him.

Whether we consider the Eucharist as an action, the great enterprise of Transubstantiation, or as a thing, the reality of Christ's Body and Blood, He it is who authorizes and explains the undertaking of the Mass and its success. If the Church acts, this can only be through the impulse of her Head who gives her life and movement, and so under the immediate influence of Christ the Priest, commanding His mystical body, president of its Members. The victim himself again can be none but Christ, the only intermediary of religious union between ourselves and God. Thus Jesus on the Church's altars is both Priest and Victim.

But if the great and only Sacrifice has taken place already, if it is finished, *consummatum est*, there can be no question of *doing* it again, at least historically, only of *having* it. Such is precisely the relation of the Mass to Calvary: it does not begin the Redemption over again, but it takes hold of it, possesses the sacrifice, communicating to us all its fruits. Or rather there does remain something for us to do: the victim already exists, but yet we have to make it ours.* Such, to repeat, is the power of the Mass through Golgotha and the Cross—with bread and wine and a word or two, in other words by a liturgical action, it finds the means to *have* the victim. If, on the one hand, it were content with *having*, like the tabernacle with the Blessed Sacrament reserved, it would be no longer a true sacrifice. On the other hand, it has not to invent a sacrifice, for this already exists and, besides, could neither be created nor replaced. But it can *do* a liturgical action so that it may *have*, and then it is a sacrifice and the Cross's sacrifice.

To that the Mass does no injury, for without that it would itself be nothing. It does not cause in Jesus Christ a fresh immolation distinct from that of Calvary, but it has Christ at its disposal as the victim, making Him to-day our victim, on this altar built by us for our own purposes; which presupposes that we have taken the initiative, placing the matter of our offering on this stone or table.

Only a Transubstantiation can realize these combined conditions. If the bread and the wine were not changed into

---

* The expression *to make ours* has a double meaning—"to get possession of" or "to do again on our own account." Applied to the Sacrifice of the Mass the expression is accurate in both these meanings, and finds its justification for them both in the doctrine of the Head of the mystical body.

the Body and Blood of Jesus Christ, they would join on the rubbish heap of dead or outworn things all the impotent sacrifices offered for centuries on all the useless altars of antiquity. But if we succeed in gaining Christ as victim, especially *under convenient species picturing and recalling to us His historic immolation,* we could say that *we possess upon our tables the sacrifice of Christ through a representative liturgy, beneath an efficacious sign.* And, also, the bread and the wine are transformed truly and in substance into Christ's Body and Blood (to employ the strict Thomist formula), *and the members share in the life of their Head.*

But, conversely, in what is known as Scotist language, if Christ's Body and Blood had not been substituted for the Church's previous offering, if our prayer had not the power to produce them, we should perhaps enjoy Christ's presence, as when two or three are gathered together in His name, but He would not be our victim, the victim of our sacrifice. Our union with Him would not involve species which are also the *sign, the figure, and the reminder of our expiatory and religious collaboration* in the great work of our Redemption. *And the Head would not visibly share in the life and the sorrows of the members.*

To our joy and wonder the Mass resolves in an instant all these heaped-up problems.

The Church begins by celebrating a rite which by itself alone would be only a useless sacrifice of bread and wine. But by the order and impulse of Christ her Head, whose words she repeats, she at once begs the Father to change this sacrifice into the very sacrifice of Calvary, that is into the victim of Golgotha, into Christ's Body and Blood. The sacrifice of the Church then becomes in reality the Cross's sacrifice, since she has this upon the altar-cloth and even in her hands.

And do not say that this exchange is impossible because Christ can no longer be an immolated victim in His glorious resurrected body. How absurd this objection would have seemed to the ancients! All the better, they would have replied, now that Christ has risen. Is He not risen as an accepted victim? To possess Him risen must always mean to possess Him as victim, indeed in the perfect and definitive sacrificial state, the object of men's search and longing, in which the victim completes His course, meeting with God and seeing the seal set upon all this movement.*

What has made this synthesis possible is the theology of the sign, applied successively to sacrifice in general, to the sacrifice of the Cross and to the sacrifice of the Mass.

To gain this position we have tried to steer a middle course between two opposed conceptions of the holy sacrifice of the Mass which seemed to us to falsify the traditional perspectives, one by excess, the other by defect. So we rejected first, and energetically, all systems which have looked for and thought to find in Christ's Body on the altar some fresh immolation, *distinct from that of the Cross*. It was no great credit to abandon such opinions after the decisive criticisms made of them by Billot and by de la Taille: they were unknown to Christian antiquity, to S. Augustine and S. Thomas, to the great tradition which has always made the bread and wine and not the Body and Blood of Christ the subjects of transubstantiation.

On the other hand, we have had to part company with more hesitations and regrets from certain more recent teachings, offered by authors who are our masters and to whom the present work owes, if not its inspiration, at least almost all the doctrinal and documentary solidity that it may have. It is no doubt true, first, that our Lord in a single

---

* A kind colleague who approached this question as a metaphysician rather than as an exegete reached similar conclusions. "We must not overemphasize", he wrote, "the heterogeneity of act and object, especially when there is question of a victim offering himself; nor that of movement and a term which is its end, but a largely immanent one. In our present matter the act of the will, the act of charity, is essentially required within the intellectual possession of the end as the everlasting source from which the latter flows. . . . The restitution of the whole self to God, which is the soul of sacrifice, is implied and achieved in the act of charity which supports the intuitive vision, and this act itself must not be kept separate from the movement of our whole existence which has produced it. Thus it is that the end resembles the means: our whole life is found there, in act and energy. So the Passion of Christ, in which His whole earthly life is condensed, is still found in His definitive state. But the merit is existent there, no longer comes into existence. By the same token there could not be a second act [another sacrifice], any more than one could speak of a second movement when movement is compared with the term where it maintains itself in all its energy. . ."

gesture on the eve of His death announced, accepted, explained and inaugurated His mystery of the morrow, when He made known in His Body and His Blood the victim acceptable to the Father and the sacrifice of the new alliance; and, secondly, that He authorized the Church to take bread and wine to find there when she desired, following His example and so by transubstantiation as on that last evening, the victim of this sacrifice or, if you will, that very sacrifice.

With what emotion then should we remember each morning that we are to renew that same gesture with which, on the eve of His death, the Saviour declared His irrevocable decision to offer and immolate Himself as an acceptable sacrifice for the redemption of our sins! What He then did, we, with the same words uttered in His name and on His behalf, are to repeat—and to bring into action all those spiritual values, all that great movement of religion which reached its culmination at that time. We are to *sign* His sacrifice anew—and with an efficacious sign because it is His before becoming ours. So we are to seize upon Him in His state of victimhood as He first constituted Himself definitively therein, once and for ever. Thus the gesture of the Cenacle is prolonged throughout the centuries, and it renews, thanks to the sacramental sign, the invisible realities of charity and religion which were perfected in Christ from the beginning, but which, in His mystical body, need always to be declared, resumed and, we may say, begun afresh.

But we have thought it undesirable to make too great a distinction in this mystery between an oblation and an immolation, the latter taking place only on Calvary, with only the former renewed upon the altar, coming to us from the Cenacle or from Heaven. This parcelling out of our riches seems to us regrettable. Here Billot, though working with a different vocabulary and perhaps a less profound conception of sacrifice in general, had thought and spoken more precisely: the Mass is not the repetition of a detached fragment, however essential, of the sacrifice of Calvary. Thanks to the double transubstantiation, and so beneath a suitable and efficacious sign, it is the taking possession of a complete sacrifice, both oblation and immolation, in fact of *the* complete and only sacrifice.

Since Easter morning we have Christ's Body and Blood in their glorious risen state, and so it is certain that we have them as they are to-day at the right hand of the Father. Here the theology of the French School keeps all its value. It is right to speak of the heavenly sacrifice placed upon our altars, if by sacrifice is meant the victim Himself together with those properties of victimhood henceforth inherent in His essence, once immolated (by reason of our sins) *in order* to be glorified, now glorified *because* once immolated, and so eternally a victim, and a victim to-day upon our altars.

Lastly we must never forget that the Church is the skilful worker and blessed beneficiary of this great act. It is her sacrifice which is changed into that of Calvary so that this may be not only multiplied but given a date and time in our present calendar and a particular intention. It is for us that Christ gave Himself and gives Himself to-day. In the words of Trent it is our daily sins, to-day's and not to-morrow's or yesterday's, that He comes to expiate. And how is this? It is because on the altar He is the victim of all those who offer the Mass that day through His priesthood's power. In agony until the end of the world* in our agonies, *made sin* we may even say, though not a sinner, in the sins of His members, it is at Mass above all that He is sacramentally our Head, gathering up our sufferings in His Passion, our energies in His Resurrection, our journey to the Father in His Ascension. It is His mystical sacrifice because His daily ritual sacrifice, ever made afresh—but this sacrifice though now ours is no less His, identical with the one and only sacrifice, promulgated or inaugurated at the Supper, immolated on Calvary, perfected in Heaven, and in all its phases always the self-same because the sole sufficient, the sole eternally fruitful, *the Sacrifice of Christ our Head.*

* [A phrase of Pascal's—Trans.]

Printed at The Chapel River Press, Andover, Hants.
2.47